T0366583

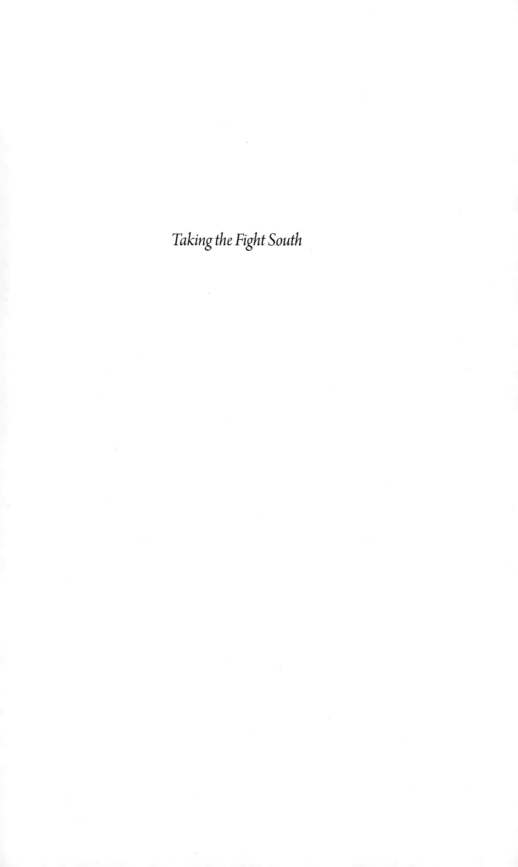

Taking the Fight South

TAKING *the*
FIGHT SOUTH

Chronicle of a Jew's Battle for
Civil Rights in Mississippi

HOWARD BALL

University of Notre Dame Press

Notre Dame, Indiana

University of Notre Dame Press
Notre Dame, Indiana 46556
undpress.nd.edu
All Rights Reserved

Published in the United States of America

Library of Congress Control Number: 2020950325

ISBN: 978-0-268-10916-5 (Hardback)
ISBN: 978-0-268-10919-6 (WebPDF)
ISBN: 978-0-268-10918-9 (Epub)

This story of a Jewish kid from the Bronx tenements

who moves his family to Starkville, Mississippi, to teach

and try to do justice would not have been told but for

the loving care provided to me by my sole tutor in

possum-ology and other South-isms, my dear friend

and spiritual brother-in-arms for justice,

DR. CHARLES D. LOWERY, of blessed memory,

professor of history, dean emeritus, at Mississippi

State University—and a talented woodsman

Contents

Foreword

Jennifer A. Stollman

The Mississippi specter haunts the minds of individuals and communities who do not call it home. I grew up understanding that the state, so far away from my reality, was like the other side of the world. It was the antithesis of America. Mississippi and other states in the Deep South represented the loud and frightening death rattles for white supremacy. Mississippi was Goddamn and Burning. Mississippi was Till, Schwerner, Goodman, and Chaney. Mississippi was also Freedom Riders and Fannie Lou Hamer.

When I accepted the privilege of writing the foreword for *Taking the Fight South*, I assumed, following a routine that I had done previously, that I would read and write a few pages about what Mississippi was and wasn't, is and isn't, and how the state has changed and how it hasn't. Curiosity and deep respect for Howard's social justice work in Mississippi and around the world encouraged me to accept reflexively the task of writing the foreword. What should have been a few days of work stood me still for weeks. His reckoning and recounting of his work and life in

Mississippi caused me to face my personal Mississippi experience. I sat with Howard Ball's work, and I expect that readers who are committed to social justice will experience the same responses. As he carries us along his journey, you will recognize the familiar signposts of success and strategy and fear and failure in the labor for justice.

I first came to Mississippi in 2002, almost three decades after Howard. Similarly, I arrived as a visiting professor at the University of Mississippi. Like Howard, I was cautioned by my Jewish family and friends not to go. They were frightened. Mississippi remained in their minds as a space of unreconciled violence. They could not understand why I would take this job when, back then, the job market was a bit easier for newly minted academics. Admittedly, I was curious. My Ph.D. focused on ante-bellum southern Jewish women and their complicated religious, regional, and racial identities. In my research, I followed nineteenth-century southern Jewish migration and settlements and traveled through Louisiana, North and South Carolina, and Georgia. A one-year position drew me to Mississippi, but a call to action awakened my lifelong journey fighting racism. During that year, I worked with like-minded individuals, traveled in the Delta, offered workshops on storytelling and interviewing for high schoolers, and created a tiny nonprofit dedicated to highlighting through the arts the lives of often silenced and ignored individuals. Like Howard, I learned to seek out and work with others who wanted to make a change. At the time, our impact was small. But we had dined at the welcome table of freedom and justice, and we were never going to leave.

After the reelection of Barack Obama, I returned to the University of Mississippi as the academic director for the William Winter Institute. Mississippi had changed. The campus was full of brave, outspoken, and action-oriented faculty, staff, students, and Oxford residents. In my six years there, we collaborated with folks across the state using our numbers and adopting others' models to push for civil rights for Black, Indigenous, People of Color, women, immigrants, and LGBTQIA+ individuals. The struggle was filled with victories followed quickly by defeats and then victories again. We continued the work that Howard and tens of thousands of Mississippi citizens and transplants initiated, all of us linked to a dedicated ancestral chain of action aimed at decentering white supremacy.

Howard's work debuts while the United States is in the midst of its most recent human and civil rights movement. On the heels of the COVID-19 pandemic, continued police brutality, and the murder of Black men and women, both cis- and transgender, pushed the second phase of the Black Lives Matter movement into the forefront of American hearts and minds. With much of the country shut down, Americans are forced to confront their country's pernicious historical and contemporary legacies and the impacts of systemic, institutional, and interpersonal white supremacy. An endless news feed, combined with an absence of live sports and new television series, earn us a front seat to demonstrations in support of civil rights and fearful and violent responses against shifts in economic, political, and social status quos. In the past, many of us turned away from these realities, but the present does not allow us to do so easily. More and more people with extended power are joining with those who have had to scrap for every inch to create a new future. Unbelievably, a groundswell of public and private support for Black civil and human rights has moved across our towns and cities. The moral pulls of justice and empathy have driven people from their sequestered states to demand, in words and deeds, racism's end. The silence created by COVID-19 is now replaced with the sounds of stomping feet and impassioned shouts of individuals across hundreds of cities, visually spectacular street art, inbox pings, and flickering web pages detailing tens of thousands of organizational statements committed to anti-racism. Millions of Americans engage in book studies internalizing concepts like institutional, structural, and interpersonal racism, fragility, and bias, and almost a billion dollars have been committed to combating racism and in support of Black equality and equity.

These are awesome times, full of energy and promise. Change does come in an instant when we have enough people dedicate themselves to the mission and commit time and action to the movement. Leaders from the front and the rear show us different ways to express citizenship and build community. They educate and inspire. We learn to be curious about and value other people's experiences that do not match ours. We follow, carried by the thrill of change and the possibility of fulfilling our constitutional and national aspirations.

We have been here before. Those who work for social justice know that the portals of interest and enthusiasm for equity and equality open and close like a wonky elevator in an old building. It's a fast and furious push to change mindsets and convert apathy into action. We know that interest fades when ending racism requires deep and uncomfortable self-reflection and confrontation beyond anti-racism performativity.

It does not have to be this way. We can choose a different path. We know that substantive equity does not happen solely by removing symbols and statues, jawboning support, and familiarizing ourselves with the historical and theoretical underpinnings of racism and bias. We know that leaders move us but cannot force us to act when we experience discomfort, are risk-averse, or do not wish to return unearned power and privilege. Sustainable change is not made in big moments and by prominent people. Change happens in our everyday conversations and actions. Change happens when ordinary people accomplish extraordinary things.

Howard's memoir demonstrates this brilliantly. Committed to equity and justice from his days in a Bronx tenement to now, as a retired professor, Howard understands that succeeding at racial justice is a lifelong endeavor and a daily struggle. His work lays out all we need to know to make deep and lasting impacts on equity and against racism. To enter the fight, as he did when he accepted an academic position at Mississippi State, we need curiosity and a desire to see if we can effect change. To step into complicated and seemingly impenetrable struggles where we are told we do not belong, as this Jew did in a profoundly Protestant land, we need faith. To break the cycle of norms, as he did when he became a football referee, we need to learn to play their games and defeat their injustice To stop the trampling of civil rights protection, as he did when taking on the Mississippi chapter of the ACLU, we need a deep understanding of existing rights and the aspirational goals of said rights. When wolves come to devour crucial policies meant to protect vulnerable populations, we must bring our intelligence, as Howard did during his testimony on the 1965 Voting Rights Act. We must view historical, present, and future landscapes with both wide and narrow lenses. When our families and neighbors, for altruistic or nefarious reasons, want us to stop fighting, we must summon our bravery and moral strength and push on. When our hearts, minds, and bodies are weakened from the fight and we are called else-where, we leave. But as Howard demonstrates, you never leave the fight, you take it to other battlefields. When a victory against evil happens, you return to the field and celebrate, for you must acknowledge the wins, or the defeats will surely push you out of the fight. Like Howard, I was in the courtroom when Edgar Ray Killen was convicted and sentenced. It was frightening to be so close to so much evil, but it was a good day.

Howard Ball, in sharing his experiences while living and working in Mississippi, confirms what we all know about making change, fighting racism, and achieving equity—we must rely on ourselves, concentrate on our immediate environments, and avail ourselves of every opportunity daily to make the deaths of racism and other forms of inequity a reality. We must accept that we can and must end racism. We cannot wait for others. We must step forward. We must model moral leadership for our children.

We make the mistake of viewing Mississippi as an anomaly, thereby excusing many of us from reconciling our relationships with inequity and racism. Howard's narrative and subsequent activity affirm that Missis-sippi and the rest of the country are kin. I recommend reading *Taking the Fight South* with an eye to how you can make anti-racist change as a parent, community member, citizen, and laborer. Pay attention to How-ard's work and explore the efforts, risks, and sacrifices made by his family and his fellow activists. Train your eyes on how Howard skillfully un-does the faulty and frail logic used by white supremacists he encoun-tered. Honestly self-reflect to see how you resemble the people in *Taking the Fight South* who pretend to be neutral, resist anti-racism efforts, or are belligerently against change. During his time in Mississippi, Howard's dedication and commitment to justice never waned. He understands and we should all understand that we have the power to make permanent and positive change. Stand up and march forward and live by the axiom that Howard lives by—extraordinary change comes through ordinary efforts.

Preface

Jewish communities, throughout history, wherever my people have lived, have always been, and still remain, some of the most reviled, hated, and despised minority groups of religious "outsiders." We Jews have been targeted as "enemies of the people" by most governments, whether democratic, monarchical, or autocratic. We Jews have been marked, by most people, both the learned and the ignorant, and their religious leaders, with a scarlet letter "J," forcibly crowded into ghettos, exiled, or—for millions of European Jews—crowded into empty cattle cars bound for the "east" in order to take a last shower.

When one reads a history of any period of world history, one generalization about my Jewish ancestors—and my Jewish friends today—was, and is, ever present. In a multitude of languages, the message was the same. "The Jews would always be outsiders, for somewhere in the roots of [nationalism,] populism and fundamentalism lurked a foreboding distrust of the foreigner, anyone who was not [say, Austrian, or] Southern, and not Christian and therefore alien to the sameness all around."[1]

We Jews are different because of our religious beliefs. Throughout history, as a well-known tribe of "outsiders," we have been marginalized and assaulted in so many ways. We have been denied citizenship rights.

There have always been, everywhere Jews wandered, employment prohibitions. We have been the scapegoat for all disasters that befell the country we were living in. And we have been banished from nation after nation because of our religious differences.

Through "all of modernity," before catastrophes engulfed them in their shtetls, Jews were asked the "Jewish question" by *goyim* (and asked it of themselves), a question that, in reality, "hovered menacingly over Jews in the West." What makes you Jewish? A majority casually mention religion, pointing "to rituals and prayers like the ones associated with the High Holy Days."[2]

For other Jews, "not so much. 'Religion doesn't play any part in my life in terms of how I live my life,' the comedian Larry David has said. 'But I don't think I've ever gone through a day in my life without hearing someone say the word "Jew" or saying it myself.'"[3] There is no agreement on the answer, other than saying, "I have absolutely nothing in common with Jews who answer incorrectly." (An old story reflects this reality. It is "about the Jew who is stranded alone on a desert island and builds two synagogues—the one he goes to, and the one he wouldn't be seen dead in.")[4]

We Jews are different in another fundamental way: we think differently. Judaism asks a Jew not only to observe and obey the law but also, much more important, we are charged to vigorously debate, discuss, and disagree with each other and, more dangerous for those who take their argument to the next level, oppose a public policy by taking political or legal action challenging its "constitutionality." There is, at the core of our religion, a moral belief, Albert Einstein reminded us, that is "incarnate in the Jewish people, that the life of the individual has value [only] as it aids in making the life of every living thing nobler and more beautiful."[5]

Einstein's epigram captures a major concept in Judaism, *tikkun olam* (repair the world), that has been interpreted by rabbis, over many centuries, as an elemental prescription for Jewish behavior. It is the idea that Jews bear responsibility not only for their own moral, spiritual, and material welfare but also for the welfare of society at large. Many contemporary rabbis tell their students *tikkun olam* refers to doing "Jewish social justice" and working for "the establishment of godly qualities throughout the world."[6]

Tikkun olam is, for me, always joined with my answering a few questions raised by the great Rabbi Hillel, who was a teacher in the first century BCE. Among his many teachings, two have stood out for me: (1) "Do not separate yourself from your community," and (2) "If I am not for myself, who will be for me? But if I am only for myself, who am I? If not now, when?"[7]

These two Jewish guides to behavior should be the symbiotic theme of a rabbi's conversation welcoming Bar and Bat Mitzvah young adults into the Jewish community. My rabbi, David B. Hollender, conveyed them to me in 1950 during my Bar Mitzvah. I was standing on the bimah[8] of the Mt. Eden Jewish Center, in the Bronx, listening to the rabbi's sermon. In wonderment, I realized that on this same Shabbos[9] morning, other young Bar Mitzvah *bochrim*,[10] all over the world, were reading the same weekly Torah *parsha*,[11] as we all, together spiritually, officially became Jews.

However divergent our answers are to the *goyim*'s "Jewish question," one response is never offered: race is not what makes us Jewish! Being Jewish is not a racial differentiation—although I know that untold millions across the history of the world believe that Jews are racially inferior compared to them. One really cannot take a caliper to a face to measure "Jewishness" in a person—although that, too, has occurred across history.

Tzvi Freeman, in a lively, perceptive essay, "Are Jews a 'Race'?," posted on the Chabad website in March 2019, starts with the assertion that a DNA test demonstrating typical Jewish DNA is "not a blank pass into the tribe. . . . Today there are African Jews, Japanese Jews, even Inuit Jews. It seems difficult to call such a mixture a 'race.' While there is a definite cluster of Jewish genes, plenty of people have these genes but aren't Jewish, and plenty don't have them and are. DNA does not make you a Jew. It is something much deeper."[12]

I am a Jew. My response to that "question" has not really changed. Prior to moving to Mississippi, my wife, Carol, and I were "Larry David Jews." But I realized at the Mt. Eden Center in 1950 that *tikkun olam* was in my DNA and in my soul. After we arrived in Starkville, Mississippi, this principle manifested itself mightily in the Magnolia State. There was a great need to restore justice before we arrived, and, sad to say, the need was still there after we left. But Carol and I knew and took comfort from the fact that our responses to the wrongs we saw in Mississippi were sincere efforts to "repair the world."

The core of my Jewishness is centered on the rabbi's words to me in 1950, more than seven decades ago. It is my belief in and commitment to *tikkun olam*, accompanied by my answering Rabbi Hillel's existential questions, that defines me as human and as a Jew.

The reality for us Jews—the "others," the forever wandering, and wanting, Jews—is the struggle to live as humans should live. As one of history's infamous religious "outsiders," we Jews have found that no matter how hard we worked "to be accepted by the dominant [political, social, and religious] culture," it has not worked. The earth rejected our attempts to plant our roots. The *goyim* see our labors, but all they see is that it "looks like you're trying too hard. [Jews] always feel, or imagine others feel, that you're still a bit . . . funny."

This continual misunderstanding, fear, and hatred of the Jew has a name, anti-Semitism. The word was first coined by a European in the 1880s, but its essence is ageless. Even in America, it is well known. It is not a stranger to us Jews. America's history is replete with examples of all kinds of discriminations against Jews and other unwanted "outsider" religious, racial, and ethnic immigrant groups, including state and national discriminatory laws and customs, and not excluding violence, arson, and murder.

Beginning with the passage of a 1924 discriminatory immigration bill, the Johnson-Reed Immigration Act, Congress established a national origins quota system restricting immigrants from southern Europe (Catholics) and eastern Europe (Jews). The law reflected the nation's racism, its anti-Catholic and anti Semitic prejudices, its fear of anarchists, socialists, communists, and all the "others" seen as different, as inferior to, the citizens of America. (In the late nineteenth century, Chinese and Japanese were barred by Congress from entering the nation.)

It wasn't until 1965 that Congress, spurred on by President Lyndon B. Johnson, passed a landmark bill, the Immigration and Nationality Act, which changed the immigration law, replacing the country quota scheme with a qualitative system that favored unifying families and attracting skilled immigrants. (In the past decade the federal government has shifted backward to using religious [Islam], ethnic [Hispanics], and country-of-origin [majority Muslim nations] indicators to restrict or deny entry into America.)

The legislatively enacted restrictive immigrant and refugee quota was, of course, not the only discrimination. Quotas, categorical rejection, discrimination, and murder of the feared "others" continue to be major features of American culture and politics. Restrictive quotas against Jews and other minorities (including women) were employed at Harvard, Yale, and other elite institutions of higher learning, including admissions to medical, law, and other professional programs. They were lifted only after World War II.

Outright racial discrimination, however, was, and still remains, the center of gravity for our nation. America was a "Jim Crow" nation until Jim Crow laws were formally ended when Congress passed the Civil Rights Act of 1964, the radical Voting Rights Act of 1965, and the Civil Rights Act of 1968 (especially Titles VIII and IX, commonly called "the Fair Housing Act"). (America's local customs and folkways still account for private prejudice and discrimination.)

Up through the 1970s, across the country, signs and humans greeted Jews, Catholics, Blacks, Asians, Muslims, and all "others," including animals, entering hotels, motels, movie theaters, country clubs, and restaurants with a humiliating message: "No Jews, Negroes, etc., or dogs welcome." My father, a plumber in New York City, was barred from joining the union because he was Jewish. It was only in the twilight of his life, the 1970s, after the union rules were changed, that he was allowed to get a union card.

Growing up in New York City in the 1940s and 1950s, I did not run into the strident anti-Semitism my father and my relatives experienced a decade or so earlier. For four decades I lived in Jewish ghettos in the Bronx and on Long Island. Most of that time, I was shielded from hate and discrimination.

I went to a campus (Hunter College, Bronx Campus, now Herbert Lehman College) of the very egalitarian City University of New York

(CUNY). There, from the mid-1950s to 1960, I initially experienced the hatred people felt about Blacks; in 1959, for example, I was spat upon and called a "n****r lover" when I, along with some other college students, picketed Woolworth's on Fordham Road in the Bronx in support of Black university students who were sitting in at a North Carolina Woolworth's demanding integration of the lunch counters.

My second searing encounter with discrimination—racial and, for the first time, religious intolerance—was when I went to basic training at Lackland Air Force Base, San Antonio, Texas. While at Hunter College, I joined the Air National Guard, and in the summer of 1958 I went to Texas for two months of training. This was my first trip outside the shtetl. It was the first time I flew in an airplane. It was also the first time I saw "creepy-crawlies" ten times bigger than our Bronx residents, the tenement-dwelling cockroaches. And at Lackland Air Force Base for the first time I experienced racial and religious bigotry.

My barracks contained sixty airmen: eight of us were from New York State (including me and three other Jews, counting Bruce Farkas, whose father owned a major Bronx department store, Alexander's), eight young strong airmen were from Hawaii, and the rest, more than forty, came from Mississippi and Alabama. For the very first time in my life, I found myself experiencing very different cultural, religious, and racial attitudes, as well as trying to figure out how to respond—or not—when their actions crossed the line.

From the get-go, the Southerners began to curse the "n****rs" in their very own unwarranted drawl. By the next midday, however, before chow, the Hawaiians gave all of us a short presentation of their proficiency in the martial arts by splitting a number of two-by-fours in half. After a few minutes, the group's spokesman offered their services to their new and dear Southern friends. No more verbal harangues were directed at the Hawaiians afterward.

I was their next target. In basic training at that time, each barracks selected "chapel guides," one airman each from among the Protestants and the Catholics. When Jews were among them, they, too, had a chapel guide. I was the chosen Jew. All denominations wore the same small badge, a blue tag, with white lettering spelling "CHAPEL GUIDE" in capital letters. It had to be worn at all times; suddenly I became the only Jew guide during that particular basic training cycle. Our tasks were mostly honorific: we worked with the minister or rabbi to prepare weekly religious activities on base, and nightly each guide said a prayer from their holy book before "lights out."

Based on the number of coreligionists, I was the last to offer a meditation. Using the tiny, brown-cover military WWII edition of the Old Testament (with a brief message from the commander-in-chief, President Franklin Delano Roosevelt!), I began reading a verse. As soon as I began, the anti-Semites began calling me names I honestly had never heard directed at me ever: dirty kike, Christ killer, among other nouns. What to do? I read my verse, and then the next one, and then the next, until someone shouted, "shut the fuck up, shit face!" As that slur did not contain an overt condemnation of my religion, I quickly said: "I'll stop when all of you shut up!" Amazingly, they shut up and I stopped praying.

But I figured they knew that I would drone on and on while they threw epithets at me in the darkened billet. The upshot: some of us, the "others," were in a hostile environment, although one (a large military base) that I hoped minimized the threat of violence. The Hawaiians and I had sent messages to our fellow comrades in arms that suggested that we, in our own manner, would not tolerate their behavior. The Southerners were smart enough to be aware of what we could do to silence their mouths: break two-by-fours and conduct a Jew filibuster until pitch black silence prevailed.

This was a pivotal moment in my life. Although I experienced racial hatred when I marched for racial justice for southern Blacks, I had never confronted anti-Semitism! I had to travel to Texas to witness a mass of forty Southern racists, in a darkened barracks, ginned up for the verbal assaults on Jews and Blacks. I did not know it then, but our move to Mississippi nearly two decades later provided my family with an exponential enhancement of this clash of personal history experiences and values.

My first teaching job, in 1965, was as a faculty member of the political science department at Hofstra University, in Nassau County, New York. It was a campus primarily of first-generation Italian and Jewish students, and many Jewish faculty. Initially we lived in Hempstead, and in 1968 we moved to Stony Brook, in Suffolk County, while teaching at Hofstra, about thirty-five miles east of the campus.

Ironically, just a month before we moved to Mississippi in 1976, the Stony Brook Fire Department (a volunteer department of one hundred members, including me and a Jewish friend, Bob Weinstein) received a signal 13, house fire. It was a night call, in the early a.m.

A farm building, the main house, was on fire. We arrived quickly but by that time the house was engulfed in flames and there was little we could do to save the residence. At the scene the owner found a crudely printed note attached to the mailbox from the Ku Klux Klan's Suffolk County Klavern.[13] They burned the house down because the owners just sold the property to "n****rs"! I remember thinking that fear and hatred of the "others" was not limited to the South.

I read that in the South, as one native white Southerner wrote, there existed an

> unthinking prejudice [that] extended not only to blacks but also to Jews, Catholics, and Gypsies. . . .
>
> [In the South] we feared others who were in any way different from us. I didn't even know a Catholic or Jew until we moved to Atlanta. . . . And although blacks lived among us, they were fundamentally, profoundly [inferior], or so I was constantly told."[14]

But it was only when I was offered a tenured position as professor at Mississippi State University that I began to examine the reality of anti-Semitism in the South. My family was not very religious; we rarely went to synagogue for services. Indeed, Carol and I quit the local reform synagogue because of a disagreement we had with the rabbi.

However, we wanted our girls to have religious training and to become Bat Mitzvah when they were thirteen years old. And they were rapidly approaching that age. Too, in New York we were members of a large Jewish ghetto in the "M" section of Levitt homes in Stony Brook.[15] With the exception of the men and women of the fire department, most of our friends were Jewish; all of them were white. Moving to Mississippi would be a radical change in these social demographics for all of us.

So Carol and I examined the question of anti-Semitism in the South intensely. Did it exist in Mississippi? Was it a manageable place to live and work for Jews? Or was its racism as palpable as the virulent racism in other Deep South states?

I decided to ask my dear friend (since 1966) Tom Lauth, a colleague at Hofstra who had moved to Georgia to teach budgeting and politics at Georgia State University. Tom, his wife, Jean, and their four boys camped with us in New York; whenever our teaching schedules aligned, Tom and I shared the drive into Hofstra from our Suffolk County towns. (During a few winters, when Tom drove, we cracked the car windows because we suspected there was an exhaust leak somewhere.) They are devout Catholics; they are also civil liberties and equal justice defenders; and they were living in the Deep South for a number of years.

We spoke at length with our friends about how the "others" functioned in a very different cultural environment. Their advice was very helpful: racism was an integral part of Southern life. It was tangible. You could not escape it if you were a minority. Blacks, Catholics, Jews, and all "others" had two choices: (1) to moderate their deepest feelings about race and religious hatred and discrimination across the social, cultural, political, religious, and economic environments, but not to abandon those feelings totally, or (2) to leave the South as soon as they could because it was too grating to live and to raise kids in such an alien and alienating environment.

Not being Jewish, Tom and Jean could not give us insights into the Jewish experience in the South. For that reason alone, it was important for Carol and me to visit Starkville and the Mississippi State campus to try to find answers to these questions. After I was offered the job, we drove to Georgia to drop our girls off at the Lauths. Carol and I then traveled to Mississippi on I-20 and US 82, passing through Birmingham and then Tuscaloosa, crossing the Tenn-Tom Waterway into Mississippi, finally arriving at Starkville.

Once there, we sought out folk who could respond to our questions about the Jewish community in this part of the state and about anti-Semitism in Mississippi. We spoke to some of the few Jews living in Starkville as well as other religious minorities living there, especially members of the local Catholic Church (some of whom were faculty in the political science department), about life in the Magnolia State.

Most told me that although there was visible intolerance, it was directed primarily at the Blacks living in Mississippi. The "others"—that is, we Catholics and Jews—were generally tolerated by the Protestant majorities in Oktibbeha County only because we were white. However, Eli Evans, in his classic book *The Provincials*,[16] did indirectly warn us about the pervasive attitude of a majority of Southern whites. They believe, he wrote, that the "Jew is just a n****r turned inside out."[17]

Southern Jews attribute the lack of personal anti-Semitic incidents to the presence of the Negro, whom they refer to as "the lightning rod for prejudice. The poor white feels an economic competitiveness with the Negro that he does not feel with the Jew. . . . Whatever else one can say about gentile attitudes toward Jews, Jews are considered white men first and live most of their lives as part of the white majority."[18]

The noted Southern historian W. J. Cash, decades earlier, had this to say about Jews and Catholics in the South: "The Jew, with his universal refusal to be assimilated, is everywhere the eternal Alien[, while] the Catholic, even more than the Jew, has stood as the intolerable Alien."[19] We wondered whether this view of these two minorities was still a valid one.

One young Jewish mother we met in Starkville told us about the Jewish Camp Henry Jacobs, located in Utica, Mississippi. Throughout the year, there were "small temples weekends" for Jewish parents and children. On these weekends, four or five a year, Jews from across Mississippi and Louisiana and southern Arkansas would meet and enjoy interacting with their coreligionists.

During the summer months, the camp was open to Jewish children from these states. Across the South, I found out, there were a number of these regional camps—in North Carolina, Georgia, and elsewhere—that provided these very important programs for relatively isolated Jews living in small towns and cities.

This information was encouraging, though it raised questions. Why was it necessary to send children to the Jewish camps? Was that a reflection of the "otherness" Jews experienced elsewhere? Would Jewish youngsters find it difficult or uncomfortable to attend non-Jewish camps?

What about toleration of Jews and other minorities in Brownie or Girl Scout troops?

These questions were unanswered when we left Stony Brook for Starkville. But still, after four days in Starkville, meeting with members of the town, a few native Jews, and the university communities, we picked up our trio of soon-to-be Southern belles and returned to Stony Brook.

This book tries to answer these and other questions dealing with how and whether religious and cultural and political outsiders, "others," like my family, could manage our lives in Mississippi. While we knew we had to adapt to some of the cultural norms and behaviors of our new community; we also knew that there were some situations where we could not change our behavior at all. Life in Mississippi was a very human balancing act for the five of us. We found out so much about life and living in what we saw as frontier Judaism. We not only experienced a very different kind of religious experience; we also experienced life, joy, sadness, living, and death, in totally different cultural, political, social, and racial front lines.

Living in Mississippi we experienced the raw, naked power of the white power elite working 24/7/365 days to evade, avoid, and delay doing the right thing for the Black citizens of the state. When we left, I said, "Thank God that in 1982, Mississippi is an outlier state." It was one of a small number of states that had no difficulty using state power to destroy the lives of tens of thousands of Black people and poor people and other "undesirables." But segregation time was running out. The events since then have disproven my hopes and belief in the arc of justice. And I and many other Jews in America are reminded, almost daily, that our constitutional system, with a vast array of individual rights, liberties, and responsibilities, is not necessarily permanent.

Our solid, safe, permanent system of equal justice under the law is perishable! We have to do more than hope that our society will rebound and return to decency. We have to activate again and again a commitment to *tikkun olam*.

Life in Mississippi was never boring. Every year we had to resolve new issues of importance that tested our commitment to our basic values. However, as they say in Mississippi, the "good Lord [was] willin' and the creek didn't rise" for us during our Mississippi years—although our poor car found many of the ever-popular Oktibbeha County drainage ditches to back into. Let us all do what we can to avoid the much bigger obstacles to safety than the ditches in Mississippi.

Howard Ball
Richmond, Vermont
January 2020

Acknowledgments

I have written a number of books since 1970. All had an acknowledgments section that followed the scholarly norms and protocols. Included were thank-yous to special collections librarians, who always seemed to find a document I was not aware of, and to scholars who helped me in all phases of my research, from the very beginning of my project, to reviewing preliminary drafts of book chapters presented at the annual regional and national political science meetings, to, finally, giving the manuscript a final critical review before my publisher's fire-breathing copyeditor seized control of my work and did a job on it. Finally, I always thanked my close friends in the academy who shared my good and bad days with me in this business of writing. It always ended (as does this book) with a loving appreciation to my dear family—including a number of dogs, horses, and, in Montana, a grateful nod to the brown and rainbow trout in the magnificent Rock Creek—for allowing me the time to travel, re-search, write—and rewrite—the book.

Taking the Fight South: Chronicle of a Jew's Battle for Civil Rights in Mississippi is a very different book in a number of ways. What follows is a retelling of the conception and the birth of this book—an almost four-decade-long pregnancy. First of all, it is a story about *my* life experiences confronting racial, ethnic, and religious discrimination—in my family, in college, in the US Air Force, in the Bronx, in Stony Brook, New York—but especially during our family's six-year stay in Starkville, Mississippi, where I taught at Mississippi State University. I do have a small number of footnotes in *Taking the Fight South*, but they are used to provide a social and political context for—to *bear witness to*—my experiences as a Jew confronting hateful racial and religious bigotry and discrimination in Mississippi.

Second, unlike every other book I have written, *Taking the Fight South* had a very long gestation period, toward the end of which there were, figuratively, a few near-miscarriages.

In 1982 we left Mississippi for the University of Utah, where I was hired to be the chair of the Department of Political Science. During our near-decade-long stay in Utah, I regularly confronted my Mississippi experiences because I continued my volunteer work as a member of the board of the Utah affiliate of the American Civil Liberties Union (ACLU). The case work of the Utah ACLU organization was very different than Mississippi's litigation. In Utah, the prime focus was litigating cases involving the First Amendment's clause prohibiting "establishment of religion" ("the Establishment Clause"). Very few voting rights or double-celling cases were entering Utah state and federal courts. There was, however, a glut of cases involving hiring of Mormon faculty without following the hiring protocols of the US Equal Employment Opportunity Commission (EEOC).

I got into the habit of jotting down stories of my Mississippi battles. Why? The Utah "establishment" cases were easy, noncontroversial ones that our affiliate won easily and for which we received legal fees mandated by the court. This financial reward we garnered paid the ACLU's bills.[1] Frankly, while sitting and listening to the same kind of case repeated over and over, I was bored and began writing memos to myself about Mississippi's powerholders' unwillingness to even symbolically move the state toward accepting equality and equal justice under law.

Very soon, I began to understand the dynamics behind our family's responses to the open, blatant inequities surrounding the five of us in the Magnolia State. I realized that we had encountered hateful thoughts and actions of "true believers" in bigotry, that we responded with fear or anxiety or anger, and that our anger sometimes triggered confrontations.

Years later, I began to edit these notes, which documented our experiences with our Jewish community; with my refereeing; with Black educators, parents, and college-age students; with university colleagues who criticized my efforts to recruit more Blacks and females into our graduate program; with the Klan and with the political behavior of the ACLU's leaders; and, centrally, with the ways in which Mississippi's governing class—the hundreds of mayors, city managers, local government lawyers, and legislators—creatively, proudly, and boldly used the "states' rights" argument (embedded in the Tenth Amendment of the US Constitution) to maintain a political, social, and economic society whose foundation was violent, raw, and unadulterated racial discrimination.

By the last decade of the twentieth century, I was the dean of the College of Arts and Sciences at the University of Vermont with a first draft of my battles for justice in Mississippi that no one had asked for! Now what was I going to do?² Since I was not asked by an editor to write a book based on my experiences, I pulled together a manuscript and sent it, over a decade, 1995–2006, to two types of publishing houses: (1) two companies publishing Jewish series touching on Jewish culture, religion, anti-Semitism, and sociology, and (2) two university presses in the Deep South, University of Alabama Press and University Press of Mississippi. None showed any interest.

And so I went on with my life; however, I did pull together another version, called *Hey, Rabbi!*—Rabbi was my football-officiating nickname—printed a few copies, and over the years shared the manuscript with friends in Vermont and Arizona.

My book, I have been told, is a memoir.³ *How does one write a memoir?* I had no inkling. I had never even thought of writing *that* kind of book! In bookstores, I rarely picked up a memoir of a movie star or some other notable public figure. I never purchased one, never read one. This genre was way beyond my reading comfort zone, which was limited to nonfiction books and only *very good* mysteries or spy novels.

At this time, 2018, I was a reviewer of a book the University of Notre Dame Press was interested in publishing. I was in communication with the editor-in-chief, Eli Bortz, and we passed a few pleasant emails. I decided to ask Eli for some advice about this *Hey, Rabbi* "memoir" kicking around my study. "Could I send you an outline of the manuscript," I asked Eli, "in order to get some words of wisdom about it?" He agreed and I immediately sent him the table of contents and the first chapter. He liked the material and asked me to send him the manuscript when I finished it. I simply said, "It's finished, I'll send it to you today." These interactions with Eli began in late July 2019, more than one year ago! And only thirty-eight years since we left Mississippi.

————

My "thank you" list is for all of you who have partnered with me in my family's wanderings across America for a half century or more. Hofstra University was my first professorship. And it was there that, in 1966, I met one of my two "brothers," Tom Lauth. For more than fifty years, we have camped together with our families, team-taught political behavior wearing white lab coats, ridden together from our towns in Suffolk County, New York, to the Hofstra campus, and shared the high and low points of our lives and the life of our constitutional republic.

I met my other "brother" ten years later, when we led a two-RV caravan[4] from Stony Brook to Starkville, Mississippi. Charles Lowery was the associate dean of the College of Arts and Sciences and a history professor at Mississippi State. We were the same age, born in 1937. He and his family, Suzie and the three boys, were our neighbors in a delightful area of town called Sherwood Forest. And it was "Chaz" who took a New York City Jew under his wing and taught me how to survive in the state, how to identify possums, or how to use a chain saw to chop a tree down, even though, at times, Charles's falling trees took down a power line or two. Most of all, he taught me what courage means when one confronts white racism. Charles supported the department's innovative efforts to recruit Blacks and women into our graduate program. He and Suzie were compatriots in these continuing battles. (Suzie recruited me to join her on the board of a small Black church in Starkville.)

After leaving the state I found out about the Lowery's battles against white racists who sought to maintain racial intolerance in Mississippi.

One effort was a plan to destroy the public school system in a draconian response to the 1954 *Brown* opinion of the US Supreme Court invalidating separate public schools for Blacks and whites. After *Brown*, the Mississippi legislature, supported by the governor, proposed a state constitutional amendment that would dismantle the public school system.

When that failed, the racists moved to plan B, the establishment of a private school system for white students. Between 1966 and 1970, 115 private schools opened across the state. A Mississippi legislator told a *New York Times* reporter in 1970, "What we're going to wind up with eventually, is a private school for the white kids and a state-subsidized school system for the n****rs." In 1969, the Starkville Academy opened, with the goal of destroying the public schools in the city. Charles and Suzie were towers of strength as they organized a Citizens Committee for Public Education to rally good citizens of the school district to support Starkville's public schools. More than 1100 residents signed a petition supporting public schools.

The upshot: the Starkville public school system has become one of the finest in the state. For more than a decade my "brother" and Suzie fought to protect and to improve public schools. Ostracized, they felt the bitterness their townsfolk threw their way; they had to find yet another church that welcomed them. At the memorial service after Charles died last year, I noted that Charles, Suzie, and I were "ohavi zedek," the Hebrew phrase meaning "lovers of justice." Both Tom and Charles, with Jeannie and Suzie, were lovers of justice. I adopted them because we all just *had* to confront the evil of racism.

A postscript: While I was still in Starkville, Starkville High School had its very first integrated senior prom. A Lowery was involved in this shocking event. But it was Charles's oldest son, Tom, a basketball star, who persuaded his Black teammates and their dates to crash the segregated senior prom at the Starkville Country Club. That event ended Starkville's practice of holding segregated proms; however, the Country Club did not host the senior prom afterward.

I had other friends in Starkville, both in the department and beyond. Two men helped me greatly when I became head of the department in 1978. One was Bill Collins, director of the John C. Stennis Institute of

Government. While at the University of Georgia, he was one of the founders of the national Public Administration Association. He provided me with the information and values associated with the discipline of public administration when I took over the helm. Always genuine, sensitive, and responsive to the inequities in the public service, he was my invaluable senior mentor.

Bill Giles was my other department mentor, the junior partner. He, too, came from the University of Georgia's PhD program in public administration. But he is from New Orleans and is the top chef of the delicacies of the sea, creole style. He taught me to appreciate the essential ethical principles professionals must possess when they go to work in government. He was also a preacher for a good earth before it was "in." Whenever I returned to Mississippi, I always had a place to call home.

Dale Krane was a colleague of mine at State who joined Tom and me in our ongoing examination of how the 1965 Voting Rights Act was being implemented in Georgia and Mississippi. His area of expertise is intergovernmental relations, and he provided the insights that enabled us to factually examine the interactions between state and federal agents responsible for managing the law in each jurisdiction covered by the Voting Rights Act.

He was a good friend; I will never forget one Friday night during football season. The three of us were presenting one of the first assessments of how the Voting Rights Act was implemented. The Southern Political Science Association was meeting in New Orleans, and our presentation was scheduled for Saturday midmorning. Tom flew in on Friday morning. Dale and I didn't because I was a football referee with a game scheduled Friday night. I convinced Dale to drive with me to the game I was officiating and then, after the game, drive the rest of the way. We stopped in time for the 7:30 game. I was in my black and white striped shirt, white pants, yellow penalty flags, with my whistle in my hand. By 10:00 p.m. the game was over, and without me changing my uniform, we hit the road south to the meeting. We arrived four hours later, checked in close to 3:00 a.m., and dashed up to the room and, for me, a desperately needed shower. Tom was asleep and when we were ready to call it a day, Dale and I noticed that there was only one bed. I grabbed the bed and

Dale was left with the couch. We slept well, and at the meeting we had a very good discussion with the group attending our presentation. On the drive back, Dale said that he enjoyed the night-life in rural Mississippi, but for him once was enough.

Meryl Schmitt was another Mississippi friend. He was the pastor of the Catholic Church in town, St. Joseph's, and we always found time to talk about religious matters, including the horrors of racial hatred. He signed me up to talk to his annual confirmation class about the Jewish perception of the Messiah. Merle attended services when our two older daughters were Bat Mitzvahed in Temple B'nai Israel, in Columbus, Mississippi. And he was the coach of the St. Joseph's softball team; he gave me my special softball shirt: it had a Star of David between the "St." and the "Joseph's." I wore it with pride for another decade, until it literally wore out.

Marilyn and Al Cohen are two other Southern friends. Originally from New Jersey, they moved to Tupelo years before our move south. He owned a Hallmark Gift Shop in the mall, and the two of them worked hard to lose their money when they went to Las Vegas. We got to know them very well when we inquired about attending Jewish High Holy Day services in their conservative synagogue in Tupelo. They graciously hosted us when we attended services. We met on occasion to visit the Henry Jacobs Camp in Utica, Mississippi. It was the meeting place for Jewish families living in small towns across four southern states to get together for a weekend. Their two children, along with our Sheryl, went to the Jacobs summer camp while we were living in the state. We still bump into them at Bar Mitzvahs and weddings.

My students, in New York, Mississippi, Utah, Vermont, New Hampshire, and overseas in Sofia, Bulgaria, and Szeged, Hungary, were always and everywhere the providers of my greatest happiness in the academy. Whether it was the banter in a bus filled with my Hofstra students on the way to my annual three-day visit to the US Supreme Court (where, on the bus ride, they were forced to watch *Casablanca* because none had *ever* seen the greatest movie of all time) or, decades later, discussions with my Vermont Law School students on a bus to the same destination (whom I did not require to see my favorite movie), I always loved to talk with students. On the latter bus ride, we talked about the new justice, Clarence Thomas, and the spectacle of the clash between him and Anita Hill during his confirmation hearings a half year earlier. Little did I know that one of my best students would end a discussion the students were having with Justice Thomas by standing up to stop the justice with a cry-out.

What led her to interrupt the jurist? Thomas was talking about his own law school experiences, and he was telling my students how his law school buddies would talk incessantly after classes, until "the beer got warm, and the pizza got cold!" When she heard these words, she stood up and cried out: "You're a liar! You told the senators you never spent time with your friends talking about the law and legal issues facing the court!" With that, Justice Thomas stood up and quickly exited the room. One of his law clerks, Laura Ingraham, held the door open for him. The young law school student was terribly embarrassed about her outburst, but I laughed and said, "But you were right to call him out." On the way back to Vermont we discussed the politicization of the judicial nomination process and the evident need of some nominees to lie to get a lifetime appointment to a federal court. Wonderful ride back to the Green Mountains.

The most fascinating students were the many undergraduates in my civil rights classes at Mississippi State. Coming to the Deep South after living in assorted Jewish ghettos in New York was an absolute mind-blowing educational experience for me. I learned so much about the dynamics of the white and Black students sharing the classroom. So did the students. We held serious class discussions on the laws and the cases we were analyzing.

Beyond discussing case law and the meaning of the Fourteenth Amendment's "equal protection" clause, both Black and white students expressed unadorned feelings—anxieties, fears, and hurts. Some of my students were related to the Klansmen who went to federal prison for conspiring to take the liberty of civil rights workers in Mississippi. Sid Salter was one of those students. He grew up in Philadelphia, Mississippi; I first met him when I officiated a football game in town. He was not talkative about his relationship with Klansmen. But he did share stories about growing up in such a hostile environment. I have known Sid since that game in 1977; I've visited him whenever I was in Starkville. He has been one of a number of my students who were of immense help when I was writing about "Preacher" Killen, the Klansman who orchestrated the murders of the trio of workers from the Congress of Racial Equality (CORE) in June 1964.

Donna Ladd was another student in my classes at Mississippi State. She was the daughter of two illiterate parents (her dad was an alcoholic womanizer who seriously mistreated Donna's mom). Donna's mom, who never attended school, insisted that Donna get the education her mother missed. Donna's focus on education was laser-sharp. She excelled. She had no known relatives in the Klan, but she knew Sheriff Price growing up in town. He was the watch repair person in Philadelphia, and over the years, Donna and her mom would visit Price to buy batteries for their watches or purchase an inexpensive watch.

She was then, and still remains, a strong activist for civil rights. Donna hated how brutal the white power holders were in their near total control of the Black community in Mississippi. However, at that time, the 1970s, there were no state newspapers that spoke truth to power about the bigoted and discriminating white men who ran the state.

After graduating from Mississippi State in 1983, she went to New York City and earned a graduate degree at Columbia University's journalism school, then worked two decades as a reporter for the *Village Voice*, a fiercely independent newspaper in the city. Donna's goal was to return to Mississippi and, in Jackson, create an alternative weekly newspaper. In 2002, she did just that. As she said on her website, "I write about racism/whiteness, poverty, gender, violence and the criminal-justice system. I regularly contribute long-form features and essays to The Guardian, and I'm the editor-in-chief of the Jackson Free Press [an award-winning freely distributed community newspaper], which I co-founded in 2002 after returning to my home state after 18 years in exile."[5] I've spent time in Jackson with Donna and a few of her muckraking reporters. We also worked together in 2005, when we were covering the Killen murder trial in Philadelphia, Mississippi. Donna is a human dynamo for justice. She is a dues-paying member of my Ohavi Zedek group. Way to go, Donna!

I have also been a matchmaker for a number of students from the South. Two very bright prelaw students at State, Adrienne Pakis and Bill

Gillon, tied the knot after graduation. I have known the two of them and their two children since their 1981 graduation. Adrienne is an active Democratic Party leader in the Memphis, Tennessee, area; Bill has worked as a lawyer for the US Department of Agriculture and is now a senior official in the Cotton Council. We were continually in touch with them when they were visiting their daughter, an undergraduate at Dartmouth. They have also visited us at our home in Vermont.

Some of my students invited Carol and me to their weddings. One invite in particular stands out in my mind. One of my students at Vermont Law School invited us to her wedding. While in Montego Bay with my sister, I bumped into her in a restaurant. She joined us for dinner and reminded me of the wedding. I told her we would be coming. We never made the wedding. She was scheduled to fly in from Jamaica on September 11, 2001, for the nuptials a few days later. There were no flights; the wedding was put off!

Still other students eagerly volunteered to work with me on research projects I was engaged in at the time. At the University of Utah, students assisted me while I was researching a controversial legal issue in the federal district court in Salt Lake City. Downwinders, a large group of Utah citizens who lived in southern Utah "downwind" of the 100 above-ground atom bomb tests at the Nevada Test Site in the 1950s, north of Las Vegas, brought a wrongful death suit against the federal government because the federal Atomic Energy Commission (AEC) "lied" to citizens when the agency said, in print and on radio, that watching an atomic bomb test was as dangerous as having your dentist take an X-ray of your teeth. "Enjoy the spectacle," was the message. Very soon, University of Utah epidemiologists were finding clusters of leukemia in southern Utah, leading to the deaths of many downwinders.

Ken Verdoia, a graduate student in political science (who was also a well-known broadcaster with the Utah PBS affiliate), volunteered to investigate the AEC while working in Washington, DC. I accepted his offer and had him try to look at the AEC documents in Washington that addressed the public health dimension of the testing program. His work provided me with a host of papers showing that the AEC had known that exposure to the radiated fallout would lead to health hazards but had considered the cost acceptable because America was distancing itself from the Russians.

Ken, a wonderful guitar player, was a godsend for me. So was another PhD student, Kate Greene. She had followed me to Utah after receiving a master's degree in public administration at Mississippi State. Knowing of my keen interest in the downwinders tragedy, she volunteered to do some interviews with a few of the downwinders. She also had an excellent interview with Utah's governor, Scott M. Matheson, about remedies for the injured citizens.

Another student of mine at the University of Vermont, Laryn Ivy, was a brilliant young scholar. She loved the law and went to DC with my class to visit the Supreme Court. After graduation, she entered the University of Virginia School of Law. While in the area, Laryn became my go-between with Associate Justice William J. Brennan. I was in the process of writing my biography of Justice Thurgood Marshall, and Justice Brennan was his very close friend. Laryn was able to assist me with my interactions with Brennan. We have continued our friendship. Carol and I were invited to her wedding in Newport, Rhode Island, and every year we exchange cards greeting the new year. She has three lovely children and still finds time to dip into books about the federal courts.

I have had the good fortune to know a handful of academic leaders and have learned much from them about the important values of integrity, patience, good humor, honesty, and the courage to do what one believes is right. Three remain in my memory and in my being: Dean Harry Levy, President Jim McComas, and Academic Vice President Irwin Altman.

Harry Levy was the dean of students at Hunter College–Uptown in the Bronx[6] when I was an undergraduate there in the late 1950s. I was a student activist, primarily focused on the horrors of race discrimination and the raw, unapologetic violence employed by the white supremacists to maintain the Southern states' racial oppression. He had a standing agreement with activists like me before an event took place. Sit down with Harry and talk about the activity: How many people? All of them from the Hunter College community? Any townies? Time of day, activities? Need for extra security? And other such questions. It was a very

xxxviii   Acknowledgments

comfortable session; he was always soft-spoken and courteous, and they were generally short, fifteen-to-twenty-minute sessions. In chapter 4 I discuss an incident that occurred during my last semester at Hunter that illustrated the character of my dean.

I always remembered the way this humane college administrator handled a person all himself. He knew how I felt, standing there, lonely, beneath the American flag, protesting the take-cover-exercise required by the state. And so, intentionally, Dean Levy slowed his pace so that the all-clear siren beat him to me. While I was not the best budgeteer in my years as administrator, I regularly applied Dean Levy's playbook when I had to deal with a situation involving someone within a hair of losing control. Dean Levy was a true *mensch*.

Jim McComas was the president of Mississippi State University during my entire stay. We both arrived in Starkville in the same year. (We were part of the entering class of professors of 1976.) I did not get to know McComas until I became head of the Department of Political Science. After that promotion, I was making plans to renovate our master's program in public administration. He very quickly heard about our efforts to recruit Blacks and women to enter our graduate program, and he supported the costs we incurred when traveling to predominantly Black undergraduate colleges located in states surrounding us. He also hosted weekend gatherings we ran for the senior administrators of the historic colleges that were part of our new network. And when students from these campuses visited Mississippi State, McComas was always available to meet our young visitors. He and the office of the dean of the College of Arts and Sciences were the strongest supporters of our efforts to integrate our degree programs. Indeed, on some occasions, given resistance from some administrative quarters, it seemed like McComas, Lowery, and Dean Lyle Behr were the only backup support for our efforts.

We became friends. The president appreciated all our efforts to expand the minority population attending State. And it wasn't until one of my last days on campus that I found out about Jim's decency. It was a final/goodbye visit in his office, and we were talking about the difficulties my family ran into because our Jewishness was not hidden. I told him how, over the past two years, we received wake-up calls from the local Klansmen in the early morning. But, I remarked, we received hardly any threatening letters. McComas laughed loudly. Walking to his desk, he pulled out a file at least four inches wide with hate letters demanding that he remove the "Jew n****r lover"[7] from campus, or else the writers would! I was flabbergasted. I asked why he didn't speak to me. He said it was his responsibility to handle the haters. He simply did not want to bother me with this junk mail!

We continued to talk after I left. He invited me to visit him at his subsequent administrative venues, as president of Virginia Polytechnic Institute and State University and president of the University of Toledo. His last position was as president at Ohio University. While there, Jim succumbed to cancer and died in 1993. I received a "farewell" note from him weeks before he passed. I cherish it.

Dr. Irwin Altman was the social sciences dean when I arrived in Utah in 1982 to chair the political science department. He was promoted to academic vice president less than two years later, and I was selected to be the next dean of the Social Sciences College. I remember a comment made by one of the staff in the political science department when these appointments were made. She wasn't surprised at this turn of events, because, after all, "they're both from the Lions of Judah tribe!"

Little did she know the real story! Irv and I are natives of New York, both born in the Bronx, both Jewish, and, topping the list, both graduates of the same high school, Taft High School, 170th Street, right off the Grand Concourse. Of course, we did not know each other at the time. (Irv was older and graduated from Taft eight years before me.)

For me, Irv was both a master problem solver and a resolute person after he reached a decision. He carefully marshaled all the facts and measured the character of the humans involved in the problem. These two factors were needed and had to be in front of him before he made a decision. He was like a scientist working to find the cure for a chronic illness. Find the facts. Know the environment. Weigh the data. Reach judgment. Gather data and analyze carefully, check and recheck your findings, and then let the result speak for itself.

He was, when we met, an internationally recognized behavioral psychologist who assiduously made time for his first love, research. We shared a commitment to doing research while doing the necessary administrative work in a way that met the expectations of the two tasks. It was unusual for administrators to carry a briefcase loaded with *both* research files and budget data; the ability to manage these two responsibilities concurrently was, I mentioned to Gloria (Irv's wife) on occasion, owing to an elixir found in the Bronx: "the pure water we drank when we were going to Taft."

I took many of Irv's qualities when I became a dean, both at Utah and at the University of Vermont. One word of caution I received from him has stayed with me. We were on a search committee to find the new director of the University of Utah's prestigious Hinckley Institute of Politics. There were two finalists for the very public position: a former, *extremely popular* mayor of Salt Lake City and a very personable senior political scientist with a sterling C.V. and experience in state politics. We discussed the two men for some time. My mind was made up; it should be the professor. However, others—including Irv—saw great merit in the mayor. I was on the wrong side when the vote was taken. The mayor became the new director of the institute and, over the decades, became a very good leader.

At the time, I didn't know how he would turn out. As we walked out of the building, I asked Irv about his decision. In an earlier meeting, he talked about the strengths of the professor. What happened? He stopped and said, "There are times when one forgoes the reasonable path for the politically expedient one. The mayor is a good member of the Mormon community. He has friends in high places, and, looking at the committee make-up, I knew the mayor would be chosen as the next director." He was saddened by his decision, but he told me, "I will go home and wash the corruption off my body. Then I'll dry off, pour some wine, and talk about the vote with Gloria. Will go to bed, and then start up again next day. The shower's the key." He suggested that there were occasions when hard choices had to be made, ones that I would be opposed to because of my value hierarchy. "We all live with red lines we cannot, in good conscience, cross over," he said. He said that I had a decision to make, either justify the crossing or say no and resign. The person has to make a hard choice. And, as Irv reflected, when you cross the red line you *must* go home and take a hot shower to clean your body and your soul. "Who said life was a big bowl of cherries?" Irv Altman was an excellent academic scientist who taught me, a political scientist, about politics. Hail Taft High!

We have lived in Vermont for thirty years. Setting aside the tumultuous times in the dean's office during the first half of the 1990s, I was involved in a number of volunteer activities over these decades. I was a Ronald McDonald House volunteer, an aide at the University of Vermont Medical Center, one of the oldest first-year members of the Richmond EMS squad after I retired in 2002, a therapy dog handler, with Carol, who visited the hospital to cheer patients up, and finally, a food server at the Vermont Respite House.

However, my close friends were members of the Ohavi Zedek synagogue. Over the years, I have met many friends—at Shabbat services, weddings, Bar Mitzvahs, and weekly meetings on Wednesday mornings at 7:30, open to all persons regardless of race, religion, or ethnicity, which have been ongoing since 1991 (now, because of advancing age, we meet Wednesdays at noon). A few of us have met for lunch or drinks and dinner, and these gatherings have led to some very rewarding friendships. One of these is the monthly "Three Musketeers" lunch, where Michael Bukanc, Richard Bingham, and I meet and talk about *everything* for two-plus hours. We usually order the soup of the day, some artisan bread, and lots of coffee. They have given me solace when I had problems. We talk about politics and religion (Richard is Christian) and so many other matters that flit across our minds. They have been with me as I worked on this book, suggesting titles, commenting on segments I shared with them, and being general cheerleaders.

Others who shared life with me are Laura Merit, a ninety-plus avowed communist from New York City who still fights in defense of battered women every Thursday in county court; Michael Schaal; Dr. Arthur Kunin and his friend Mary; Barbara McGrew and her friend Fred Childs; Joe Henry Nunes, a gay Portuguese Jew who served in the US Air Force, raises prize cattle, and parents numerous foster kids; my preacher friends, Rabbi Joshua and Rabbi Amy; my longtime friends the vintners Ken and Gail Albert; and so many others I have known and loved over these prime years of life.

I would be remiss if I didn't thank my friends in Tucson, Arizona, Carol and Charles Sumner. We have known and befriended these dear friends from New York (the Bronx) and New Jersey since our first winter trip to Arizona, back in 2005. We are both mixed pairs: Charles, the IBM engineer and my Carol, the logical mathematician and horse maven, and on the other side the passionate political junkies, Charles's Carol and I. The two of us go at it for hours on end at our irregular breakfasts at Beyond Bread. We also all go for dinner and an occasional play or concert from time to time.

We also have our friends in our monthly *Chavurah*, where a dozen of us gather on Friday evening to celebrate the coming of the Sabbath. Karen, Mike and Wendy, Ester, Joan, Jane and Randy, Joe and Sandie, and Ilene and Alvin are from different professions and have a variety of experiences, but we enjoy Friday nights with you all. Shabbat Shalom.

Finally, I must thank my wandering Jewish family for working together as we managed living in Starkville, Mississippi. Thank you, dear Susan, my oldest daughter, for forthrightly dealing with slights and insults in a very direct manner. Thank you, Sheryl (and Lila and Nathan), for your perseverance on the soccer field as well as sharing some interesting activities with mom and dad, like going to a Bat Mitzvah in New Orleans but sleeping in a houseboat, many miles away from the synagogue. Thank you, Melissa (and Sophie and husband Tim), for not grumbling too loudly when we moved just before your Bat Mitzvah in Temple B'nai Israel, in Columbus. Cantor Lawrence Loeb was waiting for you to come to Utah! Thank you, Carol, for your love for nearly sixty years. We ran the gamut of personal joys and hardships everywhere we lived since 1963. You were always focused on each problem and we were able to continue our travels because you always found a solution.

We all shared as a family so many experiences while living in the South; but each of us individually also experienced fear, joy, stress, and humor. I hope that your fond memories of life in Mississippi outweigh the other kind of remembrance. Thank you, all of you, who shared life with me in the piney woods of Mississippi.

JUSTICE

That Justice is a blind goddess
Is a thing to which we black are wise:
Her bandage hides two festering sores
That once perhaps were eyes.

—Langston Hughes

CHAPTER 1

Going Down to Mississippi

After living most of my thirty-nine years in one of the Bronx's many Jewish ghettos of the 1930s, '40s, and '50s, and then in Nassau and Suffolk Counties, New York, in the 1960s and '70s, in 1976 I took a job in Mississippi. I was going to be professor of political science at Mississippi State University (MSU), located adjacent to the city of Starkville, in Oktibbeha County, Mississippi. My responsibility at MSU was to teach four courses in constitutional law and civil rights and liberties during the academic year. It was the kind of job description I had wished for over the past decade at Hofstra University. I thought I was ready for this new teaching environment.

I immediately called my mother to tell her the news. Her response was very loud and, for her, terse: "You are *meshugenah!*"[1] She truly believed that Mississippi was an evil third-world country. It was a place where Jews were eaten after being boiled to death. And if that did not happen fast enough, you were damned because you had to eat *trafe*[2] food like fried pickles with pulled pork and—ugh—a chocolate milkshake, before you were boiled! Tearing up, she begged me not to move, asking me again and again, "*Why* would a nice Jewish professor from the Bronx, with a beautiful wife and three precious daughters, even *think* much less *move* to *that place.*" Why, indeed?

3

GROWING UP IN THE BRONX

My father, Abe, didn't offer any opinions about our moving plans, nor did he ask the *why* question. It didn't surprise me at all. His life had been a continual struggle, one in which the encounters seemingly never subsided. Abe's struggles began early in his life. Three years after he was born in Poland in 1911, his mother—physically a *very* tiny woman but *also* a *brave heart*—took Abe and his older brother Al, on foot, *across war-torn Europe* on a harrowing, years-long journey from Poland to Hamburg, Germany's largest seaport city. Her husband, the granddad I never knew, had crossed the Atlantic Ocean before the Great War began, and she and the children were joining him in America. Which she did! All by herself!

My father left school after the third grade because the family, which now included a little sister, Rachel, was quite poor and he had to go to work to help out. He worked long and hard hours, eventually mastering the plumbing trade. Because of an injury to his right arm suffered on a job, he could not serve in the army during the Second World War. Instead, he worked at Todd Shipyard's facility in Hoboken, New Jersey, the largest plant on the East Coast, installing toilets and showers in a variety of naval vessels. It was labor-intensive and dangerous work in an environment laced with asbestos, the then-largely-unknown carcinogen. As with the other shipyard laborers, asbestos was his daily intimate buddy aboard his ships. Every day for four years, at work's end, he wrapped the pipes and the joints with his silent mate. Abe was sixty-nine years old when he died of cancer in 1980. It was caused by an undiagnosed mesothelioma. My mother, devastated by his death, not yet aware of the underlying cause of death and unwilling to go through the trauma of litigation once we found out why he died, never joined a class action suit against the shipyard.[3]

After the war ended, he continued to ply his trade; but because he was Jewish, Abe was a hardworking nonunion plumber until a few years before he retired. That discrimination became a financial and a mental albatross around his neck, because he worked—as he always growled it—"for a *momzer*."[4] Every day he would come home, dirt on his clothing and his hands, tired and perpetually angry, cursing that "God-damned bastard Uberstein," especially his miserliness—and the fact that he was Jewish, to boot.

Growing up and living in New York City and Long Island for four decades, I lived in Jewish ghettos in the Bronx and on Long Island. I was shielded from the hate, prejudice, and discrimination my father and my relatives, whether in sales, or plumbing or sheet metal trades, or in all the military services, experienced.

Until I went to graduate school in New Jersey, I lived in the second-floor three-room apartment (2D) in an old, small tenement building, 322 East 173rd Street, just east of the Grand Concourse. Inside there were six other members of my family: my three sisters, Carol, Sarah, and Brenda; my mother, Fay; my father, Abe; and my grandfather, my mother's father, Max Kintish. I was the oldest and the only boy in the apartment. Until I was a Bar Mitzvah, I shared a small two-bunk bedroom with all my sisters. When I was thirteen, I was moved into a tinier room inhabited by my granddad, who was beginning his final sad journey accompanied by a common traveler, dementia. It became a somewhat difficult time when, at night, Max would get up, grab a slipper, and, very weakly, start hitting me with it, yelling at me in Yiddish. Until he passed, when I was a first-year student at Hunter College, it was just a heart-wrenching experience for me and for my mother.

Most of my parents' siblings (my aunts and uncles) and their children (my cousins) lived in the Bronx and Brooklyn. I was surrounded by familial love, cheerfulness, alongside the occasional petty, but very long-lasting, quarrels engaged in by one of the mishpucha[5] toward another. All of us were poor growing up, and there were times when job loss was a dismal reality. But we were part of a very large family, and these dilemmas were shouldered by our own little kolkhoz.[6]

When I began college work, I had to find a place in the apartment to do my schoolwork. There was only one spot: at a pulldown worktable that extended from a secretary standing in the family room. Occasionally I was working at the desk when my father came home, exhausted and angry. Most of the time, he'd yell at me, telling me "to get a job and make some money to help us out!"

Very infrequently, because I knew what happened next, I would ex-
claim, "Please just let me finish my . . ." Before my plea ended, he pulled
off his belt and quickly cornered me by the dumbwaiter next to the apartment door and gave me a couple of whacks. They stung, but he calmed
down afterward and got ready for dinner. He never apologized, but I
never expected it from him. He did not attend my high school, college,
or graduate school commencements, nor did he come to any of my Taft
High School football games.

Abe bitterly disliked the *schvartzes*[7] "invading" the Bronx from, he
swore, Puerto Rico. His prejudice extended to my Black friends on the
football team with me at Taft. He was furious when he found out that
one of my good friends and a study hall partner, Olive Bowles, who was
the head Taft cheerleader, was a *schvartze*!

This dread my dad felt toward another discriminated-against minority group never abated. He was infuriated when he found out, from
a photo of us in the *New York Daily News*, that I was one of the Hunter
College students who participated in a protest march on Fordham Road,
across from Alexander's department store, in support of the Black college
students protesting at a Woolworth's lunch counter in North Carolina.

Although my mom's fears and concerns about my family's moving to
Mississippi were profound, they never came close to my father's anger,
chagrin, and embarrassment that his only son was moving to the South.

My father claimed that his anger emerged after he was robbed and
assaulted twice by Blacks, two who had worked for him. However, his
antipathy toward persons of color was a hallmark of his life before these
muggings and robberies. The second attack occurred when he was in his
sixties. It led to his retirement. He was brutally beaten up by two Black
men when he interrupted them burglarizing his small plumbing store.
He wound up in Bronx Hospital. He never pressed charges against the
two men. He knew who they were, but he feared what might happen to
him and mom.

After he was discharged, he quickly—at a financial loss—sold the
hole-in-the-wall business and, with my mother, moved into their first,
and their only, "house." It was a no-frills mobile home in Monticello,
New York. (He did visit us in Starkville, just months before his asbestos-

induced death, on the occasion of my oldest daughter Sue's Bat Mitzvah in 1980.)

I was working in Mississippi when my father died. Before then, I had been teaching at Hofstra University, in New York's Nassau County. It was my first job after receiving my PhD from Rutgers University. Our next move was to Mississippi State University, Starkville, Oktibbeha County, Mississippi.

TEACHING AT HOFSTRA UNIVERSITY

When we moved to Mississippi, I was a tenured associate professor of political science at Hofstra University in Hempstead, Nassau County, Long Island. It was my first teaching job after graduate work at Rutgers University. I had been married thirteen years to Carol May Neidell, a Jewess of Carle Place and Westbury, Long Island (although she lived her first six years in Brooklyn). I was the father of three young daughters, Sue, Sheryl, and, the youngest, Melissa. We had lived in Stony Brook since 1968, and I commuted sixty-six miles daily (round trip) to teach my political theory, civil liberties, and constitutional law classes at Hofstra.

I had begun to seriously think about relocating around the time I received tenure at Hofstra in 1972. I enjoyed researching and writing and having my work on the US Supreme Court and constitutional issues published. While at Hofstra, annually I would take my Supreme Court class to visit the Supreme Court in Washington, DC. It was a three-day event: day one, attending oral arguments; day two, meeting a sitting justice of the court (over the eleven years, these meetings included Earl Warren, Hugo Black, Tom Clark, Potter Stewart, and William O. Douglas); and day three, meeting with law clerks, staff from the solicitor general's office, and the marshall of the court. (My students loved these trips, and I continued them when I moved to Vermont three decades later.)

And I loved interacting with my students in the many courses I taught at Hofstra. It was a "teaching" university, and I did a great deal of teaching, five different courses each semester, in two very broad subsets of political science—constitutional law and political theory.

This teaching load meant that, regularly, I taught ten different courses a year. It made research, writing, and scholarly publication very, very difficult. If I wanted to research and write, I had to spend evenings and weekends away from my growing family. (By the time I left New York, however, I had two books published and a third, *No Pledge of Privacy*, on the 1974 Watergate tapes litigation in the federal courts, in press.)

I longed to teach at a university that provided me with a different kind of scholarly environment: fewer courses to teach, colleagues who enjoyed doing research and publishing their findings, research support, and a genuinely supportive climate for social science research and publication.

The Hofstra milieu reminded me of Eugene O'Neill's powerful play *The Iceman Cometh*. There was the always-busy faculty lounge, where, day after day, for the eleven years I was at Hofstra, small groups of faculty, each clique never more than six to eight persons, would sit at round tables. They would generally be hunched over their tea and coffee in the morning, and over lunch later on in the day, always talking and shouting about the same issues and personalities. Always talking about what they would do if the school had another president, if their department had a different chairperson, and so on.

If one visited the group in the lunchroom only once a year, the overheard conversation would be fully understood. It was as if the onlooker had been sitting at the table the day before. Eerie, yes; frustrating, yes; encouraging, never. (When one of the *regulars*, a somewhat effete historian who smoked cigarettes inserted into an ivory cigarette holder, heard that my first book had been published, he remarked, "I didn't know *you* could write!")

AN INVITATION TO VISIT MISSISSIPPI

For three years, 1972–75, my job search did not go well at all. Frankly, nothing happened. However, in late 1975, I received a positive letter and a number of telephone calls from Barbara Teters, the head of the Political Science Department at Mississippi State University, inviting me down to campus for an interview. Hoping that Harvard would give me a call, I delayed responding to the Mississippi invitation.

When Harvard's Department of Government didn't make me an offer I couldn't refuse, I returned the Mississippi calls and somewhat reluctantly visited the campus. The flight down was an experience I'll never forget. I really was not eager to visit the Magnolia State, but my curiosity got the better of me. On the flight down, I was surrounded by all the horrible visions I ever imagined about Mississippi.

And they were pretty horrid specters, involving violence and death, all taking place in dark, moss-shrouded forests and swamps. And the villain was Count Dracula in the guise of a burly redneck wearing a filthy, green John Deere baseball cap, holding a shotgun ominously in both massive hands, and with a noose slung over his shoulder. By the time my plane landed at the Golden Triangle Regional Airport, servicing Starkville, West Point, and Columbus, Mississippi, my mind had done its job on me and I was *very* eager to return as quickly as possible to New York's comfortable bosom and continue my job search.

However, I quickly found out that there were no dark swampy forests in Oktibbeha County (only cool piney woods). Also, I did not see one single John Deere type during my two-day visit. (This was a good omen at the time, although once we moved, I found other, darker realities in Mississippi, including plenty of John Deere talking—and spitting—heads.)

The MSU campus was very big and quite pretty, and the people I met seemed very decent and quite gracious. And there were a greater percentage of Black students on this predominantly white Southern campus than there were on Hofstra's campus in New York.

The department needed a person to teach in only one area of political science, constitutional law/civil liberties. The teaching load was less than half the number of courses I taught annually at Hofstra, and the courses were all in my favorite subject area. And I would get a promotion and a higher salary if I took the job. Most of all, I would have the free time to do some serious research into the status of civil rights in the South. For me, I thought, Mississippi would be my laboratory!

I was invited to visit the campus to interview for the position. It was a brief visit, one full day of interviews, sandwiched between two nights in the Ramada Inn.

The university was one of three predominantly white major institutions of higher learning in the state, and scholarly research was encouraged and supported in a number of ways. (The other two institutions were the University of Mississippi and the University of Southern Mississippi.)

There were and still are eight institutions of higher learning in Mississippi. Three of them are still predominantly Black (Jackson State, Alcorn State, and Mississippi Valley State Universities). The only predominantly white colleges, Mississippi University for Women and Delta State College, were smaller liberal arts campuses.

Litigation introduced by Black plaintiffs in the 1960s challenging the segregated system of higher education in the state had still not been concluded when we arrived in July 1976. The legal controversy finally arrived at the US Supreme Court in 1991, in the case of *United States v. Fordice.* The Rehnquist court unanimously labeled Mississippi's higher education system an unconstitutional, racially segregated one and called on the state to take definitive steps to end the de jure discrimination.

The final steps had not yet been taken by the Mississippi State Board of Higher Education when I visited in 2005, having retired in 2002. The politics of higher education reform anywhere is tough, hardball politics because so much is at stake. Each of the campuses has thousands of employees, from carpenters, to cooks, to maintenance workers, to faculty and administrators. Each campus locale has dozens of small businesses who cater to the needs of the thousands of students who attend them.

Smaller campuses, whether predominantly Black or white, also dreaded the possibility of consolidation or closure. And throwing the race factor into the mix compounds the dilemma of higher education reform in Mississippi and other states that have had a dual higher education system since the beginning of Jim Crow segregation. For more than four decades, therefore, higher education has been in legal and political turmoil in the state.

The MSU Political Science Department, unlike Hofstra's, did have two small master's degree programs. There were fourteen faculty in the department, twice the number of faculty at Hofstra. Also, with the exception of three senior professors, all my potential colleagues were "outsiders" like me, from Missouri, Washington State, New Jersey, Wisconsin, and other "Yankee" states. There was only one woman in the department, and, with the exception of Professor Chris Bhansali, all were Caucasian.

I returned to New York with a different, somewhat positive, vision of MSU and the Magnolia State in the immediate environs of the campus and Starkville, Mississippi.

THE JOB OFFER

A short time after I returned to New York, I received a letter offering me the job. After I talked it over with the ladies in my family, we all decided to visit the campus. We drove to Atlanta in March 1976 and stayed with our longtime friends Tom and Jeannie Lauth and their four young boys. Tom and I met in 1966 when he joined the Political Science Department at Hofstra.

We left our daughters with Tom and Jean to visit the MSU campus. Tom, originally from Pittsburgh, was a colleague of mine at Hofstra for nearly a decade before leaving to finish his PhD at Syracuse University. Afterward, he took a job in the South: teaching political science at Georgia State University in Atlanta and living in nearby Stone Mountain (the central locale of the second Ku Klux Klan [KKK] resurgence).[8] They and their four boys seemed to be enjoying the South. More importantly, no crosses had been burned on the property of this liberal, Northern, Catholic family who despised racism as much as we did.

Four hours later, Carol and I arrived, very exhausted, and were met by a few of the political science faculty. Since it was getting dark, we were brought to the motel and given an itinerary for the remainder of our stay in Starkville.

AN UNUSUAL START TO OUR VISIT TO MISSISSIPPI

Carol and I had a bizarre experience the very first evening of our initial visit to Starkville. It was one that the two of us will never forget. About 10 p.m., after we had finished our dinner and before we hit the hay, I received a telephone call from (as I found out a day later) the major entrepreneur/*goniff*[9] in Oktibbeha County, Sid Biddulph.[10] Somehow, he found out about our visit and wanted to show us a beautiful house that would soon be for sale—and he wanted to show it to us immediately—this evening!

"Can't we see it in the morning," I asked. Sid said: "No, can't be done. The husband's divorcing the little woman, who is home all day and night, but she doesn't know it yet. I'd like to show it to you two now because she's asleep. I'll pick you up in my Lincoln, drive around the house, car lights out, then bring you to my office so I can show you the blueprints and pictures of the house. And then we can talk turkey!"

After I spoke to an astonished Carol, we agreed to partake of this unusual house showing. "What the hell," I said to Carol, "the alternative is going to bed." He picked us up fifteen minutes later. He did have a Lincoln: white exterior with a deep maroon velvet interior (MSU's colors). And Biddulph matched his car; he met us in white: white suit, white shirt, white tie, and white shoes. We entered the car and drove west on Highway 12. It was about midnight and it was very quiet and very, very dark. "Why am I here?" was the only question running through my mind.

Just beyond the city limits there were some private homes. The car slowed down and then entered a long driveway. We slowly rode on the paved road right around the entire house. Given the time and the total lack of lit headlights, house lights, and road lights, to say we could not see very much is an understatement.

After leisurely circling the property we drove back to Starkville and parked at Sid's office. We followed him inside to a conference room where he had already prepared a blueprint and photo showing of the house for us. He unrolled the large blueprint of the house and the property and pointed out the interior dimensions. He showed us a number of pictures and sketches of the house and property, prepared by the company that built it.

A very surrealistic experience was coming to an end. We thanked Sid, saying that we could not buy a house without actually seeing it. And besides, we added, the house fronted a somewhat busy two-lane Highway 12 and we have three small children. "Well," he said, "I just don't know how I can show it to you until she's out of the house. It's a great buy but you have to go with your gut feelings on it." We agreed with his assessment. He drove us back to our hotel, but without a house sale.

Someone or some couple braver than Carol and I did buy the house sight unseen. However, it was probably only after the divorce was posted (in the *Starkville Daily News*) that the buyer(s) actually saw the house interior. Back in our room, we both agreed that, if our interlude with Sid was the norm for Starkville realtors, we would be in for some kind of wild ride in house buying if we decided to move. Fortunately, our regular realtor showed us homes during daylight hours. Biddulph was an aberration.

After our midnight rendezvous with Sid, we spent another four days in Starkville, meeting with faculty, administrators, and a genuine real estate agent. We also visited the public school buildings because our daughter Sue, nine years old, and Sheryl, a year younger, were going to be attending them if we moved to Starkville. We visited a number of small buildings to speak with the principal in each one. And we found out *why* we were seeing these schools.

Starkville's buildings were the residue of the century-old separate-but-equal Mississippi public school system and all other public school districts across the South. The Starkville commissioners, forced to desegregate decades after the US Supreme Court's unanimous opinion in *Brown v. Board of Education of Topeka, Kansas*, 1954, decided to use all the existing school buildings rather than building a spanking-new K–8 schoolhouse.[11]

And so, every two years, our girls went to a different, formerly whites-only or negros-only classroom building. Which meant that Carol and I had to meet with the school administrators to talk primarily about Bible reading in our daughters' homeroom classes. But it was something that we felt must be done and that, generally, generated little controversy within the education administration. Except, surprisingly for us at the time, for the hullabaloo we triggered within our tiny Jewish community. (More about this general issue in another chapter.)

We found a very nice, very new house in a very lovely Starkville subdivision: Sherwood Forest. And we saw the property, interior and exterior, in broad daylight! (After I accepted the job offer, we bought that house.)

I spent a great deal of time meeting with faculty, campus administrators, and students in an effort to get a handle on the character of the institution I was thinking of joining—and the character of its natives. I also checked the library, computer facilities, and other kinds of support needed for teaching and research. It was, generally, an excellent review.

Carol spoke to administrators in the Starkville public school system about a teaching job in mathematics. As we found out after we settled in, they were reluctant to hire *outsiders* to teach Mississippi kids. It was only after a mathematics professor had a heart attack and his replacement, a young man, exposed himself in one of the classrooms that the administrators asked Carol to teach mathematics. She was literally the last available mathematics teacher in Starkville at that time. They had no choice!

It took a heart attack and a "flashing" male math teacher to get Carol into teaching in Starkville. Oh, she could have had a job at the Starkville Academy, a segregated private school system (K–12). Given our feelings about racial segregation and the fact that Academy faculty had to enroll their children in the Academy, she rejected that teaching position out of hand. Until the flasher flashed, Carol and another white female outsider operated a wallpaper-hanging business. They were the "Wallflowers" for three long years, battling gender discrimination decades before the #MeToo movement emerged, until the Starkville school system ran out of mathematics teachers.

Both of us were also very interested in finding out about the Jewish community in this northeastern section of Mississippi. We were driven to Columbus one day to visit Temple B'nai Israel. It was, however, closed and there were no posted notes that conveyed information about services or other activities. However, one of the faculty we met knew a Jewish family affiliated with the university, the Rubins (the husband was a faculty member in the Department of Nuclear Engineering). We contacted them and, over lunch, found out all about the very tiny Jewish community in this area of the state.

The Rubins were, to the best of our knowledge, the only affiliated Jewish faculty family at State. Although there were over one thousand faculty at State, including its large extension program, the Rubins were the only visible faculty Jews. We were delighted to meet them—and their two children. We thought, correctly, that we would be getting together with them if we moved to Mississippi. (However, after our third year at State, the Rubins accepted a faculty position at one of the Texas universities. When they left, we were the last of the tribe working at State.)

There was a retired Jewish faculty member, Henry Leveck, who had taught in the College of Agriculture. He was very popular, and after his retirement one of the south fields owned by the university was named in his honor. He and his wife, Hortense, were the venerable leaders of the Jewish community.

While on our weeklong trip south, we were able to meet with them before we had to leave for Atlanta and home. The couple was extremely friendly and provided us with all the information we desired about the Jewish community in the area. We found out about the membership and about the services that surrounded the monthly fly-in-from-Ohio student rabbi. Frankly, it sounded great to us; it felt to me like frontier Judaism.

After we were entrenched in Mississippi for a while, we found out about the reality of Jewish life in a tiny Hebrew community (about two dozen men, women, and children) spread across two states (northwest Alabama and northeast Mississippi). Our eyes were always wide open in our time with the community. It was an experience in Jewish living that we had not expected or experienced before our stay in Mississippi—and one we'd never experience again!

After returning home, we decided that I should take the position. I would take a general (unpaid) "leave of absence" from Hofstra University rather than immediately submitting my resignation. In this way, when and if we experienced the "other" frightening Mississippi reality, we could return to the North and my job at Hofstra. It was a cowardly thought and action, but we truly had no idea about what to really expect living in Mississippi, and the two-year leave was our safety net.

TAKING THE JOB AT MISSISSIPPI STATE UNIVERSITY

When my two-year unpaid leave of absence was approved and announced on the Hofstra campus, all my faculty colleagues and friends, with only one supporting my decision, assured me that the move would prove disastrous and that I would be back very quickly. The exception was a quirky history professor, one of the few colleagues I interacted well with over the years at Hofstra, Bob Sobel. He was a highly respected American economic history scholar, someone who had been disciplined enough to do scholarly research and writing while teaching many classes and who had published a number of well-received books and articles over the years. In his sardonic way, he said that the move could prove to be an excellent experience for the family and me and that he often wished he could do the same thing. His words, along with Tom and Jeannie Lauth's comments about living in the South, were an important factor in our decision to move to the Magnolia State.

My Stony Brook friends, knowing of my lifelong active work on behalf of civil rights, joined the marching band pleading with us not to go. Echoing my mom, they said I was *meshugenah*, crazy, to leave the New York cultural oasis for the dark, misty, kudzu-infested and moss-covered forests of racism and inequality in the Magnolia State. They reminded me that Mississippi was the place where hatred of the Blacks and of Jews lay at the core of the "primitive," violent culture.

Mississippi was *the* place where Jews were second only to Blacks on the hate lists of the *fine* people (KKK members all, it was thought) of Mississippi. They reminded me of what Bob Moses, the young leader of the Student Nonviolent Coordinating Committee (SNCC), said about Mississippi only a decade earlier: it was the "middle of the iceberg [of racism]."

Carol and I thought, until very recently, that our kids had a different take on the possible move. For them, we believed, it was another, albeit extended, camping trip. (Our family had been camping since 1973. We always took two-month-long summer trips in our RV across the country and into western Canada's Rocky Mountains.) Besides, they did not have the negative perspective the adults had about terrible Mississippi. By the time they could read, the many brutal and unsolved KKK murders of local Blacks and NAACP civil rights workers, regularly making the news over the course of nearly a century, had receded into history books. I believed that our daughters knew Mississippi only because one of the *Sesame Street* characters humorously spelled it out as "m-i-crooked letter, crooked letter-i-crooked letter, crooked letter-i-pee-pee-i."

Carol was less sanguine than the kids about the move. She shares my views about the evil of racism, and she was very aware of the overt racism that existed in Mississippi. However, she has *always* been an outspoken, fearless risk taker, and she agreed to the move after I told her that I would not immediately cut my (tenured) ties to Hofstra University.

Our dear close friends, and fellow New York Jewish mafia, finally accepted the fact that we were leaving Stony Brook for Starkville. They— the Weinsteins, the Handlers, the Lubells, and the Beckermans—were as shocked as my mother about our moving away. But, unlike my mother, they stopped their pleading. Shortly before we left, they took both of us out for a happy-sad send-off party for their crazy Jew friends, complete with a small "Shalom Y'all" wall plaque (still hanging in our Vermont home). They too thought we would be back.

Bob and Gail Weinstein, our camping partners, who, with their three boys, traveled across America with us (occasionally, we were a two-RV caravan), decided to trail us down to Mississippi. They had to see for themselves where we were going and what we were getting ourselves into! The Weinstein-Ball caravan to Starkville brings to mind a remembrance of another weird "Sid Biddulph-like" encounter we had right after our two rigs pulled into our driveway on Sherwood Road, Starkville, Mississippi.

We finally rode into Starkville. I remember when, just before turning south on Montgomery Street, we saw a large billboard that read:

"Welcome Dr. James McComas and family to MSU." My oldest daughter, Susan, pointed it out to us and asked, "Where's our welcome sign?" At that point I couldn't answer because I did not know that the sign was welcoming the new president of MSU! (He and I became good friends, especially after the two of us were no longer in the state. More about McComas in chapters 5 and 6.)

We desperately needed food, and after parking and unhitching our cars from the RVs, we went in search of a supermarket. The women went in one car, with our three daughters, to pick up some groceries at a local A&P supermarket. (I confess, I thought we would find and shop in a Piggly Wiggly supermarket, but we shopped at the first store we found. It would be a few weeks before I found that adorable-named store.)

Bob and I, with his boys, followed in his car. We stayed in the car while the women shopped. Bob put on the CB radio, and we were flummoxed by what we heard. CBers were talking about the two RVs with New York license plates who had pulled into Starkville that afternoon. "Who were these Yankees?" inquired one. "Don't know," answered another, "but," he added, "they must have money 'cause they parked in Sherwood Forest!"

It was the first reality check for me about our future life in Mississippi. Starkville was *not* New York City. It was not even Stony Brook. It was a scary future for a family that liked their privacy. Upon returning to New York, I called Don Mabry, a history professor I met while visiting. He had given me his telephone number and invited me to call about any issues that troubled Carol and me.

We talked a lot about living in Mississippi and cost-of-living issues, and I asked for any words of wisdom he could impart to me that might lessen my lingering uncertainty about life for New York Jews in a small town (it was called Board Town before the Civil War) without a young Jewish membership list and without a temple. He said he would send me more information.

A week later we received a long letter from Don, including two typed pages of "Economic Indicators on Cost of Living, Starkville, Mississippi, 4/8/76." The listed items included "selected grocery prices, electricity rates, sample utility bill, state income tax, sales taxes, license tags," and so on, and so forth. The letter itself was somewhat formal, but it was a friendly read. And he provided some information about the turbulence the Political Science Department had been experiencing over the past few years. "As you know," Don wrote, [it] has been undergoing a transformation since Teters came. Until this process began, there were few, if any people, in the department interested in scholarship." The department had changed dramatically. He wrote, "Now that change has come there is increasing collaboration and contact through campus."

He ended by giving us some final food for thought. "There is a cultural shock accompanying a move to a small town." It can "be eased somewhat by the friendliness, the personal security, and the informality of this town. Social life centers around friends, family, church, and bridge is a mainstay." He did not provide any insights about life—social and religious life—for a group of New York Jews. (This book tries to answer these questions.)

Needless to say, we began to tackle a number of these social issues as they popped up. We decided that we would not return to Hofstra, and two years later Paul Harper, my good friend and the chair of the political science department, received my letter of resignation. (He and his wife, Ina, were so curious that, the following summer, they drove down to visit us.) Prior to the resignation letter, we asked the girls if they wanted to return to New York. They asked whether we would move back to our house in Stony Brook. When we said no, they agreed to stay in Starkville.

By that time, a great many events experienced by all five of us had convinced us to stay in Mississippi a bit longer. The "bit longer" turned into a six-year sojourn, one that was filled with joys, sadnesses, and successes, mostly small but visible ones, and some failures. We met some great people, and we met our share of Klansmen and bigots. We have said, time and again, when talking about our years living in Mississippi: "Our time in Mississippi, on the whole, was valuable. We were glad we made the move, but we wouldn't want to do it ever again!"

This memoir is my effort to explain what that answer meant. It contains a series of small stories about life in Mississippi for five transplanted New York Jews. It is a story, really, about a large number of very different people: native Southerners, Blacks and whites, native Jews and *goyim*, trying to understand and live with an increasing number of "outsiders" like us who sought a new life in the Magnolia State. (Vermonters refer to nonnatives as "flatlanders." I cannot imagine what the Mississippi natives called us.) These interactions were always exciting ones, sometimes fulfilling and joyous, sometimes tense intersections.

By the end of our stay in Mississippi, however, we realized the meaning of the term "others." All our experiences there (and certainly in Utah, where we lived for seven years after Mississippi as "gentiles" in a Mormon world) taught all five of us what being a minority—any minority—being "others," really means. What compounded the experience was that we—all five of us—were *visible* others. Not because of skin color but because of mouth size.

When confronted by discrimination or pure hatred, we responded as openly, as uncompromisingly as we could: fighting prayer in school, challenging town discrimination against expansion of a Black child care center, creating an integrated girl scout troop because we (and our Black friends who also had three young girls) had to because we were uninvited *others*, battling efforts by city officials to use the Voting Rights Act to deny voting rights for some citizens—these were just some of the issues we loudly engaged in to try to right wrongs in the State.

We were under no illusions about the long-term consequences of our actions. It was always like battling with a powerful, armed bowl of Jell-O: punch it in the ribs and the blob just moves away. But Mississippians, behaving like Jell-O, bounce back to the well-built racist structures. For me, it was Sisyphean: we knew the rock would rush down the mountain again and again, but nevertheless we continued with our existential activity.

We Jews, we Northern Jews, could not remain silent simply because we were an infinitesimally tiny segment of the Mississippi population, even though we knew two things about the prayer-in-public-school dilemma (and most other challenges we faced): (1) once Sue graduated from the second grade and went to another school building for third grade classes, Bible reading would immediately commence in the second grade school, and (2) we would have to visit with the third grade principal to make sure that prayer would not take place while Sue was in the third grade!

We knew what the school principals would do once our kids left the building. What we did not know, but came to realize, so sadly, was the mental pain Sue (and Melissa) experienced because of the tension our actions created. We found out when Sue was admitted to the county hospital with terrible stomach pains. The doctors found nothing physical accounting for the pain; after we discussed the prayer reading events involving Sue, another set of psychological professionals met with Sue and, separately, with us. They believed that Sue, who was quite a sensitive young lady, was hurt by being singled out as someone who did not like daily prayer reading!

Sue knew what had happened, but our oldest preteen insisted that the tension was not due to the Bible-reading matter but rather that her teacher mistakenly identified American states where natural disasters occurred and when Sue corrected the teacher, the woman ridiculed Sue again and again!

It turns out that Sue was not our only daughter that had difficulty coping with a very different culture and way of living. My youngest, Melissa, just told me (see the postscript below) that during our living in the South, she felt fear a great deal of the time. After the horse has left the barn, the sad rancher fixes the broken gate. We did not correctly assess and assist Sue to make her feel better. And we never, literally until 2019, knew about or detected Melissa's silent fear she had to wrestle with alone, starting when, in 1976, she was only a four-year-old lady.

————

The following chapters examine and elaborate on the breadth of the experiences we all had living in Mississippi, and how we, the "others," continually tried to cope with all of them during our "years of living dangerously" in Mississippi.

A POSTSCRIPT

In the past year, Melissa, now forty-seven, and my middle daughter, fifty-one-year-old Sheryl, sent me notes after we talked about this book.

Their primary recollections were of very different events that they experienced.

Melissa was four years old when we moved to Mississippi and ten when we left for Utah. After all these years, Missy wrote about her feelings when we lived in Starkville. Her remembrance was, for me, a stunning memory. And it was *her* remembrance, reflecting *her* fear and hurting. It was an uneasiness I never observed—or even thought about—while we were there. She said:

> My memory of Mississippi is greatly faded. I remember always feeling unsafe though. I guess not the best feeling to have as a kid! . . . I always worried we'd get killed by the KKK. Again, probably not a great kids' book for me to write! . . . But I do remember Shakey's [i.e., Shoney's Big Boy] and eating there and Baskin-Robbins. And horseback riding. And finding our cat Snowy and pretending I broke my arm with Julie. So, maybe all the memories aren't horrible.

Melissa's distress about Southern life and values continued and evidently deepened after her family moved to Winston-Salem, North Carolina, in the late 1990s. (She remained there until June 2019, when she, her husband, Tim, and their daughter, Sophie, moved to Hinesburg, Vermont.) Winston-Salem, she said, was not a very comforting place for outsiders. That inhospitable region was, she admitted, "probably one of the reasons I never wanted Sophie [her fifteen-year-old daughter] to get involved with Temple in good ol' Winston-Salem. Fear. I still saw a lot of hate—especially when I drove to my job in rural NC. I would pass confederate flag after confederate flag, always praying that my car would never break down." Carol and I had no inkling of Missy's fearful years while we were living in Mississippi. And since she told me, I have struggled to understand why I was unaware of her angst and what I could have done to address her anxieties.

I asked my middle daughter, Sheryl, a fifty-one-year-old occupational therapist and the mother of Lila and Nathan—all of them living in Austin—for her comments about the note I received from Missy. Her memories centered on another matter, one that did not frighten my middle daughter.

Sheryl was eight years old when we moved, and she did not have Melissa's apprehensions while living in Mississippi. Indeed, she remembers and verbalizes something quite different about her Mississippi life. Our two other daughters experienced apprehensiveness daily. Sheryl's recollection, her unique experience she ran into only in Mississippi, was one that became rooted in her memory: being segregated in a school system that had recently undergone court-ordered integration. Sheryl recently recalled this reality in her note to me:

> Hi dad, here's some of the things I remember about Starkville. I liked living there. The school for me was a regular school but I was in track one of three tracks. Track one was mainly the white kids; I think it was arranged by cognitive ability. You had track one with the highest level, track 2 middle and three was the low level. So, in my track there was mainly white kids there was a couple of black kids but pretty much all my classes had white students. The same thing with Band and Physical Education. When we got to sixth grade you chose band or PE; most of the kids who chose band were white, while most kids who chose PE were black and so we were separated by that and typically lunch periods where [we sat with] our band or PE friends.
> PS: I remember in 3rd grade I was asked if we wore clothes on Long Island!

These notes, and phone conversations with my oldest daughter, Susan, about their growing up in the South, have, much, much later, shaken me to my core. Why, how could we have missed so many of their hurts, some evidently very painful, that are still rolling in their heads. I don't know enough to solve, or to explain, or to excuse my blindness.

CHAPTER 2

The Jewish Community in Starkville, Mississippi, and We "Fast-Talkin' New York Jews"

To tell the truth, until we moved to Mississippi, we were not observant Jews—not even close! In fact, we resigned our membership from a synagogue in Stony Brook, because of our objections to some of the community's policies. Until our move to Starkville, Carol and I generally went to services once a year—during the ten-day High Holy Day period in September-October: Rosh Hashanah and Yom Kippur.

BRUSHING UP ON JUDAISM, WITH HELP FROM THE JEWISH BOOK CLUB

Even before our move, we had to reexamine our existing relationship to our religion. In 1976, the year we moved to Mississippi, two of our daughters, Sue and Sheryl, were just a few years away from being bat mitzvahed. Given that we were moving into the very heart of the Protestant Bible Belt, we recommitted ourselves to membership in a synagogue, as close to Starkville as possible.

In our visit to Starkville before I accepted the job, Carol and I were made keenly aware of the importance of religious affiliation in this part of the country. Everyone we met, everywhere, from the campus and from the larger community, wanted to know our religious affiliation. For New Yorkers like us, this was a new experience as well as an irritating one.

And when the askers were told that we were Jewish, they were perplexed. "But your name, Ball, isn't a Jewish name," they responded; "it's a perfectly respectful Protestant one—probably Episcopalian." And then I had to tell them—quickly—my family genealogy, how my Polish great grandfather, who was Jewish and without a surname because, well, because he was living in Poland, married a traveling English woman and took *her* surname, Ball. It was a double whammy whenever we were asked and then answered the question: we lost anonymity and, because of the incredible story surrounding my last name, we were indelibly impressed in the minds of all those who asked.

Interestingly, the surname of one of the secretaries in the political science department was Cohen. Evidently her husband's grandfather was a rabbi. The rabbi's son—probably because it was very prudent to be a Christian in early-twentieth-century Mississippi—converted to the Baptist faith. And so, there was a Jewish name in the department's administrative offices, owned by a very devout Baptist woman. She was a person who, every three weeks or so, came into my office to tell me that she dreamed of me last night going to hell unless I accepted Christ in my life. And as she spoke these words, tears came to her eyes. "Don't go there," she pleaded with me—every time she had her dream.

She told me she prayed for the souls of non-Christians, people like me who did not share her religious beliefs. She seriously believed that we "nonbelievers" would go to hell in a handbasket if we did not welcome Jesus Christ into our lives. Regularly, I would find on my desk gifts from her: books and pamphlets about the lord Jesus. I finally, firmly—and, I hoped, gently—asked her not to leave these guides for me. Frankly, her behavior scared me. What kind of town did we move into? For it seemed to be one where there was not too much privacy, but, as was the situation with Cohen, there was occasional intense interference in our personal lives.

Up north we had anonymity because of the immense number of people who lived in the region. We never had to answer questions regarding church affiliation. But after we visited Starkville while I considered the new job, we knew that if we moved, we were moving into a very different cultural environment, one in which our private beliefs became public through such questioning by our new, and curious, neighbors.

After Starkville's Catholic priest, Father Meryl Schmitt (who, soon after we met, became a very dear friend), invited me to visit his confirmation class to talk about the Jewish understanding of the Messiah—which I accepted—I was flummoxed! Just what was Judaism's perspective on the Messiah?

I figured that I'd better learn as much about Judaism as I could—quickly and continuously. And so, we joined the Jewish Book Club. Every month or so, I would order another book about my religion. I guessed correctly—for Carol and I and, indirectly, our three daughters soon became the de facto lay Jewish experts just as school started in Starkville. I suspect that our new Southern Christian friends were comfortable asking us questions about Judaism rather than the native, local Jews with deep roots in Starkville and the South. These fundamental Protestants, I believe, felt that we were a small group of transient Jews, "others" who would probably leave Mississippi in the near future and therefore there was no need for them to walk on eggshells when their curiosity led them to raise weighty questions.

I rapidly began studying Judaism's core principles, starting, obviously, with the Jewish view of the Messiah. By my initial meeting with Father Schmitt's Communion students, I felt comfortable about the subject and thoroughly enjoyed these annual meetings with these young students.

While I was brushing up on the Messiah, Carol and our two older young women, Sue and Sheryl, also began their teaching of Judaism in the public schools. Not with lectures about our views on whatever, but with stories, songs, and some delicious Jewish delicacies associated with

Jewish holidays. In the Jewish holiday season of Hanukkah, which generally fell close to Christmas, Carol would bring into our daughters' classrooms potato *latkes*[1] and apple sauce.

For Purim, while the students were eating *hamantaschen* pastries,[2]
she told the story of evil Haman, who wanted all the Jews slaughtered by
the king, and the good Queen Esther, who prevented that from happening. Following Jewish tradition, Carol had the kids twirling their grog-
gers every time she mentioned Haman's name. The youngsters were also
eating their second piece of *hamantaschen*, a triangle cookie made of
dough with poppy seeds or prunes or jam in the middle. (For Jewish
celebrants over the centuries, the cookie was made in the shape of the
triangular hat worn by the evil Haman.)

For Passover, the story of the exodus of the Israelites from slavery
in Egypt and their lengthy journey to the land of Israel, Carol would
bring *matzohs*,[3] the unleavened bread our ancestors carried with them
in their haste to leave their slave status behind them. Always accompanying the stories and the food delights were songs sung by Carol and our
daughters.

Our daughters, around the time of Hanukkah, liked to draw and cut
out Jewish symbols of the holiday and tape these on the classroom's windows, alongside Christmas tree and Santa Claus cutouts. In one class,
the students were so excited about coloring pictures of menorahs (the
candelabras used to celebrate the eight days of Hanukkah) that when
you drove up to our daughter's school, you knew her room immediately.

On the windows of her classroom were hung menorahs and Jewish
stars; displayed on every window of all the other classrooms were pictures of Christmas trees and Santa Claus. (While these activities were,
for our family, positive affirmations of our faith as well as the passing on
of some basic Jewish customs and religious traditions to others, little did
we realize that our behaviors greatly annoyed the dozen silent Jewish
families in Starkville.)

For most goyim in Starkville, knowing or befriending a Jew was very
rare. In our first year in Starkville, Carol joined a women's bowling league.
During the first match of the season, a teammate told Carol: "You're the
first Jewish person I've ever met. But you're not what I expected!" Carol

did not ask the obvious question: "What did you expect?" Instead, she turned, pointed to another bowling team member, and said: "You see Helen right there? Well, she's Jewish!"[4] The woman was stunned to hear this fact.

THE TEMPLE SERVICES AND THE FLIGHTS OF
OUR STUDENT RABBIS

Although Starkville and Oktibbeha County had almost fifty churches, there was no synagogue in the county. The closest places of worship for us were a reform temple in Columbus, Temple B'nai Israel, twenty-five miles east on the then two-lane highway US 82, and a conservative synagogue north of Starkville, in Tupelo, much farther away than Temple B'nai Israel.

Because the Tupelo synagogue did not have a rabbi (for services, lay members of the small community read the Torah), we elected to attend services in the Columbus temple. It had a rabbi, albeit a once-a-month student rabbi who attended the Hebrew Union College in Cincinnati. He flew in on Friday, conducted Friday night services, met with the community on Saturday night for coffee, refreshments, and conversation, conducted Hebrew School for the kids on Sunday morning, had lunch with us in the Morrison's Cafeteria in the Columbus Mall, and then caught the plane back to Cincinnati that afternoon.

The young rabbi-in-training signed a contract to serve the community from the High Holy Days' services in the fall through May of the following year. So we had a nine-visit student rabbi minister to about twenty families from Starkville, Aberdeen, Columbus, and other small towns on the Mississippi-Alabama border.

In the abstract this setup seemed like an attractive one for us. This Mississippi version of Judaism, akin to what we thought frontier Judaism was like, was quite different from our religious experiences in the New York area (infamously referred to in the 1980s by the Reverend Jesse Jackson as "Hymie-town"). We found out, again before we arrived in Mississippi, that the first Jews settled in Columbus in the 1840s and that, given the importance of the city in the growth of the state after the Civil War, there were more than two hundred Jews living in the Columbus area by the end of the century. It wasn't until 1879 that the Jewish community organized and the state of Mississippi officially chartered Temple B'nai Israel as a "Church of the Hebrew Persuasion" (as it was inscribed on the charter).

The reality of synagogue service was a shocker for us. Our first services were the Rosh Hashanah days of prayer in 1976. Surprises abounded. The young rabbi, a guitar-playing person named Mark, conducted services—mostly in English. None of the men wore yarmulkes (skull caps). There was a small choir, which positively impressed us, until we found out—on the very first night of services—that the organ player and the singers were all Episcopalians who were hired to sing the Jewish liturgy on the High Holy Days.

While we were trying to absorb that information, the matriarch of the small community, Hortense Leveck, turned to us at the conclusion of the service and said in a sweet, happy voice: "See you in church [pronounced 'choich'] tomorrow. Happy Rosh Hashanah!" "Where are we?" we said to each other with our eyes. And we knew the answer: Mississippi.

We did not really begin to know what Reform Judaism in the South was like until that first night of Rosh Hashana in 1976. We did not realize that Jews in the South, especially Jews living in isolated and tiny Jewish communities like Starkville's, wanted the religious services "to sound less Jewish—an organ, no Hebrew, rewritten music to sound like hymns, and an orderly service. And the sights—stained glass windows, no skull caps or prayer shawls, families sitting together."[5]

We tried to mesh into the small Jewish community as soon as we arrived in early July 1976. During the first year of our stay in Mississippi, two of us "young folk" in the Jewish community volunteered to reestablish a monthly publication that, for many years, had not been put together and mailed to the congregants. My coeditor, Marilou,[6] was a mother of four whose husband was a member of the US Air Force stationed at Columbus Air Force Base. The family girls were blond, blue-eyed, and very *shiksa* looking,[7] which made sense after Carol and I found out that the entire family converted to Judaism, as did probably 25 percent of the members in our tiny Jewish community.

We called our monthly publication *The Light*, the "memory of the community." It contained gossip under a "From the Community" tag. Jewish Humor was another segment; we "borrowed" the *wit* from Jewish comedians, television comics, and Jewish Joke books. The six-to-eight-page newsletter also included recipes from some of the more mature female cooks in our community. It also provided dates and places for the rabbi's weekend, and we were even able to get the student rabbi to give us something we printed under the "From the Rabbi's Desk" headline.

After the May 1977 issue, however, publication ceased because it was just too hard for Marilou and me to get information, whether gossip or jokes or even recipes, from the Jewish community to publish in our tiny newsletter. Later on, while still living in Starkville, I came to understand why most congregants were reticent about opening themselves up in the newsletter.

Were we too radical for the Mississippi Jews? Perhaps so. The small Jewish community, located in Columbus, Starkville, and western Alabama, had to improvise to continue to survive in the heart of the deep and very fundamentalist Protestant South. And they had survived for nearly a hundred years by the time we joined them. However, 1976 was the only year we worshiped in Temple B'nai Israel during the six years of High Holy Days services we attended in Mississippi.

Thereafter, while we attended services throughout the year in Columbus—there was no need for the Episcopal choir beyond the Holy Days services—we attended High Holy Days services in the Tupelo synagogue for the last five years of our stay in Mississippi. There was no rabbi conducting services, but neither were there Episcopalians singing "Kol Nidre."[8]

THE SAD STORY OF OUR STUDENT RABBI FIRED DURING
HANUKKAH WEEKEND

During our years in Mississippi, we worked with five different rabbis, including, in 1977–78, an ordained rabbi, Ronald Brown. Most of them adapted to the Southern Jewish culture without too much difficulty, although one of these student rabbis was fired—summarily—right after he concluded services in December. He had spent his previous student pulpit year leading a mostly gay Jewish community in San Francisco and then found himself in northeast Mississippi. Day into night! He was still struggling to find the right comportment with our community when he was fired.

That evening, with a small group of Catholic parishioners attending the service, he evidently went beyond Jewish reasonableness in the vicinity of Columbus, Mississippi. First of all, when he recited the blessing, which normally consisted of naming our Jewish forefathers, Abraham, Isaac, and Jacob, he added the names of our Jewish foremothers, starting with Abraham's wife Sarah, and then intoning the names of Rachel, Rebecca, and Leah. His addition to the prayer ritual shocked many in the congregation (you could hear the "oohs" clearly). The final blow for the community elders was when he followed the earlier "blunder" with a sermon that centered on the mysterious Lilith, a little-known but powerful and mystical woman in Jewish lore.

After every service there immediately followed an Oneg Shabbat, an informal celebration of the beginning of our holy Sabbath. Typically, in all synagogues, there was a table always laden with ceremonial wine, grape juice, a challah (special bread baked for the holy day), cookies, and cake. The congregation would congregate in the vicinity of the food and drink and chat about events that occurred since the last time services were held.

Well, during this "firing" Oneg, the president of the temple went about the group, polling the members of the board of trustees about the behavior of the rabbi. Immediately afterward, he informed the rabbi that his services were no longer needed for the rest of the year. He would receive the balance of his salary but was not welcome to return to Temple B'nai Israel. The poor man was absolutely floored by this judgment and left for home the following day.

For the rest of the year, the Friday night services were conducted by lay readers from our small community. There were no Saturday night discussions, nor was there Hebrew Sunday school for the rest of the year.

We were as shocked as the rabbi at this action, but we soon realized that *our* behavior was anathema to most of the members of our own Jewish community in Mississippi. We soon found out how our fellow Jews truly felt about the recently arrived New York Jewish family.

THE HUNDREDTH ANNIVERSARY OF TEMPLE
B'NAI ISRAEL, 1879–1979

We were living in Starkville when the Jewish community in northeast Mississippi and northwest Alabama celebrated the centennial of Temple B'nai Israel. The small Jewish temple was chartered by the State of Mississippi on July 23, 1879, as a "Church of the Hebrew Persuasion." The first Jewish families, immigrants from Germany, arrived in Columbus in the 1840s. Most were peddlers, carrying merchandise, off-loaded from the boats, in wagons to sell in nearby towns in Mississippi and Alabama.

For sixty years, the Jews tried to get involved in Columbus's civic life (a few became members or officers in the local Chamber of Commerce, the Elks, the Masonic Lodge, the YMCA, or Rotary Club or sat on the board of a major bank in the city). They wanted to fit into the community's merchant class because they played a major role in Columbus's economic growth.

The high tide of Jewish growth came at the turn of the twentieth century, when the number of Jews living in Columbus hovered around one hundred souls. The number grew to about two hundred Jews when the *landsmen* living in Starkville and other towns nearby were included in the count of members of Temple B'nai Israel.

Although a number of the Jewish merchants and their sons were veterans of the Confederate Army's Mississippi companies, some of them were buried in unknown graves; although they had visibility as leaders of the city's economic development; and although they were upright community citizens, the equality they hungered for never materialized.

However, their repute did accomplish something they knew all about from living in the old country: religious discrimination. Their public personae led, with increasing regularity, to a spate of anti-Semitic incidents in Columbus. By the 1870s, critics lambasted the city's Jews, calling them "clannish" and "housed up like the terrapin within his shell" in all the city's affairs. One local Jewish businessman responded to the comments, raising an issue that continues to confront Jews and other "others" during the twenty-first century: He claimed that the exclusion began "with you gentiles": "You will not admit the Jew to your home circle; your wives and daughters will not meet theirs on a footing of equality. [We do not shop in local stores because] you cater to local tastes we do not share. We Jews are not accustomed to an unvarying diet of bacon and corn meal [and] appreciated other luxuries in life than whiskey and tobacco."[9]

Such an audacious response from a very visible Jew was met with silence but not violence. However, this particularly angry contretemps took place in Mississippi in the early 1870s. It ended in 1875, just two years before a major political event impacted the country for over a century. A significant dispute arose after ballots were counted to determine who won the 1876 presidential election. The Democratic candidate, New York's governor Samuel J. Tilden, won the popular vote (51 percent to 48 percent), but the Republican nominee, Rutherford B. Hayes, from Ohio, received a one vote majority in the electoral college count (185–184), but not enough to make him the winner.

After weeks of brutal hardball politics, a resolution was announced by the exhausted and very angry leaders of both parties. The Compromise of 1877 awarded the twenty contested electoral college votes needed to elect Republican Hayes, giving him (an electoral college) victory. In return, the Republicans agreed to immediately withdraw all federal troops (nearly twenty-five thousand soldiers) occupying the South, dramatically ending the Radical Republican Congress's Reconstruction policy, which protected the Black community's efforts to achieve political, social, and economic freedom and equality. The deal "effectively ceded power in the Southern states to the Democratic Redeemers Party, who proceeded to disenfranchise Black voters" and other inferior groups for over a century. The Redeemers were conservative, probusiness Southern Democrats, who, during the Reconstruction era, 1866–77, pursued a policy of removing Black freed men and Northern carpetbaggers and scalawags from Southern politics. After 1877, they and other more violent racist vigilante groups such as the Ku Klux Klan were given a free hand and unchecked power to prevent Black citizens from participating in politics and enjoying the freedom and equality the Civil War amendments allegedly provided.[10]

After that seismic change, the position of Blacks, and then all other religious, ethnic, and racial minorities, including the Jewish community in Columbus, Mississippi, shifted rapidly. Any perceived disobedience on the part of the lesser "others" was met with swift, violent, and relentless punishment. White racists had total immunity from the criminal laws of the state. Many of them were the judges and the sheriffs and the deputies who enforced the rule of law in their jurisdictions.

If you were a part of a targeted group, you didn't need a law degree to understand the dangers that members of your group might confront if they spoke out audaciously and spoke the truth in public. Quickly, the "others" understood the options they had in such a society: either one worked hard to become an *invisible* tenant in the Jim Crow South of separate-but-equal living, or—a choice made by millions of Blacks and others—one migrated out of the region in order to escape a brutal prison called Mississippi. But many Jewish men joined the Confederacy to fight in the Civil War, and, until the 1870s some Jews were visible and spoke out imprudently when confronting anti-Semitism or other kinds of discriminatory behavior.

In the twentieth century, however, few members of Temple B'nai Israel were vocal fighters for justice. Henry Meyer, one of the senior members of the temple, was one of them. He was the editor and publisher of the *Starkville Daily News* during the terrible decades when the segregationists were fighting the battle of their lives: avoiding, evading, and delaying the enforcement of civil and voting rights and fair housing bills by any means necessary. It was also the era when a number of Mississippi rabbis joined the local White Citizens' Councils.

Henry was a very ornery and very visible *mensch*.[11] He used his daily to attack the White Citizens' Council's genteel racists as well as fearlessly attacking the Klan's unmerciful use of deadly violence. He continued until his advertisers stopped advertising and his readers stopped reading the facts that revealed the enormity of the cruelty employed to stop the civil rights movement people. He was finally forced to sell the newspaper, but he continued to fight these never-ending battles.

I will never forget Henry's words of encouragement to me while I was, during my entire stay in Mississippi, visibly arguing for the extension of the voting rights act before a congressional committee, or writing op-ed pieces for the *Times* and the *Post* attacking racism, or, as a board member of the American Civil Liberties Union's (ACLU's) Mississippi chapter, fighting the Klan's efforts to hold a cross-burning rally on the grounds of an elementary school that had just integrated, or reporting to the voting section lawyers of the Civil Rights Division of the US Department of Justice (DOJ) actions by a town or city or the state to make voting changes without preclearing them with the DOJ. "You must do the right thing," Henry urged, "whatever the cost!" Henry and his wife were the only members of the temple who acknowledged and applauded my and my family's actions confronting racial and religious discrimination in school or in the Girl Scouts administration or anywhere else in Starkville.

The Jewish communities in the towns and cities of Mississippi have slowly begun to wither away. If, in 1905, there were two hundred Jewish souls in northeast Mississippi who were members of the temple, by the temple's centennial year, 1979, the membership had dropped to nearly 10 percent of the number of Jews who were members seventy years earlier.

There were only twenty to twenty-five adult Jewish members of Temple B'nai Israel while we lived in the state. And it was an aged community. There were fewer than five families, including our family of five, that still had pre-teenagers living at home. Viewing the program of the one hundredth anniversary temple service, eighteen members are listed (other than the student rabbi, David Straus, and the visiting speaker, Rabbi Jan M. Brahms, from Nashville, Tennessee, who was the temple's student rabbi from 1973 to 1975). It was virtually the entire membership of Temple B'nai Israel.

Of that number, in addition to our three young ladies, only Ellen Sonkin had young children. There were a small number of us (perhaps three) who were in their forties and fifties; the majority were much older, retired elders who had the ailments of seniors. And none of them had children nearby, working in Starkville or Columbus, or even Mississippi.

The children of the Jewish parents wanted out for a number of reasons: a much wider number and variety of jobs; better pay and benefits; a much better and vibrant social, intellectual, educational, and cultural environment then anywhere in Mississippi. Camp Henry Jacob was helpful and needed by the younger set at a certain point in their preteen and teenage lives. But it wasn't enough for them when they were ready for college. And so they migrated out of the state, initially to attend a college with a Jewish sorority or fraternity or a Hillel Society, and to a place where there weren't many rural Southern white students.

After receiving a college education, they confronted the perennial challenge of finding a job that, hopefully, would allow them to continue exploring the world and themselves. Starkville didn't meet the needs of these young Jewish graduates. And so they continued their voyage of self-discovery, first to large cities like Memphis or New Orleans, and then went further afield, to New York City, Cleveland, Chicago, and San Francisco. Anywhere but Starkville or Columbus.

The centennial "celebration" of our church of the Hebrew persuasion was, for me, a very sad, touching, and affecting one. It occurred forty years ago, and those Jews of Starkville are all of blessed memory. Writing after so many years about these decent human beings struggling, in their own way, to retain their Jewishness brings tears to my eyes. Were my actions and words about our lives among the Mississippi Jews reckless, unfeeling, and impatient?

And what has been the history of Starkville's Jews since we left in 1982? It has been an incredible history of a small number of Jews evolving in order to provide a loving environment for the community. Temple B'nai Israel has remained the only reform Jewish temple in northeast Mississippi.

After reading its web page and taking in the photos of events and of people, young and old,[12] who are members of our old temple, I was very surprised and moved to see the spirited goings-on at B'nai Israel in a new century. Since 2007, there has been a full-time ordained rabbi, Dr. Seth Oppenheimer, serving the needs of the temple's membership. There are now Mississippi State faculty who are members of the temple, along with Jewish students of Mississippi State University's Hillel Society. In 2020, unlike when we lived in Starkville, the temple has a very active sisterhood that is, among many activities, engaged in assisting the city's needy families, for example, by presenting checks to local nonprofits serving less advantaged persons and supporting the local Safe Haven for Mothers and Children program.

It makes me happy to see a small Jewish community work to grow and, evidently, embellish its religious heritage within and beyond the congregation.

GOING TO SCHOOL TO END BIBLE READING

During our first fall in Mississippi, our family had its first run-in with a sacred, hallowed tradition in Mississippi and, at the time, a great many other states: Bible reading in class. We approached the problem very carefully. We were Starkville residents for only 1.5 months when we had to address this practice.

Carol and I met with the school administrator, and he suggested a fix for *our* problem: while the prayers were read in the classroom, Susan would excuse herself and do "busy" work in the principal's office. Then she would return to her class for the rest of the school day. After speaking with Susan, we agreed to this accommodation, although we were somewhat uncomfortable with it. We were very new residents, and we wanted to arrive at a solution without raising hackles on the necks of the Protestants.

A few months into the resolution, however, Susan found herself in the county hospital with painful stomach cramps. The doctors were puzzled because they did not find anything physiological to account for her hurting. After a few days, it became clear to the medical staff that her aches were psychological. Sue, who was ten at the time, then told the two of us about her teacher and the problems she was having. There were three problems: prayers and teacher ignorance, compounded by the teacher's cruel put-downs of Sue's "errors."

Every day, the teacher, who was also Sue's homeroom teacher, would start the day with prayer and Bible readings. Until her hospital stay, Sue never said anything about the prayers. And she did agree with the decision to have her absent herself from prayer time.

However, it did bother her a great deal and was one of the reasons that led to her hospitalization. The other issue was more wounding for Sue. For about a month the same teacher, who was not too smart, taught geography, and she would regularly state "facts" that were incorrect. Sue would raise her hand and correct the teacher. Occasionally it was spelling errors. For example, her teacher said that *parcel post* was spelled "*partial* post."

Other times it was geography errors stated by the teacher and corrected by Sue. For example, according to the teacher, the Mount St. Helens disaster occurred in Oregon. Well, because our family had visited the scene of the disaster during our annual summer RV holidays, Sue knew that it was in Washington State—and she again corrected her teacher.

The woman did not take kindly to these actions of a now-eleven-year-old and, with cruel words, conveyed her irritation to Sue. We resolved the problem Sue encountered with her teacher by suggesting that Sue write down further misstatements and that she should let us have the notes she scribbled. That seemed to work. The following year, Sue moved to another public school building and did not have any problems on that score.

After these revelations, we returned to school, this time to *resolve* the prayer issue. We demanded that the principal stop school prayers. He was very stiff-necked, unwilling to end the practice.

"How about if we read from the Old Testament, wouldn't that solve you Jews' concerns?"

We were equally stubborn.

"No, it wouldn't," I stated, "because the Supreme Court said that prayers could not be said or read in public school."

After we threatened to begin a lawsuit, with the Mississippi ACLU organization's lawyers working on our behalf, the principal caved in and agreed to stop the prayers—but only, as we found out later, in Sue's classes. It was a sort of compromised compliance with our demand. Since we really did not want to get into a lawsuit over the matter, as long as our kids did not have to face Jesus every morning, it was acceptable to us.

Compounding the problem of prayer in the public schools—or at least in our children's classes—was the reality that, in 1970s Starkville, *every* formerly all-Black segregated school building continued to be used. Instead of our daughters going to one school for grades 1–6 and then to one middle school, and then high school, they went to at least four different school buildings for their elementary school education.

This meant that Carol and I would have to visit all these administrators to object to the reading of the Bible in that particular school building when one of our children was there. It was something we had to do, not only to prevent Sue and our other two children from experiencing any untoward problems because of the Bible reading but also because Bible reading in public schools, in the 1976–77 academic year, when we challenged the practice, was still unconstitutional thanks to a 1947 Supreme Court case, *Everson v. Board of Education.*

Everson "incorporated" the First Amendment's clause prohibiting the establishment of religion (hereafter "the Establishment Clause") into the Fourteenth Amendment's clause providing for due process (hereafter "the Due Process Clause"). The inclusion meant that no state law or federal statute that established or supported (using state funds), or denied support for, *any* religious group could pass constitutional muster. The New Jersey case suit was brought by a taxpayer who argued that state tax funds distributed to parents for support of parochial school bus fees for their children were an "establishment of religion" prohibited by the Fourteenth Amendment's Due Process Clause.

Justice Hugo Black's majority opinion, however, was very controversial. The other eight justices joined Black's oration on incorporation's reach: "Neither a state nor the Federal Government can, openly or secretly, participate in the affairs of any religious organizations or groups and vice versa. In the words of Jefferson, the clause against establishment of religion by law was intended to erect 'a wall of separation between Church and State.'"

Everson was one of many dozens of watershed opinions of the US Supreme Court handed down over almost five decades, from the 1930s to the mid-1980s. During this critical period of constitutional history, the court incorporated, incrementally, article by article, most of the Bill of Rights' guarantees into the Fourteenth Amendment's Due Process Clause. Until this absorption process began, the conventional understanding of the Constitution was very clear: The amendments contained in the Bill of Rights were restraints only on the power of the national government. The First Amendment's initial words spelled out that 1789 theory: "*Congress* shall make no law . . ." (emphasis added). Article I, Section 10, was the primary limit on state actions until the Civil War Amendments.

The Fourteenth Amendment's first section states, in part, that "no state shall . . . deprive any person of life, liberty, or property without due process of law." The argument for incorporating most of the provisions of the Bill of Rights into that segment of the Fourteenth Amendment was an unchanging and self-evident one: a specific Bill of Rights Amendment was so fundamental that neither a federal or a state law that ran counter to that right could stand—unless the government was able to show a compelling national interest for the curb.

There was, however, a Supreme Court–created Catch-22. Black's definition of "no law respecting an establishment of religion" was an all-encompassing one:

> The "establishment of religion" clause of the First Amendment means at least this: Neither a state nor the Federal Government can set up a church. Neither can pass laws which aid one religion, aid all religions or prefer one religion over another. Neither can force nor influence a person to go to or to remain away from church against his will or force him to profess a belief or disbelief in any religion. No person can be punished for entertaining or professing religious beliefs or disbeliefs, for church attendance or non-attendance. No tax in any amount, large or small, can be levied to support any religious activities or institutions, whatever they may be called, or whatever form they may adopt to teach or practice religion.[13]

However, after he delivered a very broad interpretation of the Establishment Clause, Black then, on the merits of the petition, concluded that in *Everson*, the "high wall of separation" between church and state had not been violated—breached—by the state statute and that the government's use of public funds to pay the parents for such busing was constitutional because it was not a direct support of religion. But four justices dissented from Black's judgment on the merits of the taxpayer suit. They disagreed with Black's argument that public funding for paying parents for their kids' busing was indirect aid and did pass constitutional muster. If the public money had gone to the parochial schools the children were going to, then it would be direct aid that breeches the high wall of separation. This argument has continued ever since *Everson*.

By the time we confronted the issue, three decades after *Everson*, most states were dutifully obeying the rule of law. In 1950, thirteen states, a majority from the South, required no less than ten verses of the Bible at least three times a week, while another twenty-five states allowed school boards to have Bible reading; in 1977, however, only five states still required Bible reading. Naturally, Mississippi was one of the five "last ditchers."

We obsequiously visited the principal, who knew why we were visiting, and he assured us that Sue would not be exposed to Jesus and his stories every morning. And so life went on in the Starkville public school system for our kids. At no time, interestingly, before or after we fought the issue, did any other Jewish family in Starkville address the issue of Bible reading in school. But that did not trouble us. We believed then—and believe now—that we had no choice but to deal with an environment that had created visible psychic havoc for one or, as I found out recently, more of our children.

A FLEETING "RACE MIXING" SCRAP?

Another incident, involving race mixing, took place when Sue was in middle school. Before classes began each morning, many of the children would hang out in the school cafeteria. One of Sue's friends had a portable radio, and they listened—and occasionally danced—to the music. One evening we received a call from a school administrator.

"Do you know that your daughter Susan is dancing before school?" she asked.

I said: "I didn't know that, but so what's the problem? Is there a public school rule that prohibits dancing?"

After a slight hesitation, the woman said, "Well, Sue was caught dancin' with a negra boy, and that's not acceptable!"

"What!" I exclaimed. "Where is it written that dancing with a Black friend is somehow against school rules?"

"Well, it's not written, but it just ain't right!"

"Too bad!" I said to the woman and hung up.

After I gave Carol the gist of the conversation, we agreed not to tell Sue of the phone call. We were not called again. As far as we know, Sue continued to dance with her friends before school—including her many new Black friends.

That was the first openly racist issue we confronted in Starkville. Another incident soon followed. It was a very disturbing one for all of us! Sue and Sheryl wanted to join a Girl Scout group in Starkville. We inquired about the girls joining a troop in the county and found that there were no vacancies in any of them, except for an unauthorized small group of girls who did not have a permanent adult leader. (Our kids knew and were friendly with a number of them from school.) Furthermore, it was, except for our two girls, an all-Black Girl Scout faux troop. Carol volunteered to become the small troop's leader. It immediately became the only integrated Girl Scout troop in the county!

Carol had the part-time assistance of two female students at MSU when the troop held its meetings. In addition, one of the other mothers, a Black faculty member in the education department at MSU, became the coleader of the troop. We became good friends through this Girl Scout connection.

However, this scouting experience became, literally overnight, a harrowing, fearful one. In Oktibbeha County, there was a Girl Scout camp where the youngsters spent a few weekends a year sleeping in the available tents and generally having a great time. On the first such weekend that Carol's integrated troop could participate, she was told by the Girl Scout administrators that they could not go because Carol was not "familiar" with Girl Scout regulations.

We went anyway. Using our two cars, a blue Chevy Suburban and a yellow Dodge station wagon, we crammed all the girl scouts into the autos and drove to the camp for the weekend with all the other troops. Joining us was the Black troop coleader. Her husband was still working, but he would join us that evening for the weekend. Well, we had a great time unloading and setting up the tents, playing, eating, and then roasting marshmallows and making "s'mores" around the fire.

Our friend's husband, however, was still missing when we all turned in. Around 2 a.m. I heard some noise outside the tent area. Taking my flashlight, I went outside to see what was going on. It was the missing husband, wandering around the area, with no flashlight. I called him over and brought him to his wife's tent. She was up in an instant and beside herself with fear and anger about his early morning arrival.

"Are you crazy," she yelled. "Do you want to get yourself shot wandering around a Girl Scout camp at 2 in the morning? Don't you have any brains? Fool, do you really want to get yourself killed?"

He didn't say a word when he entered the tent. I had not seen such fear and anguish in a woman's voice until that night. I went back to our tent. Carol was up. I told her what happened. She didn't say anything.

BECOMING A BAT MITZVAH IN MISSISSIPPI

The once-a-month religious services were always a surprise, for we never had a clue about the student rabbi's stay this time. He would fly into the Golden Triangle Regional Airport on Fridays about three in the afternoon. His host for the weekend picked him up, brought him to their house, had an early dinner with him, and then brought him to Columbus for the Friday night service. Saturdays were set aside for visiting with elderly or infirm members of the congregation during the day, and then, in the evening, the rabbi-in-training would lead a discussion group of the members about some aspect of Judaism's history.

These sessions were held in Columbus, and when the school ended, everyone went to lunch at Morrison's in the mall. After lunch, the host family drove the rabbi back to the airport for his return flight to the Hebrew Union College.

It was in this setting that Sue, in 1980, and Sheryl, the following year, became Bat Mitzvah, "woman of the commandments," woman of the Jewish community. The day is special because, in the Jewish religion, when a young man or woman turns thirteen, the Bar/Bat Mitzvah is the ceremony that formally, religiously, welcomes the young person into adulthood in the Jewish community.

Preparations for both of our daughters for their special days were quite different from those for their friends still living in New York and very different from the preparation for Bat Mitzvah that their youngest sister, Melissa, went through after we moved to Salt Lake City. First of all Sue and Sheryl had no three-times-a-week Bat/Bar Mitzvah class to attend from August until their actual Bat Mitzvah many months later.

Sue and Sheryl did not have to attend weekly Shabbat services in Mississippi, because there was only one service a month. There was no taskmaster they had to meet with weekly to show the progress they were making in their Bat Mitzvah studies, in reading their Torah *parsha* in Hebrew, and in writing their speech.

They were largely on their own to study the service, review the words of the service they had to say, learn enough Hebrew to be able to read a small part of the Torah portion that was uttered in their specific weekly Bat Mitzvah Shabbat service. They also had to write their own little sermon, which called for them to incorporate the religious ideas in the weekly Torah reading with their own ideas about their meaning. I was the taskmaster during Sue's year of preparation, and an Israeli couple in residence at Mississippi State University helped Sheryl prepare for her special day.

Student rabbi David Straus was their monthly teacher (he was rehired by the community after the first year in Mississippi, 1979–80). While I and the Israelis helped Sue and Sheryl with their Hebrew, Rabbi David worked with them on their Torah reading and on the speech they had to make. Sue's Bat Mitzvah was on April 19, 1980. It was a joyous occasion with friends and family from the North visiting and sharing the occasion with us. (It was my father's only visit to us in Mississippi; a few months later he died on the operating table in a New York City hospital after another mugging. The pathologist discovered Abe's mesothelioma during the autopsy.)

After the service in Columbus, guests, mostly goyim friends of our children from the Starkville area, came to our home in Starkville for a lovely reception. Sheryl's Bat Mitzvah, on May 9, 1981, was equally enjoyable. (I must proudly note that in 1980, our youngest daughter, Melissa—Missy—was also featured in the *Starkville Daily News*. She was one of four youngsters, all between the ages of four and nine, who were winners in the Starkville annual doll show. Her entry was the winner in the "Most Unique Stuffed Animal" contest. She was as thrilled as we were, and she carried the ribbon—and the photo of her published in the *Starkville Daily News*—around with her for a few weeks.)

Melissa had her Bat Mitzvah in 1985, under very different circumstances. We were living in Salt Lake City; I was the dean of the College of Social and Behavioral Sciences at the University of Utah. There was one conservative synagogue in Salt Lake City, but it was a large one, with more than three hundred families, a full-time rabbi, and a full-time cantor—who was also the taskmaster for all the Bar and Bat Mitzvah students.

Unlike her two siblings, Missy had to go to Hebrew School three times a week and regularly attend Saturday services. She hated the rigid Bat Mitzvah routine and continually complained about the unfairness of her situation. "It's not fair," she would tell us weekly. "Sue and Sheryl never had to go through all this for their Bat Mitzvahs! Why me?" she would wail. I had my hands full making sure she went to her classes and to the Shabbat services. It was a tougher time than my worst hours as dean of the college—and I had many of those!

She barely made it through the process and protocol and did become a Bat Mitzvah in the spring of 1985. We even taped her synagogue performance—but don't ask to view it because, a few years later, I mistakenly taped a New York Giants football game over Melissa's Bat Mitzvah video. I think Melissa has never forgiven us for moving out of Mississippi before her Bat Mitzvah.

On occasions such as our daughters' Mississippi Bat Mitzvahs, we broke into our stash of precious bagels imported from Atlanta through Carol's brother Les. Whenever we traveled to that metropolis, to visit our best friends, Tom and Jean Lauth, and their four boys, we always returned with twelve dozen assorted "New York" style bagels. And during the five-hour drive back to Starkville, the five of us in the car devoured a number of the still-warm delicious bagels. The bagel aroma in the car was pure heaven for us—as were the bagels. Once home, we would freeze these delicacies and defrost them for special occasions such as Bat Mitzvah receptions.

We could never accustom ourselves to buying and eating those soft, miserable bagels sold in plastic bags at the local supermarket. We would buy a package when we were truly, truly desperate for a bagel. No matter what we did to try to make it a reasonable facsimile, nothing ever worked. Local bakeries did not bake bagels, and so, it was either eating the "Lenders" plastic-encased soft bagel, or doing without, or importing the real stuff from Atlanta. This was a no-brainer.

When Carol's brother Les, who taught at Georgia Tech University, in Atlanta, had to travel west, he would always take US Route 82, which took him through Starkville, in order to visit his sister and us. The unspoken reason was that he was carrying our twelve dozen bagels, our manna, from Atlanta. When we moved to Salt Lake City in 1982, there were no bakeries that made and sold bagels in our vicinity, and we were still not able to enjoy Lender's bagels.

In 1998 I visited Starkville to give a talk about the first Black person to serve on the US Supreme Court: Justice Thurgood Marshall. (I had just finished a biography of Justice Marshall, *A Defiant Life*, which would soon be published by Crown/Random House.) Ironically, I was invited to give a talk because I was selected as that year's John C. Stennis Distinguished Lecturer. My friend and former colleague in the political science department at MSU, Bill Giles, had a surprise for me. At long last there was a bagel place in Starkville! The owners baked the bagels and then, in their always-packed dining facility, served a variety of bagel sandwiches.

It was, for me, an eye- and mouth-opener. Eating a warm onion bagel with cream cheese and lox and tomato, baked and smeared right in downtown Starkville! I looked around. None of the Jewish community members that I knew were in view, but a great many goyim were eating their bagels with gusto, just as we did. It was a great sight. And the bagels were quite delicious, much better than the Lender's, almost on a par with those delicious bagels we imported from Atlanta, but, alas, nothing close to the bagels made in New York City!

EMBARRASSING STARKVILLE'S FIFTEEN SILENT
JEWISH FAMILIES

Starkville's Jewish community was a small one in the 1970s. A few—two in addition to me—were associated with the university. Another was Henry Meyer, the former publisher and editor of the *Starkville Daily News*. Most of the congregants were retired businesspersons, who ran jewelry stores, shoe stores—one couple even ran a "Christmas Tree"–type store year-round.

Many of our coreligionists had roots in the South that went back more than a century; they had kin in Memphis or Atlanta or Greenville, South Carolina, or New Orleans. Jews in the South, I soon realized, had kin all over the region. The grapevine was always working, and its stories were about the good times and the bad times of the family, the *gansa mishpucha*.[14]

All of the Jewish families had lived in Starkville for generations and had developed working and social relationships with the goyim in the town. For example, during the holiest days of the year, Rosh Hashanah and Yom Kippur, there would appear in the *Starkville Daily News* small paid announcements stating, "Kleban's Shoe Store will be closed for a religious holiday." These announcements never mentioned the Jewish High Holy Days or said "closed for Rosh Hashanah, the Jewish New Year." The community was generally tolerated by the goyim, and to my knowledge no overtly anti-Semitic incident was ever experienced by that small group while we were living in Mississippi.

I was told the story of the only time the Jewish community of northeast Mississippi was collectively frightened by outside events. It occurred during the High Holy Days of Rosh Hashanah, some years before we arrived. It was a time of great tension in the area because of federal court orders to integrate Mississippi public schools. There was also the heroic civil rights movement, led by Black men and women, some rabbis, ministers, priests, and young students, which challenged racial discrimination throughout the South.

Well, during the Rosh Hashanah services during this turbulent, violent time—with the Episcopal choir singing—a group of military personnel entered Temple B'nai Israel with their weapons prominently displayed. After a moment of pure fright, the congregation realized that these were *Jewish* airmen from the Columbus Air Force Base who came to the services directly from guard duty. After storing their weapons, these airmen joined the congregation for the New Year's services. In short order, that incident became a memorable "rural legend" in the Jewish community.

If any anti-Semitic incidents were experienced by individual members, they were absorbed by the family and not discussed with others in the community. Oh, there were slights, some intentional, others probably not. I remember an occasion when I had students over to our house for a get-together where we discussed the upcoming final examination. One of my students, a fine, affable young man, began talking about a stereo system he had purchased for his apartment. "Well," he said, "I really Jew'd the guy down and got a real good price. You really have to Jew-down to get a bargain." One of his friends kicked him in the shin, trying to dislodge that phrase from his conversation, at least while he was in my house.

To no avail. He must have used that phrase another two times before his buddies switched the subject to the recently ended college football season of the Southeastern Conference. As the kids were leaving, the shin kicker apologized for his friend, saying the friend was just unaware of the term's offensive meaning to Jews. That was not the only occasion when we were privy to that language, but I just never got angry enough to counter. I figured I was in the South and that the phrase "Jew-down," like other insensitive slurs, especially "n****r," was an old expression ingrained in the subterranean corner of most white Mississippians' psyches.

Until our already-discussed effort to combat prayer reading in the public schools, to my knowledge, my coreligionists never tried to limit Bible reading in public schools. Indeed, during the height of the anti-civil-rights movement in Mississippi and other states in the South—the 1950s and 1960s—some loud segregationist voices came from members of Mississippi's Jewish community, including a few rabbis in the state who were members of the local White Citizens' Councils that sprang up and spread like kudzu after the 1954 *Brown* school integration decision. On the whole, however, Southern Jews "watched the civil rights crisis hoping not to be harmed themselves." As Eli Evans recalled, a rabbi who served in the South for over thirty years said, "Jews just don't want to stick their necks out."[15]

We found out—directly—how our fellow Hebrews felt about us during the course of one of those Saturday evening congregation get-togethers. Carol and I were prepared to listen to a discussion of the "Archaeology of the Old Testament." The student rabbi was the discussion leader and was preparing to use maps and photographs of ancient structures in the conversation. However, we never did get around to the planned conversation because, by that time, our open defiance toward public school administrators during the past few weeks concerning religious practices had an unexpected consequence.

During the preceding week, Carol and I had another occasion to visit with another principal to talk about Bible reading in yet another public school Sue was attending for the first time. The conversation had gone well, and we did not have it on our minds when we met with our fellow Mississippi congregants that Saturday night. However, for our fellow Jews—most of them—what we did once again was too much. We were branded as civil rights activists by our coreligionists. We were both a threat and an embarrassment to the Jews in our town.

"God damn," said one of the community elders, "can't you two just keep quiet and let the goyim read their stupid prayers! You're just makin' waves for us in Starkville with your god-damned demands. And sooner than later you're goin' to move out of Mississippi but we're left here having to deal with all the bad feelings you're stirring up in *our* town!"

Carol and I were shaken and perplexed at this outbreak.

Before we could respond, another elder, one of the women, spoke up. "And you talk too damn fast, for us, and for the rest of the people in Starkville. And you wear your religion on your sleeves, goin' to schools with Jewish foods, and talkin' to the goyim about Jewish ideas, and Jewish holidays. We don't want *visibility*; we've lived here for generations without doin' things that bring attention to our religion."

She stopped momentarily to take a breath and began again. "We like being white and invisible. It's a safety device. Let the goyim pick on the n****rs, we say, and we'll get along as we have been getting' along for over a century! We're all happy livin' the way we live, and we don't get into trouble with the goyim. At least, not until you two came here with your kids!"

And then it really began. Many of the Starkville Hebrews present, with a few exceptions (Henry Meyer and his wife and the revered leaders of the community, Henry and Hortense Leveck), sat down and chastised us for our activities and behaviors, actions that brought them into our vortex because we were all Jews. We realized that there was not going to be an Old Testament discussion this night.

The evening was also not simply a venting of spleens about the behavior of two New York Jews in their midst. True, we were the horrible barbarians—by virtue of being Jewish and by opening our mouths—whose behavior had rubbed off on them. Without uttering an angry word, these coreligionists saw their once-invisible gates protecting them thrown open. They were very frightened because our actions threatened their peaceful coexistence with the goyim of Board Town, Mississippi.

We returned home, thoroughly taken aback and upset by the hostile words we heard. We knew that we were visible Jews, but we were doing things that we felt were important to our family's mental health as well as worthy. This venting took place early during our stay in Starkville. The Jews were right on one important point. We would, probably in another two to three years, leave Starkville and Mississippi, while most of them would never leave.

But we couldn't just remain quiet about our newfound Judaism. And it went beyond our religious beliefs. I was on the board of directors of the Mississippi chapter of the American Civil Liberties Union (discussed in a following chapter). Carol was the Girl Scout troop leader of the only integrated troop in the county. She went to the schools annually to celebrate Hanukkah and other Jewish holidays with stories, food, arts and crafts, and songs. These were some of the other very visible behaviors of ours that upset many persons in Mississippi—Jews and goyim alike—in temple, in the local school administrator's offices, and beyond, in the town itself.

I was also crisscrossing the state researching and examining whether Mississippi towns and cities were complying with or disobeying the 1965 Voting Rights Act. Most of the Mississippi cities were ignoring the statute, and the US Department of Justice was made aware of these noncompliant behaviors by myself and a very small number of other unofficial—and unpaid—monitors who would call the Voting Section of the Civil Rights Division of the DOJ to report these nonimplementation behaviors to the senior lawyer of the section, David Hunter.

I was also one of only two Mississippians who, in late June 1981, were called to Washington, DC, to testify regarding the continuation of the Voting Rights Act. I forcefully argued that the Voting Rights Act had to be continued because racial discrimination in Mississippi was still a stark reality. My appearance before the House Judiciary Committee was covered in every paper in the state, from the *Starkville Daily News* to the *Columbus Commercial-Dispatch* to the *Jackson Clarion-Ledger*, the state newspaper.

Carol, who finally was hired to teach mathematics in Starkville High School, was as vocal as I was regarding civil rights issues generally. She was immediately labeled a white liberal, and she, another woman so tagged, and the only two Black teachers were assigned the same lunch breaks, the same lunch assignments, and a single faculty office to share. These four "outsiders" also shared the same free period.

All of our activities were tied together by our Judaism; they were not unknown to our neighbors and to Starkville's Jews. It was an interesting, at times tense, environment for us until we left the state. Although I was somewhat immunized from the gossip and the less-than-friendly interactions with Starkvillians, my wife was not. She had to leave the high school because of her discomfort living in the small ghetto. However, she was able to teach college algebra at State, thanks to the efforts of Jimmy Solomon, the head of the math department. For the last two years of our stay in Mississippi, she taught at State, and that was a great joy for her. (Carol also received her master's degree in mathematics at State; she collected an A in *every* course she took!)

THE PHONE CALLS FROM OUR GOOD FRIENDS,
THE LOCAL KLAN KLAVERN

What we could never really deal with were the terrible phone calls we began receiving in the last half of our stay in the state. Invariably, they would come late at night or early morning, between midnight and 3 a.m., and would essentially be just one message. "Get out of town or you're gonna find out what we can do to god-damned Jew-N****r lovers!" At first, we were terrified. We changed telephone numbers to escape the harassment. The callers quickly found out the new numbers, and the calls came back. Here we were, in Mississippi, in 1980, and we were receiving these horrible phone calls. After a tepid response from local law enforcement persons, we simply stopped reporting and took the phones off the hook.

Fortunately, these threats never amounted to anything; no crosses were burned on our lawn on Sherwood Road. No rocks were thrown into our windows. Other than the phone calls, no actions were ever taken by the Klan.

The only dead bodies found on our front door were rabbits killed by our pussy cat, Snowy, and a phantom animal that scared the girls one day before school. I came out and swatted the *thing* to death, but when I went out to dispose of the body, it had disappeared!

That evening, Friday night, was football time in the South. On the way to the game, I mentioned my murder of a small animal and its subsequent disappearance. Had I not been driving, there would have been a terrible car accident. What happened? Laughing hysterically, the group informed me that I had killed a "possum." The tenement Jew met the Shadow!

PITCHING FOR THE ST. JOSEPH'S CATHOLIC CHURCH SOFTBALL TEAM

Most of our close friends in Mississippi were members of the local Catholic church, St. Joseph's. Many of the Catholics in Starkville were faculty at Mississippi State. A great many of them came to the South from the Northeast, especially the New York metropolitan area. In many ways, they were our *landsmen*,[16] our family, more so than the local Mississippi Hebrews. A number of the members were also colleagues of mine in the political science department—and most of them had kids our daughters' ages.

The parish priest, Meryl Schmitt, was an absolute hoot. He always spoke softly, except at softball games, and had a radiant smile. He was truly loved by his parishioners. He was the priest for the entire six years of our stay in Mississippi. He attended our girls' Bat Mitzvahs and insisted that I participate in his church's confirmation classes by giving talks about, for example, the Jewish understanding of the Messiah. I was delighted to do this for Schmitt, who once told me that he would have been proud if he had been born into a Jewish family. He, along with my dear friend Charles Lowery, a historian and associate dean of the College of Arts and Sciences, was a brother to me.

Oktibbeha County had a very well-organized slow-pitch softball league. All the teams in the league represented their churches. Because of its small size and its advanced age, accompanied by many knee, hip, and back aches, Columbus's Temple B'nai Israel was not able to field a team in these athletic activities. However, St. Joseph's invited me to play on their softball team. I agreed, with a great deal of pleasure. And they presented me with a special shirt. On it was the name of the church, St. Joseph's, but they added one item that set me apart from my teammates. Between the "St." and the "Joseph's," there was plastered a white Jewish Star of David. I wore that shirt proudly every game I played for and with the Catholics.

Perhaps the greatest day of my softball life in Starkville was the day St. Joseph's played the powerhouse of the league, the First Baptist Church team. Because of the large number of congregants, the church fielded a number of teams in the league, but the team we were playing that day was the major league group. (The other First Baptist teams were basically minor league quality.) They had really neat polyester baseball uniforms, white with scarlet red lettering on their chests that proclaimed, "First Baptist."

St. Joseph's was outfitted in our blue T-shirts with white lettering across the chest. We took the field and began to play ball. I was the pitcher for St. Joseph's, and that day I had an extremely effective very, very slow pitch. It absolutely baffled these trim Baptists, and by the last inning it was—very surprising—0–0. We were up first, and I was first up. On the second pitch I swung and really connected. It was an "in-betweener" and the left fielder and center fielder both ran to chase the ball down. I huffed and puffed (age forty-one and not in great shape) and found myself barely standing at third base. I thought briefly of trying to score, but I was plum tuckered out, as they say in Mississippi.

There I was at third base with no one out. This was the stuff dreams are made of: last inning, man on third and no one out. Scoreless game. However, sadly, I never scored, and in the bottom of the ninth, the Baptists teed off on me and we lost.

I have always regretted not trying to score when I had the chance. I could have been hit by the relay throw and scored; the throw could have been wild, and I scored; the catcher would have dropped the ball after I plowed into him—and I scored, and so on and so forth. Every scenario I imagined had me scoring with an inside-the-park home run. There are nights, even now, when I dream of that top of the ninth. I should have tried for home plate, even though I probably would have crawled the last fifteen feet. I really regret not trying to score.

However, my years with the St. Joseph's players and their families were very happy ones, much happier, sadly, than my years with Starkville's Jews. My big mouth was an embarrassing abomination to my *landsmen*; fortunately, it was not seen in the same light by my St. Joseph's Catholic Church friends.

While the Jewish community in Starkville was for the most part an elderly community (where grown-up children moved to Memphis or Atlanta), and very *Mississippi*, the Catholic community we knew was, demographically, very different. Many of the Catholics were faculty at MSU; they were our age or younger. And many of them, like us, were outsiders. They came from New York and Massachusetts and Wisconsin and other states outside the South to live and work in Mississippi. And we, Catholics and Jews, were equally a part of the society of the "others"!

Whenever I recall this paradox, it saddens me. I understand the reasons for this irony, but it still bothers me that most of my religious brethren saw and derided Carol and me as fast-talking damn New York Jews who were totally insensitive to the feelings and the fears of the Mississippi Jews. We never fully understood the Starkville Jews' intense desire to stay out of such frays. Evans's recollection of a rabbi's joke about this tendency of Southern Jews sums up their antipathy regarding involvement in human rights crises in their state: "[The rabbi] then told a joke about an all-Jewish jury accidentally selected for a civil rights trial. When the judge asked the foreman for his verdict, the foreman announced, 'Your honor, we've decided not to get involved.'"[17]

Looking back, I realize how much our civil rights actions instantly created trepidation in the hearts and minds of our fellow Jews in Starkville. Although we tried to be more circumspect in our behavior after that Saturday night venting by our coreligionists, we never stopped responding to events we felt were demeaning or discriminatory or racist or just plain unfair and unjust. These actions, we realized, were so unlike the behavior of many Southern Jews when confronted with a crisis. We were, it turned out, outsiders—aliens—to both Southern Jews and Southern Protestants.

CHAPTER 3

"Hey, Rabbi"

Refereeing Football Games in the Magnolia State

I confess. I love the game of football. I did not know how much the game meant to me until we moved to Mississippi in the mid-1970s. I played in high school and, after graduating in 1955, played exactly one half of one game in a semiprofessional league in the Bronx. (I remember that game well because I almost lost my upper front teeth on the last play of the half. I was on defense and was a late substitution. As I was lining up for the play, still standing upright, the ball was snapped and a hunk-of-meat of an offensive tackle threw his elbow into my face, causing the pain and the fear that I no longer had front teeth. For a few weeks it was touch and go but my teeth and I survived, though my football career was over.)

During my college years at Hunter College–Uptown (in the Bronx), which was one of the campuses that made up the City University of New York, I was a fanatical New York Giants football fan. (After I graduated in 1960, Hunter College–Uptown was formally separated from the Hunter College Manhattan campus. It is now called Herbert Lehman College of CUNY.) In those days, the Giants had a superlative team, on both sides of the line of scrimmage. The classic confrontations in those years were the days when the Giants played their bitter enemy the Cleveland Browns, led by quarterback Otto Graham and, later, the great fullback Jimmy Brown.

For us Giants fanatics, Sundays in the fall meant going to their home games. In those days, they played at Yankee Stadium in the Bronx. For us, that meant getting up early, packing a hefty lunch, buying a hefty Sunday paper—the *New York Times*—taking the subway to the 161st Street station on either the "D" train or the 3rd Avenue "El," and, when the doors opened at 9 a.m. (for the 1 p.m. game), purchasing bleacher tickets (cost: five dollars) and running to the area in the bleachers that overlooked the Yankees right field baseball bullpen. We wanted that location because it gave us a fairly unobstructed view of the field from between the 10-yard line and the 15-yard line.

We bought the hefty *Times* because, after some reading, we used the pages to light fires in the available fifty-gallon oil drums spread about the bleachers. After all, we were standing, and then shivering, in the cold, sometimes bitter New York winter weather, for four hours before kickoff. We needed some heat to get us through to game time. After quickly reading the papers, we then started fires in the oil drums, huddled around them for some warmth, and kibitzed for a few hours.

The fever we caught at these Giant home games was not contracted by others. With a few exceptions, there were no heated, passionate rivalries between city high school or college football teams. It was only when we moved to Mississippi that I saw and heard the raw emotions—the passions—in the high school stands and on the field.

WATCHING GIANTS FOOTBALL IN DIXIE, WHEN I FORGOT MY THREE LADIES

I must also confess to some bonehead behavior on my part when we moved to Mississippi in 1976. Unlike Giant watching in New York, where all the away games were televised by the local CBS affiliate, there were very few Sundays when the New York Giants appeared on Sunday afternoon television in Mississippi. When that happened, I was captured by the television screen and did not move away until the game ended. It was probably akin to the condition of some manic-depressive person on lithium: my limbs weighed a ton, and I simply could not stand up and leave the confines of the television room—unless, of course, it was to go to the bathroom or to get another pop.

One Sunday, *knowing* that my Giants were not on television, I took my three daughters to lunch at a local Starkville eatery, Shoney's Big Boy. After receiving the check, I realized I had not taken my wallet. Dutifully, I explained my predicament and told the hostess that I lived only a few minutes away and would quickly return to pay the bill. As a token of my honesty, I left my three young ladies at the restaurant. The three "hostages" were happily sipping sodas and noshing French fries when I left.

When I got home, I quickly found the wallet and, before I left, turned on the television just to see who *was* playing. To my shock, dismay, and then happiness, the Giants were on, playing their bitter rivals the Eagles of Philadelphia. Needless to say, I was instantly detained. Sitting down to watch the game, I was oblivious to the fact that my lovely darlings, my three young maidens, ages nine, eight, and four, had been left sipping soda in the restaurant. I remained that way until the *very* exciting game ended, two hours later. Momentarily I was euphoric, for not only had I caught that rare treat, the Giants on television in Starkville, but the Giants beat the Eagles!

At exactly that time, my wife Carol, who had been in Columbus to meet with friends, came home. "Where are the girls?" she asked in a gentle, unknowing tone. I did not answer for fear of immediate, vengeful retaliation by a very strong, and very beautiful, Jewish mother bred in Brooklyn. Instead, I raced out of the house, got in my car, and headed for the Shoney's, hoping against hope that it was still open, that my precious children were still there, and that the police had not been notified.

And there they were, still eating and sipping what I found out were their third round of Big Boy's fries and soda pop. "Hi, dad," my oldest, Sue, yelled out. "We were wondering what happened to you." I quickly paid the bill—which had increased in the hours I was gone—grabbed my precious ones, and headed home. (Once again—as when I videotaped a Giants game over Missy's Bat Mitzvah—the Giants walloped me at my daughters' expense!) Carol did, of course, find out. My youngest lady, even at such an early age, was the family's "tattler"! The episode, since then, has become one of our family's favorite rural legends.

THE "RABBI": THE FIRST JEWISH FOOTBALL OFFICIAL IN NORTHEAST MISSISSIPPI

High school football in the South is unlike the game called football in New York, where I had come from, and definitely unlike the game played in Utah and other Western states, where I went after my sojourn in Mississippi. In the North and the West, it is, generally, simply a game, and when it is over, the two teams exchange handshakes and other goodwill gestures. For the most part, their stands are filled with two hundred spectators at most. And no fistfights break out during and after the game. The attendees do some cheering during the game, eat hotdogs and drink soda, and then quietly file out of the stadium, much like they do when they leave Sunday morning church services.

I became a football official because my three children, all young ladies, *chose* not to play football.

I myself played football at William Howard Taft High School in the Bronx. For two years, the team played single wing football under a small, wiry coach from the Pennsylvania coal fields named Joe Consagra. (We found out that Coach Joe was a cousin of the great professional football player Charlie Trippi.) Playing football in a Jewish ghetto in the Bronx was a burdensome, tiring activity. Taft had no home field, so all games were away games. Nor was there a practice field at the school. And so every day, four days in a week, going to practice meant packing our equipment in a large war-surplus duffel bag, catching a bus after school, and then, after about a half-hour drive, walking from the bus stop to Crotona Park to suit up in the park's small dressing room. After two hours or so, practice ended, and we traversed the path in reverse. After the bus ride and the storage of our gear in Taft's lockers, we walked home, which was, for me, about another twenty minutes.

In my senior year, another major problem confronted the players. Coach Consagra took another job, and a new coach, Sy Kalman, came on board. He had played T-formation college football at New York University; his position: quarterback! This news meant that a fundamental change to our playbooks was coming. That was very unfortunate because the team studied, practiced, and played single wing football, using Coach Joe's single wing power playbook. (This formation emphasized grinding power-runs, with our offensive linemen opening holes in the defense for our strong tailback to power through the gaps.) Coach Kalman introduced us to the T-formation playbook, which stressed quickness and required a quarterback who was a sharp, strong thrower and quick on his feet. When he arrived at Taft, Kalman faced the players, about two dozen of us, and he soon found out that we did not have a player who could very quickly switch gears.

Although we were losers playing single wing, we were *horrible* losers in the new system. We had a decent quarterback, but he wasn't a speedy leader who could run the basic run-pass option that was at the core of the T-formations. We had one good, tall end and one average running back. All of us had no speed to speak of, and speed and quickness were what was needed in the new system. That season, we wound up with a 1-8-1 record.

But, hell, the parties we had after the games were great affairs. And besides, there weren't that many people watching us play football. So our humiliating losses had few witnesses, and we wore our letter jackets—rather, our girlfriends wore them—proudly. Even though the team won only three games and tied in another in my three years on the team, they were a wonderful three years, for two and a half reasons.

First, *because* of our predicaments—that is, no home field, no practice field, an abrupt change from single wing to T-formation football, and a horrible won-lost record—we bonded together soon after we joined the team. We were a band of brothers, Jewish and Catholic, Black and Caucasian, slow and slower, sharing all the bad situations with good humor. Even when events got us down, our locker room banter drowned out the funky stuff that was out of our control. I always remember how they shouted out to me, "Hey, Ballsie, how're you hangin'?" And my response was nearly always the same. I intoned, in a baritone tone, "Mighty low, mighty low!"

Second, those three years gave me an opportunity to play and cavort and learn from my Black teammates. There were only a handful of them on the team, and we got to know each other as human beings. At home, at this time, was my father, who continuously belittled and joked about the *schvartzes*. For me, his language was always grossly racist. Obliquely, I tried to express my disapproval by talking to him about Cornelius, a Black offensive lineman who also played my position, center. My friend had a great sense of humor; I recall one of his classic shout-outs at practices. When a kick or a pass went awry, a shout would always follow. Cornelius's "misguided missile" warning gave rise to his moniker MM, and so Ballsie and MM were our nicknames all during high school. After graduation, he joined the Air Force and I went to college. We lost contact, but his and Olive's humanity powerfully countered my father's racist beliefs.

Who was Olive? Olive Bowles was the captain of the Taft cheerleaders. She was a lovely Black senior who was in a number of classes with me; we generally sat next to each other because our last names started with *B*. We studied together with a few other friends. One of my few academic strengths was economics; Olive had difficulty only with that subject, and so we spent time on that subject. And before our games, I would stroll over to the cheerleaders to say hello to them and to Olive. I even invited my father to games so I could introduce him to Olive, Cornelius, and other teammates. He never attended a single game during my three years on the team.

Oh, about the half reason for my positive remembrances of the woeful Taft football team: that was our only tie game during my three years on the team. The tie became the occasion for absolute joy for all of us. Taft, with probably the worst football record in the city, was playing our one *real* archrival, DeWitt Clinton High School, then the best team playing in the city. The game took place at the very end of my second year on the team, and we were still using Coach Joe's playbook. We were 1-8 going into the game; Clinton was 9-0. Of course, it was another road game for us. When the buses left for the game, there wasn't the usual pregame rabble-rousing.

Clinton scored first but missed the extra point. The 6–0 score held until well into the fourth quarter, when, miraculously, our wide sweep around the edge of the formation led to a tying touchdown! Pandemonium! On both sides of the field! Long story short: we also missed the extra point, and the game ended in a 6–6 tie. Clinton's record was now 9-0-1. We delighted on our *winning* record of 1-8-1. That joyousness we experienced atoned for all the bus trips to practice fields and for our miserable won-lost record.

I grew a lot because of the team's raucousness and because of the friendships that emerged from this noise. For the first time in my life, I got to know and become friends with men and women with a different skin color, ethnicity, and religion. I always think of my father when I recall these high school years. I wonder whether his view of the *schvartze* would have changed, even slightly, if he had met my friends even one time. I am troubled by my answer to that "if" question. For, by then, I did not foresee a time when my father would give up using the derisive word *schvartze*, to label an*other* discriminated-against minority.

My vision for my family's future, because I was—and am—a football addict, was to coach my three *sons* when they were old enough to play the game. Things didn't quite work out that way, and so, after my third daughter came along, I decided to go into officiating football games in Suffolk County, New York. That was as close to the field as I would ever get as a participant, given that my lovely wife Carol refused to eat the ends of rye bread my mother foisted on her at every opportunity. (Fannie, my dear departed mother, believed in the old Jewish fable that eating the end slice of a loaf of rye would enhance the chances of a male person—who would someday play football—emerging after the requisite nine months in the womb.)

I have always blamed Carol for the state of affairs that led me to officiate rather than coach football. One consolation though: my young ladies grew to enjoy and play integrated soccer—male and female as well as Black and white—in Mississippi, with me and my colleague Tom Lynch coaching. They were regulars on "The Force" until their bodies—well, my girls "blossomed" into teenagers. (The film *Star Wars* was the rage when they played ball; hence the team name.)

THE JEWISH REFEREE, WEARING GLASSES, WITH A BEARD,
AND TALKING FUNNY

When we moved to Mississippi in 1976, I had been officiating high school football for four years. Very quickly after our move in July 1976, I sought out the secretary of the Northeast Mississippi High School Football Officials Association. He was an employee of the local road maintenance system in Starkville, Mississippi. I had an official letter from my New York officials' organization summarizing my experience as a high school official.

Almost all of the men officiating in the association were Southerners. They grew up in Mississippi or Alabama or Texas, played football in high school, and some even played college ball. Most of them were in their thirties and forties, lean and tough-looking. Many, like the association secretary, worked for their municipalities, as road men, water men, laborers. To my knowledge, only one other official was a professor at Mississippi State University. Probably seventy officials worked in the organization—all white and Christian. No one, I quickly found out, was Jewish.

It was quite the reverse in New York, where games were played during the day, either Friday or Saturday. Many officials were educators, secondary as well as university, because we could juggle our teaching schedules in order to officiate. And I was not the only Jew in stripes working games on those days.

As I mentioned earlier, Starkville residents quickly found out a newcomer's religion. One of the very first questions always asked was, "What church do you belong to?" That was the question I was asked by the association secretary when I gave him my documents. I quickly answered: "Billy, I'm Jewish." To which he replied—with a wry smile: "Oh, damn, we got us a rabbi!"

I grew to like and greatly respect this man. For Billy, the task of the official was to let the kids play good, hard football and to make sure the game was kept as safe as possible for the "chillen," as he would call the players. That meant that we had to fairly employ the rules of the game to avoid the preventable actions that caused injuries. Therefore, major penalties such as spearing a player, punching, biting, and other unsportsmanlike conduct, and late hits, clipping, roughing the passer, and personal fouls were penalties we had to call. For if we were not vigilant and did not enforce the rules, one or more of the "chillen" could be injured, occasionally severely injured. Billy's philosophy has always been my philosophy: protect the players from unnecessary and illegal actions by players on the other side.

And so I instantly became known as the Rabbi, and I suppose my facial and vocal features strengthened the "rightness" of my new moniker. I had a beard, wore spectacles, and spoke funny. Sid Salter, a former student of mine at State and a columnist for the *Jackson (MS) Clarion-Ledger*, recently wrote a column about his first meeting with me. It was when he played football for Philadelphia High School.

> The first time I ever met Dr. Howard Ball, he was wearing black-and-white stripes and tossing yellow unnecessary roughness flags during a particularly bruising high school football game between my old Philadelphia Tornadoes and the cross-town Neshoba Central Rockets. He got nose-to-nose with us—taking control of the rivalry. I didn't know his name then, but I remembered "that Yankee referee" as we came to call him behind his back. He was tough, but fair. To Mississippi country boys, the Yankee accent was identifiable, and it was clear that he was an educated man. A burly, bearded fellow with piercing eyes, it was also clear that Ball wasn't intimidated by even the largest lineman on the field when extracurricular contact continued after the whistle was blown.

My religious, physical, and linguistic attributes, as I soon found out, separated me from all the other officials working in northeast Mississippi during the late summer and fall during my years in the state. I remember a game played at Gillespie, Mississippi, where, after the coin toss and before the opening kickoff, the Gillespie coach came over to me, stood inches from my face, and said in a hushed voice: "My kids think you're drunk or something; they say you talk funny and that your breath smells. What're you up to," he asked. I quickly replied: "Well, as you can hear, I'm a Yankee, so I suppose that's funny talk and as for my breath, well, I'm sucking on a couple of mentholated cough drops." I proceeded to breathe in his face and show him the package of cough drops. He smiled and turned, and the game began a few seconds later.

I really grew fond of being called "Rabbi." I was, I realized, a very different kind of official in the association. But, after all, we were all in the profession because we loved football and enjoyed the responsibility—even though there were at times some "interesting" events that occurred during and after the game. And I never detected any hostility on the part of my fellow officials when they greeted me at Shoney's after our Friday evening games.

AN ETHICAL DILEMMA CONFRONTING A JEWISH REFEREE

Playing games on Friday nights posed another problem for me as a Jew. In many small Jewish communities, especially in the South, it was impossible to hire a full-time rabbi to lead the congregation. Although there were forty-seven churches in Oktibbeha County in the 1970s, there was no synagogue or temple. The nearest congregation was in Columbus, about thirty miles due east of Starkville on Highway 82. The congregation, Temple B'nai Israel, once had a large Jewish community (when, in the nineteenth and early twentieth centuries, Columbus was a bustling economic center on the Tennessee-Tombigbee Waterway).

But, by the late 1950s, economic conditions had changed significantly, children moved away to larger cities in the South, and the community could no longer support a full-time rabbi. When we moved to Mississippi, we found that since 1962 student rabbis had been flying in from the Hebrew Union College in Cincinnati to serve the community one weekend a month.

In 1979, on the one hundredth anniversary of its founding, Temple B'nai Israel consisted of about two dozen adults from Starkville, Columbus (including the Columbus Air Force Base Jews), and Ackerman, Mississippi, and a few Jews living in small towns in western Alabama. Of course, the religious service was the first task for the student rabbi, and the religious service, in our reform temple, was on Friday nights.

But because I worked football on Friday nights, I faced a conflict of religious conscience at the time. (In 1977–78, I was appointed president of the temple even though I could not be present for the monthly Friday night services during football season. I was reluctant to accept the honor, but the board insisted, and so I became the "half-year" president.)

The crisis was, I rationalized at the time, easily resolved, hopefully with God's approval: when the invocation was rendered—and it always was!—before the game started, I had my hat off but instead of praising Jesus, I was saying the "She 'ma Yisroel" and another short blessing. When our crew officiated Choctaw football games on the reservation, they, too, had an invocation. However, every word was in Choctaw except for "Jesus" and my whispered Hebrew words.

No one knew of my praying, no one was bothered by my prayers, and I always felt relieved when I said it—as if I captured the hours-long temple service in less than two minutes. And then I was the official on the field who blew the whistle to start the game. But my choice to referee bothered me then, and even now, even though I am a Saturday regular at Shabbos services, I grumble when I recall the decision I made on Fridays during football season.

FOOTBALL AS THE OVERARCHING RELIGION IN MISSISSIPPI

Football in the South is very, very different. It is a serious activity in Mississippi. It is not so much a game as it is a war between towns, cities, and counties, played every Friday evening from August through November. It is a war experienced by nearly the entire population of both towns. Literally thousands of militant fans attended the war. Unlike New York high school football games, in Mississippi there was always capacity—standing room only—attendance on Friday nights.

The visiting team's supporters would come to the game in private cars and, for the majority, in buses operated by that community's Baptist or Methodist or Church of Christ congregation, or by any other Christian denomination that had a serviceable bus or buses (which meant, in the larger towns, the local Methodist and Baptist churches). While the stadium seating was formally integrated, as were the teams when I refereed in the '70s and early '80s, the church buses were not, because most Mississippi churches remained segregated institutions.

In Mississippi, unlike New York and Utah, the other two states I worked as a football referee, an official is assigned to a crew of five persons, led by the referee, and including the clock operator. The referee is the leader of the group and can ask a member of his crew to leave the crew if there is something amiss about that person's field coverage or personal behavior during the contest.

I will never forget the Friday night drives to the towns where my crew was officiating. It was always pitch black. Rural, two-lane roads in the state in the 1970s were poorly marked. No overhead lamps lit the roads, and for the most part the road markings had disappeared. If you somehow lost your headlights, you were cast adrift in a very dark place.

And so we would drive along for miles and miles, and then, as if the North Star turned on, the stadium lights—our target—appeared in the distance. We followed the beacon to the football field, parked our car "nose out" (so we could quickly exit to escape the wrath of the families and friends of the losing team), and began our pregame protocols: checking field conditions, speaking to coaches about any plays we should be on the alert for, checking cleats, examining wraps and casts on players' hands, and so on.

And after the whistle was blown to end that week's war, there is a bloodied and battered winner and an equally bloodied and battered loser. No handshaking after the game, no hurrahs for the other team, none of that effete stuff. The same was true for the townsfolk in the stands. No matter the records of the teams, losses were felt deeply and painfully by the onlookers, and they were not able to control their emotions, their blood pressure—and their anger—for days after the defeat.

I learned this reality in a painful way. We officials finished a particularly desultory exhibition of football by two teams with horrible won-lost records. One team was 1-7 and the other team was 0-8. The "better" team won by the lopsided score of 48–0. Toward the end of the first half, with the score 28–0, the losing team had the ball and was moving down-field. With about thirty seconds left, the quarterback threw an absolutely beautiful spiral pass at least forty yards to his receiver. The youngster caught the ball and was tackled on the 8-yard line.

However, I had thrown a yellow flag on the play because the quarter-back threw the pass when he was almost ten yards *beyond* the line of scrimmage. Clearly, it was an illegal forward pass. Instead of first and goal on the 8-yard line with about twenty seconds left in the half, it was first and twenty-five yards on about their own 40-yard line. Needless to say, the team did not score; needless to say, again, the townspeople were in-flamed about the call and let us know their feelings at halftime and during the second half.

The game ended and immediately our crew was surrounded by about five policemen to escort us to our car. However, I needed to re-trieve my warm-up official's jacket from the losing team's bench. One of the deputies offered to get it for me. Not yet fully aware of the sociology of Mississippi football, I thanked him, but I didn't see any problem in my getting my jacket.

Not a smart move. I slowly walked over to the bench, alone, without an escort, and picked up the jacket. The townsfolk were still in the stands booing me and instantly began throwing bottles, cans, and other debris at me. Given their love for, and expertise in, hunting all kinds of animals, their aim was unerringly on target. I was being stoned by a group of people who had seen their 0-8 team lose 48–0 to the now 2-7 victors!

That night I learned that perceived "taunting" by an official, even if the taunt was in the form of a jacket retrieval from the losing team's bench, is a serious lapse of common sense and, in some Mississippi counties, grounds for commitment to the local hospital. From that game on (the stoning occurred during my first refereeing season in Missis-sippi), we always parked our car "nose out" and jogged quickly to the vehicle after the game.

Also, whenever the home team had a gun raffle going on that night during halftime, I would buy at least twenty tickets in the forlorn hope

that I would win the rifle, not some bitter, drunken father of the losing
team's quarterback—or water boy! I never won a rifle but never grew
tired of buying as many raffle tickets as I could as a sort of insurance
policy. Obviously, since I'm still around, the winners of the rifles, thank
God, evidently were townsfolk whose team won that night.

After the game, we headed toward the Shoney's Big Boy in Starkville.
After leaving the city or town limits, the driver (we would rotate the driving among the four field officials) would pull over, stop, open the trunk,
hoist the beer/pop cooler, and bring it into the cabin for our postgame
refreshments before we arrived at Shoney's.

BEEF AND BEER WITH MY CREW—AND OFFICERS OF THE LAW

On a few occasions, rather than go to Shoney's, we would pull into a
local barbecue establishment, located on the patio of a home of one of
the local chefs in the county. They were middle-aged Black men whose
specialty was barbecue pulled pork and beef, served with coleslaw and
fries. Instead of the Shoney's burgers after the game, we would gorge
ourselves on unbelievably tasty dinners.

The first time we avoided Big Boy for the pulled pork—and, yes, although Jewish, I just loved that delicacy—I found myself in a potentially
embarrassing—indeed, critical—situation. It was during the first few
months of my teaching career at State, where I was a professor of political science. We stopped in a local establishment in Oktibbeha County,
which was, at that time, a dry county—the prohibition applied only to
beer drinking, however. (It was a local law aimed at preventing the thousands of Mississippi State students from enjoying themselves when the
weekend partying began—on Wednesday evenings.)

Hard liquor and wine sales, on the other hand, were permitted so
that the good ladies of the Confederate Warriors auxiliary were always
able to make their mint juleps. We ordered our meats, and while the
plates were being prepared, the beer cooler was brought in and we all
took out cans of beer. We were going to dine on pulled pork, coleslaw,
biscuits, and fries and wash everything down with our Budweisers.

As soon as we started to eat our dinners, two Mississippi Highway Patrol officers pulled up and entered the porch. They, too, were stopping for the barbecue fixings. Well, needless to say, I panicked when I saw them enter the eating area. Flashing in my mind were the headlines in the next day's *Starkville Daily News*: "MSU Professor Arrested for Drinking Beer, Taken to the Starkville City Jail." My god, I thought, I'm going to be locked up in the same jail cell Johnny Cash inhabited some years ago and immortalized in his song "The Starkville City Jail."

In my haste to hide the can of beer from the officers, as is my habit, I clumsily tipped it over and the cold, delightful nectar spilled all over me and my pulled pork dinner. And, surprise! They all laughed uproariously, the chef, my crew, and the two officers. It was at that point in my life that I truly understood the old legal principle that, at times, "the law is honored in the breach." I retrieved another can, and then two more for the officers, blotted my pulled pork, and continued my meal. It was another unforgettable experience.

FRIDAY NIGHT POSTGAME BURGERS AT THE
SHONEY'S "BIG BOY" IN STARKVILLE

More often than not, however, after the game ended, we would head for the Shoney's "Big Boy" on Highway 12 in Starkville. Every Friday night during football season, generally after 10 p.m., the Shoney's was packed with the seventy or so "zebras," officials in their striped shirts who had finished their work and were ready to eat some burgers and fries. In addition to chowing down we looked forward to the camaraderie and the swapping of war stories with each other about the games we had just worked.

We would joke and generally unwind for almost two hours in the crowded gathering place. Between 10 and 11 p.m. the crews would arrive. Some had to drive a great distance—fifty miles was not unusual—to the games they worked, and they arrived later than the rest of us. By midnight, the last of the more than one dozen crews would slowly leave

Shoney's for the drive home. But before we left, we would laugh uproariously at some silly happening on the field—whether it was a story like
my being stoned by angry fans or some unbelievable action by one of the
crew members, such as the time my rookie linesman (he had worked the
clock the year before) marked a runner out on the 3-yard line and then
signaled touchdown when the runner reentered and ran into the end
zone. When we saw the lineman's hands go up indicating touchdown, all
of us threw our hands up and blew whistles ending the play. During the
halftime break, he finally told us that the runner had gone out of bounds
at the 3-yard line. "Why didn't you tell me then," I exclaimed. "Well," he
said, "I saw all your hands signaling touchdown, so I figured you all knew
more about it than I did!"

On another night the best entertainment came from the referee of
the last crew to arrive. After ordering, the crew sat down and the referee
explained their lateness. "We had this terrible chain crew," he said. "They
took their damned time moving the chains after a first down and there
were a few times when they moved the chains even though a penalty had
been called on the field. It got so bad that I threw a flag on the chain crew
and marked off fifteen yards against the home team!" All seventy of us
burst out laughing.

Shoney's was such a great ending to a long night—imagine, throwing a flag and penalizing the chain crew! These always enjoyable postgame sessions capped off what was, for most of us, another enjoyable
night out with the boys. When I returned home Friday nights, I would
engage in my weekly ritual: taking four aspirin to alleviate the pain in my
knees. By Tuesday, I would be back to walking normally.

LEADING THE ONLY RACIALLY INTEGRATED FOOTBALL CREW
IN NORTHEAST MISSISSIPPI

I changed my crew only once in my Mississippi officiating career. My
umpire, a Mississippian who worked for a town road maintenance
department, had a bad habit of drinking liquor (vodka) before every

game. While he was not a staggering drunk, he was incapable of doing his job, especially during the second half of the game. As soon as I detected the drinking, I removed him from my crew and informed Billy.

Serendipitously, just one day after I fired my umpire for his drinking problem, Billy called me.

"I got good news and bad news for ya," he said.

"OK," I replied, "give them to me."

"Well, I got you an umpire to replace your drinker, and I hear that he's a good one too."

"So, what's the bad news?"

"Well, he's a nigg . . ., er, he's a Negro. Name's Dave."

"Is he good? Does he drink?" were my only questions.

"Well, he just got out of the federal prison in Montgomery, Alabama," Billy told me in a sort of a whisper.

"Does he know the game?"

"I believe so," Billy said to me, hesitantly, and then he said that the new official "doesn't drink before games."

"Well, OK, give me his number and I'll call him up for this week's game," I said.

Billy then thanked me profusely. He exclaimed that my decision had probably saved the association from being sued because no one else was willing to take the Black official. I was, it turned out, Billy's last—his only—hope. My tentative acceptance of the official, Dave, made Billy's day. The "Rabbi" saved the day!

I called Dave up and we had a marvelous time talking football. He had been officiating for a number of years until his conviction for embezzlement suspended his career. He had no hesitation talking about his stay in the federal prison on the Montgomery Air Force Base.

He was there for, I think, four years, and—get this—his cellmate was none other than John Mitchell, President Richard M. Nixon's attorney general of the United States. Dave hit it off with Mitchell, and they enjoyed each other's company until Dave left prison. He did say that Mitchell became, instantly, Montgomery's "jailhouse lawyer," readily giving legal advice to convicts who needed legal assistance.

For my part, as a teacher of constitutional law at State, I found the addition of Dave to my crew to be a double blessing. First off, he was a great presence on the field. He covered the middle of the field behind the defensive line with skill and courage. He never ran into racial problems on the field, though a number of times, after a tough game, he led us to the car in record time for our dinner at Shoney's. And second, we spent a few hours talking about criminal justice and the criminal justice system.

I was to work with Dave until I left Mississippi for Utah in 1982. He was an excellent football official, one of the best persons I have ever worked with during my three-state football officiating career. And when we did the games, the sight of a bearded, bespectacled Jewish "Yankee" referee walking beside a very Black, ex-con umpire, as we inspected the field before game time, must have stunned the entire population attending that night's game. Fans, players, coaches—everybody was astounded that a Black official was working with white officials. But no criticism was ever voiced toward the two of us as we took care of business on the field.

THE GHOSTS OF MICKEY SCHWERNER, ANDY GOODMAN, AND JAMES CHANEY

I will never forget the first time my crew drove down to Philadelphia, Mississippi, in the fall of 1977, to work a game.

Philadelphia, in Neshoba County, was the infamous locale of the cold-blooded murders in 1964 of three civil rights workers from the Congress of Racial Equality (CORE):[1] Mickey Schwerner, Andy Goodman, and James Chaney. Until 1980, Neshoba County's sole claim to a footnote in American history was that it was the home of the Ku Klux Klan members who got away with these killings. They murdered the men and buried them in the county; they lived in the county, went to church in the county, and worked in Philadelphia or Meridian. They included the sheriff of Neshoba County, Lawrence Rainey; the deputy sheriff, Cecil Price; and the local wood cutter, part-time Baptist preacher, and the leader of the county's KKK, Edgar Ray Killen. (Donna Ladd, one of my best students at Mississippi State, was a resident of Philadelphia. She recalled that she and her mother regularly visited Price's shop to purchase new batteries for the family's watches. She remembers him as a big, nice man who always had a smile for her. She is now the editor-in-chief of the independent, liberal news weekly in Jackson, Mississippi.)

On August 3, 1980, the 1964 murder case "was still a festering sore" when Ronald Reagan, the Republican Party's candidate for the presidency, chose the Neshoba County Fair as the very first stop in his general election campaign. The fair, begun in 1889 in "Redeemer" country,[2] was a weeklong festival for whites to gather to have fun and games and, throughout the week, to listen to speeches by white Democratic candidates running for local, state, and federal office. True to his word, Reagan's campaign opened in Neshoba County, "in front of a white and, at times, raucous crowd of perhaps 10,000, chanting: 'We Want Reagan! We Want Reagan!'" His opening remark was most welcome to the chanters: "I believe in state's rights!" It was understood that when politicians started chirping about "states' rights" to white people in places like Neshoba County they were saying that when it comes down to you and the blacks, we're with you. Reagan was the third contemporary Republican nominee for the presidency to employ the party's "Southern Strategy," following Barry Goldwater (1964) and Richard Nixon (1968, 1972). He would not be the last Republican to take that tack. His concluding remark placed the county in the history books a second time when he told the cheering Mississippians that if there was a clash between white Southerners and the feds, "I'm with you!"[3]

Listening to Reagan's rousing language at the time, I felt sick knowing what changes would be coming down the pike. If Reagan defeated President Jimmy Carter, he would try to undue all the good changes that had taken place since 1964: setting aside civil rights and voting rights legislation, appointing conservative federal judges and government administrators. In November 1980 he defeated Carter, and then his administration began developing a major plan to change federal laws that protected Black citizens. His initial target was the upcoming congressional debates and vote on another extension of the 1965 Voting Rights Act. The extension battle took place between 1981 and 1982. That conflict was a no-holds-barred fight, one that, in the middle of the clashes, brought me to Washington, DC, to testify before a House committee to support the extension of the Voting Rights Act.

So in late September 1977 I was coming to referee a football game in a bloody spot of violence committed by hooded Klansmen in order to maintain white supremacy in the state. Coming to the ball field, I was mute; I was saying to myself, "How can my passengers, my crew, go on as if nothing happened here a dozen years ago?" We all got out of the car, went to the ball field, and began checking the ground conditions prior to my blowing my whistle to start the game.

In a book I wrote in 2002 about the case, *Murder in Mississippi*, I mentioned this visit to Neshoba County—my first. I recalled that drive to my readers:

> For the others in the car, longtime residents of the state, the trip was uneventful, and their talk focused on reviewing football rules and such. I was not listening to the chatter because I was about to travel a historic road, one that scared the living daylights out of me. . . . We went south on Highway 25 for about 35 miles, through the sleepy town of Louisville. . . . It was another 17 miles south before I spotted the sign for Philadelphia: "Philadelphia, 18 miles. Left on Highway 19." I made the turn. I was now on Highway 19, the road taken by the three young civil rights workers a dozen years earlier as they traveled to Meridian. I remember tightly gripping the car's wheel, half in fear, half in remembrance. My body was one large goose bump, and the hair on the back of my neck and on my arms was standing upright. . . .
>
> [Finally,] for the first time in my life, I was in Neshoba County, on the road to Philadelphia, Mississippi, which Martin Luther King, Jr. called a "terrible town, the worst [he had] seen."[4]

Well, we went through the pregame checks and the invocation. Philadelphia received the first kickoff. I was back at the goal line with two young Black Philadelphia players on either side of me awaiting the kick. I was to blow the whistle and follow the play up the field after one of the players received the kick.

Before I blew, however, I heard some ugly, racist shouts from the sideline directed at the two receivers. The "yeller" wore a Philadelphia jacket, was unshaven, perhaps in his thirties, and seemed *very* intoxicated. And he was yelling "n****r this, n****r that" comments to Philadelphia players! I walked over to the nearest receiver and said: "I can't believe the shit coming from that guy's mouth." The youngster smiled at me and said in his Southern drawl: "Oh, him, he's a town drunk, we don't mind him at all!" OK, I said to myself, as I went back to my field position, and blew the whistle. The game began. And for a few hours the 1964 tragedy that took place in this neck of the woods was set aside.

Although I officiated a few other games in Neshoba County, I left the county and the state in 1982. It was nearly a quarter of a century later, 2005, when I returned to Neshoba County. This time it was not to officiate a football game but as a news reporter covering, for the *Burlington (VT) Free Press*, the murder trial of Edgar Ray "Preacher" Killen. He was charged with planning the murders of the three young civil rights workers in 1964. On June 21, 2005—eerily, the forty-first anniversary of their deaths—he was found guilty of manslaughter and sentenced to sixty years imprisonment.[5]

I loved officiating in Mississippi. Even in the tiniest towns there was always an excited crowd and some high schoolers who were damn good football players. And I had the great fortune to referee games in Neshoba County, where one of the greatest football players in Mississippi history, Marcus Dupree, set records that will probably remain unbroken for a very long time. Playing for Philadelphia High School for four years (1978–81), he rushed for an amazing 5,284 yards and scored almost ninety touchdowns. He had huge thighs and blazing speed for a person his size.[6]

As referee, I took a position on the field behind the offensive line. I generally moved up the field to follow the play. When a team had to kick to Philadelphia, I had a different plan. Knowing that Marcus would receive the kick and run toward me, I just waited for him to reach me! Invariably, he would run back a kick for either a touchdown or a long return, and there I was, waiting for him! And before such a play, I would ask Marcus which way he was going to return the kick. Given our comparative speeds, I needed that kind of information to keep up with him! He was the greatest offensive player I have ever seen.

Although some games were runaways, and some teams were not very good, and some fields even ran downhill (visit the Gillespie High School football field when you visit the state!), there was always camaraderie on the field—and, for us officials, after the game ended, there was always Shoney's on Friday nights in the fall. I still miss that friendship very much.

Somewhere in my basement in Vermont, I still have my old football official's uniform: striped shirt and jacket, pants, black shoes, white hat, a few whistles, and the yellow flags. I don't know why I carried them with me every time I moved. I suspect that, deep inside my psyche, I'm ready to take the field again to work football with the "chillen." At times, even now, I think that I'm happy Carol never ate the ends of the kosher rye breads offered to her by my mother.

CHAPTER 4

Confronting Racism While Serving the ACLU in Mississippi

"Ohavi Zedek" is the name of our synagogue in Burlington, Vermont. We have been members for three decades, since our move to Vermont in 1989. In English, the name means "lovers of justice." For me, it is such an appropriate name, for it embodies the core of my beliefs and actions as an adult. For as long as I can remember, going more than a half century back to my high school and undergraduate days at Hunter College, I have been an advocate for social justice for all persons regardless of race, religion, and ethnicity and notwithstanding whether the discriminated-against "other" is a citizen or resident or illegal immigrant.

As I noted in the preface, two thousand years ago Rabbi Hillel taught what for me are two essential principles that define my Jewish life. First, he believed and taught that we are members of one large human community. One must not "separate [oneself] from community." Second, Hillel asked all sentient human beings, living in a community, the three-part quintessential question: "If I am not for myself, who will be for me? But if I am only for myself, who am I? If not now, when?"

For many decades, the ideal of doing justice has literally surrounded me. My old BMW had a vanity plate that proclaimed "Justiz" ("justice" in

German). I tried to paint an exclamation mark on the plate after the "z," but it didn't last. Tacking on the "Justiz" plate was, and remans, my way of saying that Hitler did not succeed in destroying my people, that my Polish Jewish immigrant father survived the Holocaust (although forty-seven of my Polish relatives who remained there were gassed and incinerated by the Nazis), and that it is a Jew driving a BMW! I splurged on the plate because justice has always been my mantra and has been the trigger for my actions for eight decades, whether to ensure fairness and justice for my students or, as an administrator, to provide an atmosphere that enabled faculty and staff to function to their fullest capacity—as researchers, as support staff, as teachers, and as advisors.

As a political science chair (at Mississippi State and the University of Utah) and as dean of social sciences (Utah) and of arts and sciences (University of Vermont), I have always been committed to the justice principle. That value was the vital center of all my actions as a student, a faculty member, an administrator, and a researcher of political events, policies, and persons involved in political events. Given the human condition, wherever I was, there was injustice! My life's story, at times to a major degree, has been whether and how well I responded to a mosaic of discriminatory actions taken by private individuals alongside those taken by public lawmakers and law enforcers. I have battled unfairness, unequal treatment, beatings, and murder, in all venues, north and south, east and west, in America and beyond.

Since the 1990s, I have been researching and writing about xenophobic acts outside America—and visiting the sites of those acts in the course of my research—including genocide in Bosnia-Herzegovina, Rwanda, Cambodia, and elsewhere. In each case the perpetrators, who were powerful and ethically lacking autocrats and their followers (Hutu in Rwanda, Bosnian Serbs in the former Yugoslavia), believed that a neutral characteristic—religion, ethnicity, age, gender, sex, or something else—demanded discrimination, segregation, ethnic cleansing, and eradication.

The most dominant and pervasive inequity in my lifetime—and in the lifetime of our nation—is the evil of slavery and its offspring: segregation, Jim Crow, the Ku Klux Klan, intentional inhuman emasculation, vote dilution, and lynching. In the long history of injustice against

African Americans, the harm has come from two fundamental sources: formal, governmental actions and folkways. Governmental injustice, on the one hand, was practiced at every level: federal, state, and local. The federal government's agencies were instigators of discriminatory actions that deprived African Americans and others of fundamental rights. For many decades after the Civil War, Supreme Court majorities validated state laws that deprived Blacks of their constitutional rights ("separate but equal," from the 1880s through the middle of the twentieth century, was one of many circumscribed doctrines that made the court an accessory to discriminatory acts against Black citizens). For many decades in the early twentieth century, presidential and executive actions and regulations prevented Black citizens from entering the federal civil service. (See Woodrow Wilson's successful efforts to bar Black citizens from such employment.) More horrendous have been state and local laws and regulations that created two communities—mainly, but not exclusively, in the South—that were called, falsely, "separate but equal." On the other hand, folkways or customs or traditions of white supremacy across the country—informal but just as pernicious as governmental forces—have conditioned white people to discriminate against African Americans.

These twin carriers of invidious racial discrimination were the foundation stones for the ugly, brutal reality of the United States' landscape since the first slaves landed in Virginia in 1619. As the late US Supreme Court justice Thurgood Marshall observed, in his bitter dissent in the 1978 Bakke case: "The position of the Negro today in America is the tragic but inevitable consequence of centuries of unequal treatment. Measured by any benchmark of comfort or achievement, meaningful equality remains a distant dream for the Negro."

THE MIDDLE OF THE ICEBERG

Slavery has defined America, and it still does. It and its progeny continue to set aside the nation's core values reflected in the Declaration of Independence, the US Constitution, the Bill of Rights, and the constitutional amendments enacted after the Civil War ended. If we as a nation are to

fully affirm those values in our treatment of African American citizens—
if we are to free them from the "badges of slavery" they still wear—we
must provide them with at least four conditions: voting equality, quality
education for their children, equal employment and housing opportunities, and due process/fundamental fairness in the American criminal justice system.

For those who have attempted to deal with the cruel plight of the millions of Blacks and other minorities who still carry the scars (mental as
well as physical) and the badges of slavery, finding solutions for the inequality has been an enormous, nearly impossible, quandary. In 1914,
W. E. B. Du Bois, a major force for change, wrote that for the millions of
Black citizens in America, "today [our advancement toward freedom] is
not possible. *We can piddle on, we can beat time, we can do a few small,
obvious things, but the great blow—the freeing of ten million . . . that means
power and organization on a tremendous scale.*"[1]

As a college student, in 1960, I was one of about thirty students who
picketed Woolworth's on the Grand Concourse in the Bronx on behalf of
the Black student sit-inners in North Carolina and other states. I will
never forget the angry, hateful words about us and the Southern "Negras"
we were sympathizing with on our picket lines. Nor will I ever forget the
spit tossed by some very hostile onlookers that wound up on my face
and clothes during these protest marches. But that was all I could do to
address that wrong.

In 1959–60, I was the leader of the Hunter College Negro Rights
Committee and, for many weeks, pleaded, ineffectively, with my fellow
students to sign petitions in support of the Southern Black students' demands for equality and justice. It was difficult to get many students in that
"silent generation" era to sign any kind of petition. They had seen how
young people like themselves had signed such petitions on behalf of
Spanish victims of the Spanish Civil War twenty-five years earlier and
how, in the late 1940s and 1950s, those petitioners' lives were shattered
because they were investigated by legislative committees as communist
threats to American democracy, or because they refused to sign federal
and state "loyalty" oaths, or because during the McCarthy hearings in the
Senate they were accused of membership in the Communist Party.

All these public events had the same goal: to discover, uncover, and list the names of these purported enemies of the state for their treasonable—un-American—activities and then to prosecute them. These enemies, it was claimed by Know-Nothings, America-firsters, and other nativist Americans, had successfully wormed their way into every sector of American social, economic, and political life. In New York City in the 1940s and 1950s, a professional wrestler was banned from plying his craft in Madison Square Garden because he refused to sign a loyalty oath. And while I was a student at Taft High School, Mr. Nash, a fine senior biology teacher, was summarily fired because his name had been on a list of Communist Party members and sympathizers.

In 1965, when I joined the faculty at Hofstra University, I almost didn't! I refused to sign a required loyalty oath. Fortunately, by that time, the university was in the final stages of ending that offensive policy. The hope was that these strong governmental actions would root out communists and "pinkos" before they could destroy us.

I continued my actions on behalf of what I believed justice demanded during my graduate school days as well as my early years as an instructor at Hofstra University. And in the 1960s, for me, that meant continuing my support for racial equality in the South and vigorously objecting to the expansion of America's military actions in Vietnam. By the time I started teaching at Hofstra, in 1965, the Vietnam War had escalated dramatically.

Across the nation, in colleges and universities, the "sit-ins" and the "teach-ins" became a regular part of higher education programs of study. I was a junior faculty member who participated in these civil protests and teach-ins that tried to bring more knowledge about America's involvement in the Vietnamese civil war to our students and the general public. And it was in this hectic time that I became a member of the ACLU and, later, the National Association for the Advancement of Colored People (NAACP).

I continued my ACLU affiliation in Mississippi, in Utah, and in Vermont. Like all members of this important organization, I disagreed with a number of the organization's policy decisions regarding the meaning of the First Amendment. But, also like so many ACLU members, I agreed far more with the organization's stands on civil liberties policies.

My strong commitment to equal justice inexorably led to my affiliation with the ACLU and other organizations whose task simply is to act
to overcome discrimination, inequality, and injustice. At Hunter I pro-
tested Southern racial discrimination as well as challenged the probity of
the 1950s-era national take-cover-it's-a-nuclear attack practice drills in
elementary and secondary schools as well as public colleges. Hunter College's take-cover rehearsals, four times a school year, were mandatory. I
will never forget one particular single-person (me) protest when I was in
my senior year at Hunter (1959–60).

It is important to understand the context of my civil disobedience
while sitting under the flag at the center of the campus. Because Hunter
did not have a football team, I found other ways to pass my time as an undergraduate. I joined the Air National Guard (and in the summer of 1961
my unit was activated and sent to Germany when the Berlin Wall went
up). I was a lead thespian in the campus theater group's performance
of Bertolt Brecht's *The Private Life of the Master Race*. For a number of
months, I led small groups of undergraduates protesting racial discrimination at Woolworth's lunch counters in North Carolina. I pleaded, successfully, with the student dean, Harry Levy, to let our soccer team's
fantastic striker (who was under a one-game suspension) play in the
CUNY championship game against Brooklyn College (which we won!).
I was president of the Inter-Fraternity Council. I was one of the elected
representatives who sat on the Hunter College Student Council. And I
was the 8–9 a.m. disc jockey for the campus radio station three days
a week.

During my tenure as the jazz jockey, I became very angry about the
absolute lunacy of students participating in nuclear-attack-take-cover ex-
ercises. None of us would survive such a ghastly atomic bombing. None-
theless, in New York City, all public school and public college students,
beginning with first graders, had to take cover when the air raid horn
began its shrill siren sounds. And the students, all of them, were to meekly
walk to the designated "safe" shelter, led by teachers and administrators.

No more! Three times a week, I broadcast from my tiny studio on
top of Gillette Hall. In between jazz greats like Ella Fitzgerald and the
Dave Brubeck Quartet, I implored my listeners to ignore the upcoming

take-cover instructions. I invited all of my listeners in the café or the bridge-players room to join me in a civil-disobedience action. My plan, I informed whoever was listening, was simple. When the horn went off, I and all my reasonable listeners would walk from Gillette Hall across a manicured lawn to the flagpole. And there we would stand, defying Dean Levy's take-cover order.

I informed the dean of my plan, aware of the costs associated with civil disobedience. The dean gently explained what he had to do if we did not take cover. He would come across the grass, with campus security, ask us to take cover and, when we refused, he would instruct the security people to "escort" us to a shelter. When the exercise concluded, security was to take the protesters to his office to receive punishment. He assured me that, whatever punishment we received, we could appeal his action. Dean Levy then carefully spelled out the due process steps we needed to take if we went the appeal route. It was a very civil argument; Dean Levy was a very decent human being. He was a very reasonable enforcer of the law. I was very impressed with his coolness in a potentially stressful situation. I learned a lot during that short meeting with the dean.

The day of the drill came at the beginning of my final semester at Hunter. I had absolutely no information about who would be showing up for the protest. First of all, the radio station's effective range was very limited. I don't think a person sitting in the lounges on Gillette Hall's ground floor could hear anything or anyone, even if the person was Benny Goodman and his band. Second, my earlier effort to get students to sign a petition supporting the Southern college student sit-inners ended dismally. Very few came over to read the petition; most who dropped by did not sign it. Sure enough, when the sirens began singing, I was the only disobedient student.

I walked briskly to the flagpole and then stood there while hundreds of my fellow students began their walk—in the open!—to the shelters located in the gymnasium and other, more distant, campus structures. (The procession reminded me of a scene from a Three Stooges movie.) Now I was waiting for Dean Levy to shepherd me to a shelter. He finally appeared, exiting Gillette Hall. He saw me, looked at his watch, then looked around—searching for security, I guessed. Finding no one and noting that I was the sole protester, he decided to walk over to me to end another dismal effort on my part to get college students to do more than play bridge in Gillette Hall for hours on end. (I was very pissed at their uncaring attitude.)

The dean started his stroll to the flagpole. But it was at a dawdling gait. He was very slowly ambling over to me! When he was about fifteen yards from me, the all clear signal erupted! I sat down. I think I was disappointed. Levy finally arrived at the flagpole and sat down next to me, with a smile on his gentle face.

We talked for a few minutes about my protest. He asked how I felt now that I had spoken out against the "utter futility" of the take-cover policy. I didn't respond to his question, for I had one of my own. "OK, Dean Levy, what's going to happen to me now? I know there's a cost when a person intentionally violates a law in order to protest the policy behind it. . . . I'm OK with anything you do, so long as I can graduate in June!" He patted my knee, saying, "Since I did not get to you in a timely fashion before the all-clear signal sounded, I guess it's a wash. Let's get some coffee, shall we?" We did.

When I became an academic administrator, as chair and then as dean, and regularly had to deal with hard decisions, I always remembered and tried to embody Dean Levy's calmness, rectitude, and fundamental decency. While in graduate school a few years later, I was informed that Dean Harry Levy had died months earlier.

WORKING FOR THE ACLU IN MISSISSIPPI

When I moved to Mississippi with my family in July 1976, I carried my commitment to do social justice with me. That meant, in part, continuing my affiliation with the ACLU, which I did during the first month of our residence in the Magnolia State. As I was to very quickly find out, the Mississippi ACLU affiliate's agenda was quite different from the New York chapter's to-do list.

The Mississippi affiliate had about three hundred members when we moved to Starkville. (About half were Black residents of the state.) The chapter was formed in 1969, only seven years before we arrived. For someone coming from the North, where the ACLU membership was in the tens of thousands, the very small number of members underlined the perception residents of the Deep South had about civil rights and civil liberties: the ACLU was a very dangerous, communist-front, antireligious, atheistic organization filled with un-American types.

For the most part, the leadership and the members came from the metro area of Jackson, Mississippi. Meetings of all kinds were held at the Unitarian Church in Jackson. Fundraisers such as art auctions were also held in the capital. Most of the volunteer attorneys worked in the Jackson area. However, the makeup of the ACLU's board of trustees had to be more inclusive, so a few of us living in other parts of Mississippi were asked to serve. I was invited to join the board during our first fall in residence in the state. I gladly accepted, not knowing how different the goals and policies of the Mississippi ACLU affiliate were from those of the New York affiliate.

Beyond the size of the membership, a major difference between the New York and Mississippi affiliates was the types of cases litigated by the attorneys. In New York and throughout most of the nation, the ACLU focuses on First Amendment freedoms: it advocates for the right to speak, the freedom of the press, and religious freedom and vigorously challenges any effort by the state to establish religion. The Deep South litigation agenda was another story. ACLU affiliates in this region focused on litigation that challenged state action that allegedly deprived persons of their Fourteenth Amendment due process rights to the "equal protection of the laws." Equally relevant for the Southern ACLU boards and their lawyers was strategic planning for litigation that challenged state action that allegedly deprived persons of "life, liberty, or property" without "due process of the law."

While I was in Mississippi, these were the two primary constitutional issues litigated by the ACLU. Although the chapter took up and litigated some First Amendment cases (such as the 1977–78 KKK case discussed below), the great majority of cases dealt with the state's treatment of Blacks in the criminal justice system: before trial, during trial, and afterward, when they were incarcerated by the state.

This meant that the ACLU, alongside the NAACP, went into state and federal courts to challenge the way in which police treated Blacks; the lack of due process for prisoners; prison conditions; the condition of rural, small town jails; and the harassment of Black prisoners, including alleged police brutality directed toward Blacks. The ACLU affiliate brought litigation to challenge general discrimination against Blacks in voting and in public accommodations, as well as conditions and treatment of prisoners in the criminal justice system.

Besides attending meetings in Jackson, I was also one of a handful of ACLU contact persons who resided in the northeastern part of the state. This meant that I would be the person who brought the ACLU's legal papers to the US District Court, Northern Division, in Ackerman, Mississippi. Several times I filed paperwork that initiated litigation involving persons the ACLU was defending who lived in the jurisdiction of this courthouse.

I recall walking into the federal courthouse carrying a briefcase with the materials needed to file. I passed all the "John Deere" white folk standing outside the courthouse and wondered what they would do if they knew what I was carrying into the court. Once inside, I went directly to the clerk's office and turned over the materials to one of the clerks. With the time stamping by the clerk, the litigation process began, and I was the one who started the process. I felt really good walking out of the courthouse. On returning to Starkville, I telephoned the ACLU office in Jackson to indicate that the file was received by the court clerk's office.

Another concern of our ACLU affiliate, as well as of the NAACP, was voting discrimination. In the years before the highly controversial and radical 1965 Voting Rights Act was passed, countless complaints were filed about the immense difficulty Blacks had when they tried to register to vote. Efforts to deny them this right ran the gamut from the hated literacy test to poll taxes and economic threats to actual violence—including murder—against those who tried to register.

After the Voting Rights Act was passed, there developed a new crop of discriminatory charges against entrenched power holders in Mississippi. This time, however, the major issue was Black vote dilution. The ACLU, along with the NAACP, worked on behalf of Black plaintiffs in litigation challenging these vote dilution strategies.

Given my academic background and my research regarding Southern compliance with the Voting Rights Act, I took on the task of writing op-ed pieces supporting the continuation of the law (which was up for renewal in 1982). Toward that end, I also testified in Congress in support of the extension of the act and had two op-ed pieces published in the *New York Times* and the *Washington Post*. (Another chapter in the book will more fully discuss these activities in support of the extension of the act.)

On very infrequent occasions, I had another very interesting task as a member of the board of trustees: providing guidance for Black fugitives from justice who were terrified about the prospect of turning themselves in to the local sheriff's office. This responsibility was always triggered by a telephone call from the fugitive, asking for help in surrendering to law enforcement officials. Obviously, the best—the safest—bet for such persons was to surrender to law enforcement in the presence of an ACLU attorney. And so, when I received a call, I would provide some basic information as well as the telephone number of the ACLU executive director. Arrangements would then be made for the surrender of the fugitive.

Clearly, this situation reflected the nature of the criminal justice system in the second half of the twentieth century, especially so in the South. Blacks were extremely anxious about how they might be treated by local and state law enforcement officials. The fear was not misplaced, for in Mississippi, in this era, there was a great deal of police brutality. As discussed in chapter 3, only a decade earlier, in Philadelphia, Mississippi, a deputy sheriff was directly implicated in the brutal murders of three young civil rights workers.

For me, a person who participated in "sympathy" marches in the Bronx, the reality of my proximity to raw police brutality and general, pervasive racial segregation was overwhelming at times. Looking at the actual horrors of local jail conditions in small, rural towns in Mississippi was unlike anything I ever did in my life! The board's review of these facts led to our decision to initiate—or not—litigation challenging such conditions as a violation of the Fourteenth Amendment's Due Process Clause.

In the 1950s I participated vicariously in the civil rights movement; it was really exciting and fun to work with fellow students, many of them

Jews, some very pretty young women, on behalf of young persons actually taking actions on behalf of civil rights and equality in the South. (We met in Harlem, led by Mike Harrington, who was writing a book, *Poverty in America*, that became required reading in the John F. Kennedy administration, just a few years later.)

A decade or so later, I was a *participant*, albeit at the margin, in initiating legal actions similar to those I had been teaching in my civil rights classes. This time, unlike in my undergraduate college days and nights, I did not participate for excitement; it was *necessary* for me to act. I saw the discrimination personally, through the events that engulfed me, my daughters, and Carol. I saw the racism and the fears of racist actions when I tried to recruit Black college graduates to enroll in Mississippi State's master of public administration program.

It was not very pleasant to see how Blacks were treated by whites in ordinary social interactions, much less how they were treated in the Mississippi criminal justice system. During my years in the state, I could not get over the humiliating reality of some Black men walking on a public street, in the 1970s and 1980s, moving out of the way of white women walking the pavement. The head bowed, no eye contact, with the occasional tipping of a hat as the women passed. Nor can I ever forget the way Black prisoners were treated in small, rural county jails by their white jailers.

I quickly realized how correct Bob Moses, the young leader of the Student Nonviolent Coordinating Committee, was when, a decade earlier, he said that overcoming racism in Mississippi would take patience and continual prodding from the SNCC, the NAACP, and other civil rights groups. "Mississippi," he said, "was the middle of the iceberg."

DEFENDING THE MISSISSIPPI KU KLUX KLAN

In fall 1977, the Mississippi ACLU's executive director acted unilaterally and, for such a small organization, disastrously. Without any discussion with the board before her decision, she accepted a case brought to our affiliate by the Mississippi Ku Klux Klan. The KKK wanted to hold a rally on the public elementary school grounds (the ball field) of Saucier, Mississippi, one of the last towns to integrate its public schools.

They submitted their demand to the Saucier school board, which very quickly denied it. The educators maintained that such a rally on school grounds, including the burning of a cross on the field, would heighten tensions in the small town as it began to implement its school desegregation policy. (This initial move by the school board to end public school segregation began twenty-four years *after* the 1954 *Brown* decision of the US Supreme Court.)

The Klan immediately called our Jackson office and asked the ACLU's executive director to take their case. The argument: the KKK had a First Amendment right to freedom of speech on public land. She immediately committed the ACLU to defend the Klan against the school board ban. As soon as word got out, via the press and television, half of the three hundred members of the ACLU affiliate—all the Black members—submitted their resignations in protest.

They were stunned by the action of the director—a feeling shared by many of the remaining members—and reacted very negatively. By the time of our affiliate's emergency meeting shortly afterwards, the Mississippi ACLU had less than 150 members! And the chapter's affiliate lawyers were already defending the Klan in state court.

At this time, a majority of the members supported a move to take the case from the Mississippi Chancery Court to the United States District Court for the Southern District of Mississippi. Such a move from one jurisdiction was a golden opportunity to fully discuss our position on defending the Klan and, hopefully, to formally drop our association with this hateful, murderous organization. The stage was set for this emergency showdown meeting. Everybody was invited, especially the Blacks who had left the affiliate to protest our defense of the Klan.

Present, too, at this December 1977 meeting was the national ACLU president, Norman Dorsen. He was present for one primary—though unspoken at the meeting—reason: to ensure that the Mississippi ACLU affiliate continued its defense of the Klan in federal court.

Why? The answer was easy. At the very same time our affiliate was meeting to discuss whether we would continue the Klan defense, the Illinois ACLU affiliate was defending—successfully—the right of Nazis from Chicago to march in the city of Skokie, Illinois. The city had a popu-lation of seventy thousand: forty thousand were Holocaust survivors.[2]

In late 1976, Frank Collin, the leader of the National Socialist (Nazi) Party, wrote letters to the administrators of dozens of bedroom suburb towns surrounding Chicago. He requested a permit for his group to hold a rally in the town park. Except for Skokie, all mayors or city managers simply ignored the request. Skokie rejected out of hand the Nazi request to march. In 1977 their local government passed three anti-Nazi ordi-nances: no hate groups could use the public property to conduct a rally; no group wearing a faux-Nazi uniform could use the Skokie land to hold a rally; and a $350,000 indemnity bond was needed in order for any group to march in Skokie.

The Nazi leader, Collin, then went to the executive director of the ACLU's Illinois affiliate and asked the organization to defend its right to march in Skokie. Collin argued that to deny the Nazis a permit was unconstitutional. All segments of the First Amendment, by this time, had been incorporated into the Fourteenth Amendment's Due Process Clause.

In 1977, the US Constitution prohibited any governmental organization—federal or state or local—from passing laws barring per-sons or organizations from using public land to conduct a march and hold a rally on public property. In 1978, the ACLU successfully defended the Nazis' right to march, starting with a win in the Illinois Supreme Court. The state court overturned the ban on the Nazis marching. In so doing, the court declared that the three Skokie ordinances were unconstitu-tional because they were in conflict with First Amendment rights. The ACLU also won in federal court when the US Court of Appeals for the Seventh Circuit affirmed the state court ruling.

The decision to take the case was as damaging for the Illinois ACLU affiliate as was the Mississippi decision to defend the KKK. In Illinois, thousands of Jewish members of the ACLU quit in protest, unable to accept the reality of the ACLU defending hateful advocates of Nazism before and during World War II.

By the time we held our meeting in the Unitarian Church in Decem-ber 1977, the Illinois affiliate's lawyers were already the legal advocates for the hated Nazi Party in state court. And Dorsen, the national ACLU president (as the Mississippi ACLU board members would find out in short order), was adamant that if the ACLU had to defend Nazis in Illinois, it had to continue to defend the Klan in Mississippi.

Under these circumstances, the ACLU board members and more than two hundred interested members convened in the Unitarian Church in Jackson. It was a packed, tense gathering. Everyone attending the assembly could feel the apprehension in the air. I drove down from Starkville with my father-in-law, Sid Neidell. (He was visiting the family, and I invited him to come down with me because, I told him, it would probably be a very interesting and, for both of us, an exceptional meeting that we would not forget for a long while. I had no idea how prophetic my comments would be about that meeting!)

It was an almost three-hour drive, and we began the drive while it was still pitch-black out. By the time we arrived, a little before 9 a.m., the church was filled to capacity. Norm Dorsen was sitting on the stage, along with the board of trustees, the executive director, and Ed King. The Reverend Edwin (Ed) King, was our affiliate's representative on the ACLU's national board. A white Methodist minister born in Vicksburg, Mississippi, in 1936, he had been on the front lines of the civil rights battles in Mississippi since the mid-1950s. From 1962 to 1967, King was the dean of students and chaplain at Tougaloo College, a small private Methodist, predominantly Black college located in the Jackson area. He marched with Medgar Evers, the NAACP Mississippi field secretary (who was murdered by Byron De La Beckwith in June 1963 just moments after President John F. Kennedy, on national television, announced his plan to send Congress a civil rights bill). While the first white chaplain at Tougaloo, every Sunday King would escort small groups of Black college students to local churches in order to have both races pray together. These Sunday actions were labeled "kneel-ins" by King. Not admitted to any church, he and the students would then kneel down on the front steps and pray and block the entrance—which led to confrontations when the service ended.

He also regularly engaged in sit-ins in Jackson and other Southern cities—with members of the SNCC—in order to force major chains such as Kresge's and Woolworth's to integrate their lunch counters.

During many of these confrontations, he was beaten severely by the white onlookers. While demonstrating in Montgomery, Alabama, he was beaten by police using truncheons to smash his face. But, as he said a few years ago, "just about anybody who was involved in the civil rights movement here was probably arrested, beaten, tortured."

King was actively engaged in civil rights activities in Mississippi, and during the 1964 Freedom Summer he was selected as the vice chairperson of the Mississippi Freedom Democratic Party (MFDP), alongside Aaron Henry, its chair. He went to the National Democratic Convention in 1964 to try to unseat the all-white Mississippi delegation. Although the MFDP failed to accomplish its goals at that convention, they were instrumental in forcing changes in the protocol for selecting delegates to upcoming conventions, beginning with the 1968 Democratic Convention in Chicago. When one saw King in 1978, one saw a tall, gaunt-looking person, with a very large scar on the lower right side of his face—just above his chin.

As he rode back from another protest action, the car King was in was run off the road. It was crushed from the side by a speeding vehicle. His face was shattered, the lower part of it needed reconstruction, and he was in recovery, hospitalized several times, for months.[3]

For Ed King, the struggle had to continue until racial discrimination was defeated, however long it took. He echoed the words that Bob Moses, the leader of the 1964 Freedom Summer in Mississippi, said in one of his early speeches: "If you did not face the monster in the worst place, the dragon in the cave, then the dragon would come out of the cave and spread [its evil across the nation]."[4]

Blacks, especially Mississippi Blacks, respected this gentle and courageous white minister who continually put his life on the line in order to advance the twin notions of equality and due process for all persons, Black and white. For all of us, looking at his heavily scarred face, King was our source of strength. He had been there at the beginning and, in 1977, was still battling the dragon in the cave. King, eighty-three years old in 2020, now retired from the ministry and protest activities, was loved and admired by all of the people in the church at that terribly important meeting involving the Klan and the ACLU.

The president, Dorsen, not the executive director, chaired the meeting, which was to go on for about ten hours. It was an emotional roller coaster session. After summarizing the steps taken by the executive director and the volunteer ACLU lawyers, he asked for comments, suggestions, anything that members wished to get off their chests. There followed about four hours of commentary, essentially first-person observations about the KKK's criminality, conveyed to the attendees by many of the Black participants.

These were stark, shocking anecdotes. They were tales of house burnings, beatings and whippings, rapes, and murders—both in the dead of night and in broad daylight. And all these crimes were committed by the KKK, and all these crimes were immunized from any form of legal penalty because the crimes were committed against "n****rs." Underscoring all these stories of terror was the reality that the evildoers functioned penalty free in the "Jim Crow" white culture of impunity.

For me and, as I found out on the drive back to Starkville with Sid, for him and probably most of the whites in the group, these observations about the cruelty and bestial, murderous behavior of the Klan over the past three or so decades shocked our consciences. One after another, hour after hour, the dozens of stories about the Klan rolled from the hearts and souls of the Black witnesses telling us what happened to them, to their parents, to their grandparents, to their brothers and sisters. Beneath these reminiscences lurked the basic question: How the hell can the ACLU come to the legal defense of racist murderers? Again, and again, that question hung in the air surrounding the gruesome stories of KKK actions against Blacks and whites in Mississippi.

The meeting took another turn when, after we had exhausted ourselves with the memories of Klan violence, the president called for motions. I offered a simple motion: The ACLU must drop its defense of the KKK immediately. It was seconded quickly, and the conversation then turned to the merits of the proposal.

As introducer of the motion, I spoke first. And my words became hand grenades tossed at the Blacks in the audience—and across the state! I argued that the US Supreme Court, over the decades, had heard dozens of cases involving picketing and marching and protesting by all kinds of groups—Jehovah's Witnesses, Nazis, NAACP, SNCC, communists, and hate groups. And the court had defined First Amendment rights differently according to the nature and location of the public property the group wanted to use to voice its protest and redress grievances.

If a group wanted to protest in front of the city hall or the state capital or the steps of Congress in Washington, DC, it could do so without any limits, provided it adhered to some basic law enforcement guidelines regarding time of march, numbers of marchers, route of the march, and so on. However, if that same group wanted to protest in front of a courthouse, additional constraints were needed.

And so, for example, in order to maintain the dignity and decorum of the goings-on in the court, protesters could be placed a greater distance away from the building itself. No loudspeakers playing music could be used as part of the march and rally outside the courthouse. There is a difference between a statehouse and a courthouse, and there is a difference between a public schoolhouse and some other public property targeted for a protest march and, in our Klan case, a cross burning.

I pointed out the differences between marching to protest the actions of the legislature or the governor and marching in front of or on the property of an educational facility. Just as the courthouse is treated differently, so too, according to court decisions, is the schoolhouse. A local school board, I concluded, especially the Saucier school board, which had finally, after decades, adopted a desegregation policy that seemed acceptable to both the whites and the Blacks in the county, has the constitutional right to protect its school children from harassment by the Klan.

I then suggested, directing my comments to Norman Dorsen, that there is a substantive difference between marching down a public street to the city hall of Skokie, Illinois, and holding a rally and burning a cross on a public school ball field in Saucier, Mississippi. I concluded that the Mississippi ACLU was not beholden to follow the lead of the Illinois ACLU because to do so would ignore Supreme Court decisions regarding the First Amendment and protest marches on public school property.

Dorsen did not speak to the motion at all. However, the motion was ridiculed by the Black members in attendance. The general consensus was that it was categorically "immoral" for an ACLU lawyer to defend these murderers. The motion was a loophole escape from the responsibility of labeling something evil because it was evil!

For the critics, my motion was just as outrageous as was the initial decision to defend the Klan in court. It was wrong, wrong, wrong, for any decent person to defend the right of the KKK to spread its hatred under the protective umbrella of the Constitution. They maintained that had the KKK in Saucier wanted to march to the city hall, according to my motion and argument, the ACLU would have to defend their right to so march—regardless of the substantive evil message paraded down the streets and on the steps of the city hall. Wrong, wrong, wrong!! (Had the KKK wanted to march on the public streets to protest in front of city hall, my argument would be null and void. The critics of my motion were right, right, and right!) For them, the proposal was simply a cowardly way out of a moral confrontation between good and evil. One after another speaker condemned the proposal, and they, after another hour or so of condemning the motion, introduced a substitute proposal: the ACLU does not defend, in any court, immoral, evil behavior such as that of the KKK. Period.

It was late afternoon, around 6 p.m., when the board got around to voting on the proposals. The substitute amendment was defeated, with embarrassment I believe, by the board. Then came the vote on the motion to withdraw from defending the Klan. It passed by a wide margin. We had severed our legal relations with the KKK in Mississippi.

Norman Dorsen then spoke. "It has been an exhausting day, mentally and physically," he said. "I applaud the openness and the frankness expressed by all of you that spoke. I learned so much today, more than probably in any other meeting. As for the vote to disengage from the legal defense of the Klan, I applaud you for taking that action and will do all I can to continue to support this brave ACLU affiliate." Dorsen, the liar-to-be, then sat down. We would hear a very different message from him as well as the executive director of the national ACLU, Aryeh Neier, very soon. Too soon! After a few more comments by the affiliate president, the meeting ended. We did not convince the former Black members to return to the affiliate. They were as angry after the meeting as they were before. On the ride home, Sid was physically and mentally exhausted. He was a world traveler, but he had never, he said, experienced an event as power-ful, emotional, and important as that 1977 ACLU board meeting.

What intrigued but terribly angered him was the inability of the two sets of voters to reach agreement about the manner in which the ACLU disengaged from a common foe: the KKK. Sid, a very successful busi-nessman, knew the critical importance of talking to compromise.

Although we dropped the KKK case, we did not convince the former Black members to return to the affiliate. They were as angry after the meeting as they were before it began.

Ironically, sadly, but as expected, as soon as Dorsen returned to the ACLU's headquarters in New York City, he and Neier did everything they could to have the ACLU affiliate make an about-face and continue to de-fend the Klan. As Neier told me in a very tough ten-minute yelling match a few weeks after the meeting, "If the ACLU is going down in flames, like Kamikaze pilots, with the Nazis in Illinois, we will have to go down in flames with the KKK in Mississippi."

I responded bluntly, "Over my dead body," and hung up.

The two national leaders immediately began implementing their campaign—over long-distance telephone—to see if the board mem-bers would change their minds and take the case. That failed miserably. Then they tried to convince the affiliate's representative to the national ACLU—Ed King—to reverse our 1977 decision. That failed.

Dorsen was running out of time. The trial date in the district court had been set. The judge who was scheduled to hear the case was the no-torious states' rights jurist William Howard Cox, who had presided over the 1967 trial of more than one dozen Mississippi Klansmen who, Cox said in open court, were charged with conspiring to kill "a n****r, a Jew, and a white man." Dorsen had one option left if the ACLU was to defend the KKK.

Dorsen quickly appointed two ACLU lawyers from the New York branch, Robert J. LaBine, from Long Beach, New York, assisted by Jo-seph E. Guarino, from Brooklyn, to defend the KKK in federal court, re-placing the Mississippi defenders. They barely made it to the trial. By late August 1978, it was over but without any final judgment.

Why did it end in that manner? Before announcing his judgment, Judge Cox "suggested that the plaintiffs [Coen and Page] should make a new application including assurances that they would post a bond for costs and property damage and would not burn crosses, carry firearms, and wear hooded robes. The plaintiffs did so, and the school board granted permission for the rally. The rally was held on September 16, 1978, without violence and disturbance. Accordingly, the district court never issued a judgment on the merits."[5]

That ended a drama-packed thirteen months, from late August 1977 to September 1978. I still have not really forgiven Dorsen and Neier for their actions after our board meeting that December long ago. While I think I understood their "Kamikaze" frame-of-mind, I cannot forgive them for placing some sense of macho pride ("going down in flames with both the Nazis and the KKK") over the reality of what had occurred in Mississippi, what our affiliate's immense problems were (e.g., membership losses), and the question of how we were going to recover from the debacle.

Looking today at the Mississippi affiliate's policy agenda on its website, one still sees listed police brutality and unsanitary, double-celling conditions of local jails as two of the major issues confronting the ACLU. And Ed King, now eighty-three, is still addressing these injustices, like some other eighty-plus writers among us, by writing about his experiences of a half century earlier.[6] Things change, but in Mississippi some things either change very, very slowly or, sadly, remain the same.

POSTSCRIPT

Less than one year after we settled in Salt Lake City in July 1982, the executive director of the Utah ACLU affiliate left to take a similar job with the Louisiana affiliate. In Utah, she was a politically savvy activist and a very intelligent and strategic director. After she took the job down South, she and I got together for lunch to talk about her upcoming move. She was taking my path, but in reverse.

And so I tried to inform her about the character of an ACLU affiliate in that part of the country. "There will not be many affiliate members in Louisiana," I told her. "And it will be more difficult to find volunteer attorneys in Louisiana." Most importantly, the agenda would be very different from the ready-made First Amendment agenda of the ACLU affiliate in Utah: establishment of religion (Mormonism) in the state.

The federal courts, including the US Supreme Court, since the *Everson* precedent, had been hearing establishment cases from plaintiffs challenging state or county laws allegedly establishing religion, and the courts had been deciding many of them in favor of plaintiffs' argument that a state law passed was another effort to "establish" a religion.

"Utah's ACLU," I said, "is bankrolled by the Latter-day Saints. Their violations of the First Amendment and federal equal employment regulations pay all our expenses! Louisiana will be, like Mississippi, a tough nut to crack. And the opponents you'll battle with in federal and state courts are not the genteel attorneys of the Mormon church." I also told her, "You'll look back and long for the quiet arguments in state and federal courts regarding the Mormon Church's alleged unconstitutional interference in the legal and political life of the community." She took these observations with her, without any comments, and left for Baton Rouge, where the ACLU affiliate has its main office.

One year later, I attended a Southern Political Science Association meeting in New Orleans. Walking across the Tulane University campus with a friend, I saw the former executive director of the Utah ACLU affiliate. She ran over and hugged me and said: "You were so god-damn right about working in Louisiana. It's so fuckin' different than Utah. I'm still trying to comprehend these rednecks!" All I could say, after kissing her, was, "Welcome to the middle of the iceberg!"

CHAPTER 5

Defending the 1965 Voting Rights Act

One of the primary reasons for my decision to move to Mississippi was that it gave me the unique opportunity to examine how and, most important, whether the watershed 1965 Voting Rights Act was being implemented in the Deep South. Mississippi in 1976 was one of the deepest Southern fortresses still aggressively and effectively defending the "states' rights" racial orthodoxy against federal intrusion to terminate this age-old evil.

A century after the Civil War ended, fate made Lyndon Baines Johnson, a big, earthy, first-rate wheeler-dealer, who absolutely loved the prospect of battling for a more perfect America, the dominant political leader at a pivotal moment in the centuries-long clash between white supremacy and the constitutional demand for equality.

Johnson grew up in south Texas. He had to work while attending college, so, when he was just twenty years old, he took a teaching position in a tiny, essentially Hispanic, public school in the tiny town of Cotulla, for the 1928–29 school year. Johnson was the only white teacher in the school and taught mathematics and geography. Everybody in the town loved the young Texan: he was a stern teacher, but he cared for his students. It was at this time, in this town, that Johnson encountered the painful reality of severe poverty and its accompanying trappings, and at this time and in this town he declared war on poverty—a war he fought for the rest of his life, including his tenure as president of the United States. On earning his degree, he took a teaching job in Houston and worked there from 1930 to 1932.

In 1937, after serving as an aide to a congressman and working as the state director of the National Youth Administration,[1] Johnson moved into an arena where he would spend the rest of his life: politics. In 1938, the twenty-nine-year-old Texas Democrat took his seat in the House of Representatives. He did not return to his home in Texas until 1969. Politics was where he wanted to be working for the public. As he once said to an interviewer while president, "I loved only three kinds of work: preaching, teaching, and politics." Asked why, he said that they all put him to work directly to improve the lives of fellow human beings.

After Johnson became president in November 1963 upon the death of President Kennedy, the Texan's new powerful political position allowed him to drive a very reluctant Congress, still controlled by a seniority system that put the most senior members into chairs of every committee in both houses. When the Democratic Party held a majority in one or both chambers, the chairs of most committees were from the still-one-party South (Senate) and from large urban working-class union districts (House).

Between 1964 and 1968 Johnson urgently, strongly, and successively pushed through a trio of major civil rights bills. In 1964 the Civil Rights Act was passed, the very first substantive civil rights legislation passed since the era of the Radical Republicans, 1865–77.[2] In 1965 the radical, very atypical Voting Rights Act went through. Lastly, the Civil Rights Act of 1968 was passed. The 1968 legislation contained ten "titles," or sections: Titles I–VII, the Indian Civil Rights Act, which extended the Bill of Rights protections to all Native American tribes; Titles VIII–IX, the Fair Housing Act; and Title X, the Anti-Riot Act. The enactment of these laws reflected President Johnson's ability—even as his presidency was wounded mortally fighting the first of the nation's "endless wars"—to push, pull, persuade, and threaten legislators and to take advantage of terrible events in order to achieve necessary victories in the battles for equality. I and many millions of other citizens saw these laws as pivotal for transforming our nation into one that was fair and just—a nation of equals. We thought, sanguinely, that finally, after hundreds of years, the scourge of slavery and, after 1865, the "badges of slavery," would end.

Our family moved to Mississippi eleven years after the voting rights law passed and only a few years after the US Department of Justice finished the near-impossible task of creating the regulations that would, we all hoped, enable its staff to implement the radical law in a part of the nation where the majority of white voters absolutely, murderously, hated the essential norms embedded in the law.

The issues that frame the heart of this chapter are these three: (1) What I saw across the Deep South, shortly after we arrived in the state, at first unnerved and then angered me. (2) I responded to this anger by asking, What can I do during my years in Mississippi to address the continuing denial, by local politicians and city attorneys, of Black citizens' voting rights? (3) Finally, as I look back today, I've asked myself, How much has changed—if voting rights have in fact changed—since we left in 1982?

First, however, we must grasp the elements of what was, on paper, the most radical bill ever passed by the federal government to end local and state laws that effectively destroyed millions of Black citizens' hallmark of equality in America, the fundamental right to vote.

THE 1965 VOTING RIGHTS ACT

In a speech before the joint session of Congress on March 15, 1965, about the new voting rights bill that he was conveying to them that day, President Johnson was the angry leader of a great political experiment, a constitutional federal republic based on the rule of law. He was bristling with anger, because he knew that even a democratic government could fail if the people failed to fulfill that government's most pressing and most divisive mission:

I speak tonight for the dignity of man and the destiny of democracy.

. . . Our mission is at once the oldest and the most basic of this country: to right wrong, to do justice, to serve man.

. . . There is no Negro problem. There is no Southern problem or Northern problem. There is only an American problem.

. . . But even if we pass this bill, the battle will not be over. What happened in Selma [Alabama] is part of . . . the effort of American Negroes to secure for themselves the full blessings of American life.

Their cause must be our cause too. It is not just Negros, but all of us, who must overcome the crippling legacy of bigotry and injustice. And we shall overcome.[3]

The president was charging and challenging not only the legislators but also the millions of us watching on TV—and the entire society.

The speech came a year after Johnson signed the Civil Rights Act of 1964. It came after efforts in the summer of 1964 to register Black voters in Mississippi failed to increase the number of Blacks registered to vote—but did increase the number of persons pursuing civil rights who were murdered by the Klan that summer: nearly a dozen were lynched. It came even as civil rights groups continued—and they would continue unsuccessfully into the summer of 1965—their nonviolent efforts to register Black voters across the Deep South. It came eight days after the nation witnessed the murderous Bloody Sunday march—begun on March 7 and coordinated by the Southern Christian Leadership Conference (SCLC)—from Selma, Alabama, to the state capital, Montgomery, fifty-four miles away. On CBS, NBC, and ABC that evening, viewers saw images of white segregationists, joined by a host of state police on horses and local police on foot, armed with rifles, clubs, tear gas, and dogs, congregated on the Edmund Pettus Bridge in Selma, dispersing the protestors by charging into them and beating them mercilessly just after the march began. In the evening of that same Sunday, James Reeb, a young white minister, was beaten to death by a group of Klansmen. The march was planned by SCLC leader Martin Luther King Jr. after a young Black, peaceful demonstrator, Jimmie Lee Jackson, was killed by an Alabama state officer weeks earlier, on February 18, 1965, in Marion.

The president's speech came six days *before* the regrouped and greatly enlarged mass of peaceful protesters, more than three thousand, protected by Army National Guard troops who had been federalized by Johnson, began their march on March 21, 1965, to Montgomery. In three days of nonstop marching, continuously harassed and murdered by white protestors, the marchers reached the state capital. The speech came before the Klan killed Mrs. Viola Liuzzo, a white thirty-nine-year-old NAACP member, SCLC volunteer, and mother of five from Michigan, as she drove a Black demonstrator back to Selma during the three-day march. Four Klansmen were later arrested in connection with her murder. Of these, only two were charged in an Alabama court, and they were quickly acquitted by an all-white jury. However, they were later convicted in federal district court for conspiring to take Mrs. Liuzzo's rights and sentenced to ten years.

The president's presentation of the voting rights law on the evening of March 15 had been in the works since the previous summer, when his civil rights brain trust was putting the final touches to Johnson's speech to be given at the signing of the 1964 Civil Rights Act. The president, a man of the South, knew of Southern unyieldingness regarding civil rights for Blacks, especially the extremely successful efforts of Southerners to deny the right to vote to a large racial minority who had been freed, made citizens of the United States, and, as citizens, guaranteed the right to vote in the Thirteenth and Fifteenth Amendments, ratified in 1865 and 1870. He was itching to deal with voting rights discrimination immediately.

Even before plotting to push through the late President Kennedy's civil rights act, Johnson wanted to put an end to the even greater evil of voter discrimination because of race. Initially he relented, but from the summer of 1964 to March 1965 he and his senior officials in the Department of Justice (DOJ), including his future attorney general, Nick Katzenbach, and the assistant attorney general and head of the Civil Rights Division in the DOJ, Burke Marshall, along with close advisors in the White House, were hard at work crafting the voting rights bill. For Johnson, the historic—successful—efforts of Southern whites to keep Black citizens from "the most important function of democracy—

choosing their own representatives in government"—led him to "vent his anger" in his March 15 speech. His "sense of moral indignation was unmistakable" as he spoke to Congress, wrote a reporter who covered the president.[4]

On August 6, 1965, a bit over four months after Congress received the voting rights bill, President Johnson signed it. He was overjoyed. His remarks matched the fulfillment of his major goal: "Today," he said, "is a triumph for freedom as huge as any victory that has ever been won on the battlefield."[5] Both houses of Congress had supported the bill by large bipartisan majorities (House, 328–77; Senate, 77–19).

Naturally, the president left unanswered the question of what would happen if his charge to Americans (in his March 15 speech quoted above) about the "American problem" was not heard or not acted on in good faith. I found a fascinating piece written in 2015 by Joseph Mc-Auley on that question,[6] one that has been raised by American leaders since the eighteenth century, from the crafters of our Constitution to President Johnson to the present. In 2015 Donald Trump had not yet run for president on a platform that encouraged racism, but already, across the country, there were shocking, polarization-producing attacks on Muslims, Blacks, Jews, and other minorities, including millions of immigrants seeking refugee status in America; clearly the "American problem" had not been solved. President Johnson well knew about the good and bad angels in all humans, wrote McAuley, but nevertheless the president championed the voting rights bill. "He signed [the act] with hope, *though he feared that it would be used someday to undermine the democracy he wanted the American people to have.* But he did it anyway, believing in the future that is the American birthright."[7] When President Johnson put forward the bill, this fundamentally important "what if" question about the continuing stability of our representative government—an ongoing experiment undertaken in 1787—was not on my mind because I, and millions of Americans, were cheering the inventiveness of the president and his domestic policy advisors.

However, those who framed the Constitution and defended their effort in the Federalist Papers had that "what if" possibility constantly on their minds while drafting it, ratifying it, and, after the new system of government was operational, maintaining it. John Adams reflected on why there had to be such continual vigilance: people are not angels; they have passions that, if left unchecked, are powerful enough to destroy all governmental systems, including ours. "Avarice, ambition, revenge, or gallantry, would break the strongest cords of our Constitution as a whale goes through a net. Our Constitution was made only for a moral and religious people. It is wholly inadequate to the government of any other."[8]

Johnson shared the concern expressed by Adams and James Madison and Alexander Hamilton and all the other politicians and clerics and scholars and philosophers about the Constitution's ability to restrain human bestiality. He understood the remark Benjamin Franklin made about the Constitution soon after it was ratified: "Our new Constitution is now established, everything seems to promise it will be durable; but, in this world, nothing is certain except death and taxes."[9] What choice did Johnson have, or did Lincoln have, when confronted, one hundred years apart, with the same conundrum? Both confronted a reality that threatened the existence of the federal union: Lincoln faced the threat of the Southern states' secession, which, if successful, would destroy the union; Johnson, in the midtwentieth century, faced the risk of allowing the white Southern power holders to continue to act with impunity and immunity to deprive millions of citizens of their citizenship rights. Neither president had a choice; both had to act. Both hoped that their arguments would persuade those with power in the South to return to the union. They hoped their words could repair the damage; but were they prepared to use the power of the federal government to end the crisis each faced? Lincoln was, and he did use that power. Johnson and his surrogates in the White House and the Department of Justice were not, and they did not.

One basic reason for the failure of the Johnson administration to use the powerful federal sword to achieve compliance was the very nature of the federal system itself. To implement the key segments of the Voting Rights Act, Johnson had to convince the Deep South states to follow the 1965 law. However, the predicament he faced was significantly different from the one Lincoln faced in 1861: the use of federal force to enforce a law, short of the catastrophe of secession and civil war or a serious, violent uprising that threatens the "general welfare" of the nation, is near impossible in a democracy, and Johnson did not face such a catastrophe or threat. As will be shown shortly, if state leaders do not want to obey a federal law, the federal system's sharing of powers provides white supremacists with the institutional mechanism for disobeying a federal law, an opinion of the US Supreme Court, or a federal regulation.

Another reason for the continuing inability of the 1965 Voting Rights Act to repair the jagged divisiveness of our society is the Yin/Yang of human behavior. When Congress passed the 1965 Voting Rights Act, those who promoted it hoped that because it was radical, it would finally do the job of protecting the civil rights of all of us, but in accordance with known features of human nature, those in power in the South continued to find ways to resist implementation of the act.

The act suspended all literacy tests and other devices used to determine whether a person could vote. These literacy tests had existed for six or more decades and effectively restricted Black voters in the South from registering to vote. The act's passage in 1965 both affirmed the basic principles of a democratic society and stated the objectives the federal government had to pursue in order to end racially discriminatory voting practices in the nation, especially the restrictions very successfully used in the more than a dozen Southern states.

Sections 4 and 5 of the new legislation would, it was hoped, effectively provide a federal check on all changes in a community's voting practices (e.g., a change from a single member district to an at-large district or a change of voting venue), requiring that any change be approved by the federal government before being permitted. Each proposed voting change was allowed if it did not have the intent or the purpose of discriminating against Black voters. Under these provisions, a state or local jurisdiction would be permitted to change voting patterns only if the US District Court in Washington, DC, was convinced that the proposed change would not dilute Black voting strength. During committee discussions about the bill, the legislators had agreed to add the US

Department of Justice as a second-choice reviewer of proposed voting changes reported to the federal government. It was noted that the federal trial court judges would be swamped with requests for approval, or "preclearance," of proposed changes, leading to a backlog of preclearance requests and thus intolerable delays in the federal government's answering of the requests. Legislators also thought that the DOJ was a less expensive and less onerous method of obtaining federal approval of a proposed voting change. In the end, the act created a joint administration of section 5.

Before the Voting Rights Act was passed, very rarely did the local town clerk pass the Black literacy-test takers who needed to pass the test because they did not have a birth certificate to show their eligibility to vote. Since Blacks rarely passed these tests because racially biased town clerks graded them, very few could vote. In the year the Voting Rights Act became law, less than 7 percent of Black persons in Mississippi (where nearly 40 percent of the population was Black) were registered to vote in the state and national elections. Statistics for Black registered voters in the other Southern states were nearly as bad.

Any state or county of a state whose voter turnout in the November 1964 presidential election was less than 50 percent was covered by the 1965 Voting Rights Act. That meant that all seven Deep South states, including Mississippi, as well as some counties in North Carolina, had to take the steps outlined in the act. One radical section of the law suspended, for five years, all literacy tests used in the covered jurisdictions. That meant that between 1965 and 1970 Blacks could register to vote without having to take the dreaded literacy test.

As a consequence, the statistics shot up dramatically. In Mississippi, by 1970, more than 70 percent of eligible Blacks were registered to vote. Black registration statistics in the other covered states increased exponentially as well. In addition, however, the White Citizens' Council, an organization set up to fight public school integration after the 1954 *Brown* decision, encouraged whites to register to vote because of the dramatic increases in Black registration. So if Black registration stood at 70 percent in Mississippi in 1970, white registration in the state topped 75 percent.

VALIDATION: THE US SUPREME COURT DECISION *SOUTH CAROLINA V. KATZENBACH*, 1966

The US Supreme Court's near-unanimous opinions validating the Voting Rights Act of 1965 provided more hope to the millions who supported the act. In 1966, however, South Carolina, joined by the other Deep South states (as amici), filed a bill of complaint with the Supreme Court under the court's original jurisdiction authority, seeking direct review of the law on the grounds that Congress had exceeded its constitutional authority in that it had "encroach[ed] on an area [voting] reserved to the States." The court heard the arguments and, in record time, less than two months, announced its decision. In *South Carolina v. Katzenbach*, the justices (by an 8–1 vote), in an opinion written by Chief Justice Earl Warren, decisively bolstered the Voting Rights Act. Justice Warren dismissed the state's complaint that the suspension in all "covered jurisdictions" of literacy tests and the use of federal examiners to oversee actual voting in the covered jurisdictions' in order to protect Black citizens was unconstitutional. Noting the history of racial voter discrimination ever since the ratification in 1870 of the Fifteenth Amendment, he ruled that the act was a "proper exercise of congressional authority under the Fifteenth Amendment." Addressing the state's argument that the legislation's innovative provisions were excessive, Warren stated, very bluntly, that Congress's "inventive manner" in dealing with voter discrimination was called for given the reality of massive vote denial to Blacks in the South for the past century.[10]

The most controversial of the section 5 protections, requiring federal preclearance of all proposed changes in a jurisdiction's voting protocol before they could be implemented, pushed the anger button of every Southern city council member, lawyer, state judge, state legislator, the dissenting jurist on the Supreme Court, and every defender of the primacy of "states' rights."

Prior efforts by the federal government to remedy the racial discrimination had not been able to dent the problem, much less end it. Warren wrote that effective implementation of the right to vote required "sterner and more elaborate measures in order to satisfy the clear commands of the Fifteenth Amendment." Because of the South's "unremitting and ingenious defiance" of the Constitution, by their creation of a "variety" of cunning and effective voter discrimination statutes, and because there existed "nearly a century of systematic persistence" in devising new ways to prevent Blacks from voting, the congressional actions were themselves "ingenious" yet constitutional.[11] The Supreme Court held

> that the portions of the Voting Rights Act properly before us are a valid means for carrying out the commands of the Fifteenth Amendment. Hopefully, millions of non-white Americans will now be able to participate for the first time on an equal basis in the government under which they live. We may finally look forward to the day when truly "[t]he right of citizens of the United States to vote shall not be denied or abridged by the United States or by any State on account of race, color, or previous condition of servitude" [Fifteenth Amendment]. The bill of complaint is dismissed.[12]

The Alabaman sitting on the court, Justice Hugo L. Black, partially dissented because he believed that the radical preclearance passage in the act's section 5 was wholly unconstitutional because of its rejection of a fundamental principle of Anglo-Saxon law: legislation can be reviewed only after it has been implemented! For the senior jurist, treating the seven Southern states the way section 5 treated them was effectively turning the Southern states into "conquered provinces" crawling on their knees to far-off Washington.

> Section 5 . . . [unconstitutionally] provide[s] that a State . . . can in no way amend its constitution or laws relating to voting without first trying to persuade the [federal overseers] that the new proposed laws *do not have the purpose and will not have the effect of denying the right to vote to citizens on account of their race or color.* . . . I cannot help but believe that the inevitable effect of any such law which forces any one of the States to entreat federal authorities in far-away places for ap-

proval of local laws before they can become effective is to create the impression that the State or States treated in this way are little more than *conquered provinces*.[13]

The purpose of federal review was to ensure that no voting change had the "purpose or effect" of diluting the minority vote. The federal judge or voting section personnel (the DOJ review route, once regulations were prepared, has been used 99.9 percent of the time by lawyers for the covered jurisdiction) had to determine whether the proposed voting change would adversely affect, diminish, or effectively dilute the vote of Black citizens.

Until section 5, a Black plaintiff could challenge a new voting change that allegedly diminished voting rights and powers only after the law or regulation had taken effect. Under traditional law, to bring a suit in a federal courthouse, actual injury had to be claimed by the petitioner. Advisory opinions were not rendered by the federal courts; one needed an actual case to bring suit in the federal courthouse. Under section 5, that ancient legal tradition floundered—much to the dismay and anger of Southern town managers and their lawyers and to the disapproval of the sole dissenter when the act was challenged in the US Supreme Court, Justice Hugo L. Black, of Alabama.

DILEMMAS IN APPLYING THE PRECLEARANCE PROCESS

Hard, often very complex, enforcement problems have always confronted the implementors of the voting section of the DOJ's Civil Rights Division. They start with the extremely small size of the voting section and the near total failure of DOJ spokespersons to get congressional finance committees to authorize additional funds to increase the total number of paraprofessionals and attorneys working in the section. The voting section work was handled by two units, the submission staff and the litigative group. Almost half of the staffers, around twenty-six, were the "paraprofessionals" (young men and women, recent high school graduates); they were not lawyers and were on the lowest pay scale for government workers, G-5. Their primary task was to formally respond to all preclearance requests received. All staff had been trained to spot "red flags" such as reduction in the number and/or the location of polling places; redistricting and annexation plans had to be carefully reviewed before implemented to ensure that the new plan did not further dilute the votes of minorities. When I arrived in Mississippi, these paraprofessionals were averaging twenty-five to thirty preclearance provisions daily. The litigative unit consists of twenty attorneys and a few staff assistants.

By the time we arrived in Mississippi in 1976, the Voting Rights Act had been amended, so that twenty-two states, not the original seven, were covered by section 5. These states contained more than seven thousand smaller units of government, many more than the seventeen hundred jurisdictions covered in 1965. All seven thousand were covered jurisdictions; all were required to submit their voting changes to the voting section for section 5 preclearance approval.

If a covered jurisdiction *wanted* to follow the guidelines, it submitted the papers to the DOJ's voting section. If a city declined to send its voting changes into the DOJ and, instead, implemented an annexation or a line drawing to maximize white voting strength, the DOJ had no formal, institutional way of knowing that the jurisdiction implemented a voting change. Much more sinister was that such a noncleared local voting action was made in order to further dilute the vote of Black citizens in that town, or county, or state.

The lack of such oversight was, and remains, an endemic problem for federal policymakers and implementors (such as voting section staff). This reticence of federal officials, in the White House and in the Department of Justice, was, for me, quite a revelation. Wherever I visited in Mississippi, there was a total reliance on informal, whispered information conveyed to the voting section. However, when I researched the issue, the answer hit me in my noggin: the law of unintended consequences.

The crafters of the voting rights bill knew that if passed, it would trigger unremitting anger by the aggrieved majority that advocated for states' rights. They also believed, incorrectly, that a host of civil rights groups—including the older groups (NAACP, the Congress of Racial Equality [CORE],[14] the Urban League) as well as the new, vigorous public action groups (SCLC, Council of Federated Organizations [COFO])[15]—would continue their civil rights work by monitoring implementation of the act in the "covered jurisdictions." That did not happen. A radical example of unintended consequences was the creation of "the Indianola, Mississippi, Way" to preclear voting changes. Hope did not do the trick. More than hope was needed for realizing the dreams of President Johnson, millions of disfranchised Black citizens, and many millions who hoped for the end of voting discrimination.

From the very first steps taken by the drafters of the voting rights bill, they surrendered to the white supremacists. They had a choice to make regarding federal enforcement of the act: use all the weapons in the union's arsenal or keep the federal presence in implementing the act minimal to invisible. They took the invisible-implementation road.

Implementation moved slowly, first, because the president and his civil rights administrators in the DOJ were very aware of the strong opposition of Southern white politicians both in Congress and in state and local governments. They also knew the essential reality of federalism's limits on a president's ability to occupy the South to ensure compliance with federal law. After 1865, for twenty years tens of thousands of federal troops occupied the South in order to protect the Black citizens. The president and his policymakers were well aware of the chaos, violence, and lynching that accompanied that occupation, and they knew that federal force was used against states very rarely in America. Although a few racial crises prompted a president to use the National Guard and the army to support federal orders (Eisenhower: Little Rock, Arkansas, 1958; Kennedy: University of Mississippi, 1961; Johnson: Neshoba County, Mississippi, 1964), for the most part army troops were not deployed to enforce federal laws and court opinions. The only remedy for Southern unwillingness to follow federal law was the slow process of litigation to enforce that law.

Implementation was slow, second, because it took six years for the DOJ bureaucracy to write and then get approval for regulations that codified the process that a "covered jurisdiction" had to follow in order to get a proposed voting change precleared by the voting section reviewer. Therefore, during that delay, Southern politicians continued to create new voting changes whose purpose or effect was to dilute the votes of Blacks who were now participating in elections.

Third, once the regulations were in place in the Code of Federal Regulations (CFR), the DOJ leadership of President Nixon's administration continued the policy of President Johnson's DOJ: they, too, did not want the federal government overseers (the DOJ and the FBI) continually patrolling the covered jurisdictions to uncover and criminally charge local or state officials for violating the Voting Rights Act. (The criminal penalty under the Voting Rights Act for failing to preclear was a fine and imprisonment. It was never enforced.)

Burke Marshall, the head of the Civil Rights Division of the DOJ when the Voting Rights Act was being written and also when it was passed, said: "We must realize the constitutional rights of Negroes in states where they are denied but we must do so with the smallest possible federal intrusion into the conduct of state affairs." His colleague, Attorney General Nicholas Katzenbach, who, with Marshall, worked with the president to draft the Voting Rights Act, said, the year the law was passed: "'The federal government can't solve all the South's problems for it' and that (my task) 'is to avoid at all costs an occupation of the South by federal troops, lawyers, registrars, and marshalls.'" And John Doar, another key DOJ Civil Rights Division leader, said in 1967: "Blacks would be better off not relying on federal action to increase black political participation." Instead, all advocates of the voting rights bill believed, in Doar's words, that "a political organization at the local level is needed [to monitor voting changes]. . . . Federal [monitoring] would only reinforce the caste system in the South."[16]

The DOJ's key assumption, erroneous though understandable, was that a viable minority political community would emerge in most of the seven thousand jurisdictions (cities, towns, counties, and states) covered under the 1965 act. Of course, that was also the veritable Catch-22: Congress discussed and rapidly passed the most radical voting rights bill in American history but did not acknowledge that it was nearly impossible for a tiny number of low-level voting section staffers to effectively enforce (while white Dixie politicos knew that the small DOJ staff was unable to enforce) the law that resulted. Nor did the legislators know that the criminal sanctions provided for refusal to follow the act (section 12) would never be imposed (just as those same Southern lawmakers hoped they would not be imposed) by the Department of Justice! Nevertheless, Congress passed the legislation and never provided new appropriations to add personnel to the voting section.

No army of local volunteer monitors ever emerged. That it would was a forlorn hope of the Washington men and women who wrote the Voting Rights Act as well as those who had to implement the law. Very few local civil rights institutions (mainly large cities such as Birmingham, Atlanta, Jackson, and New Orleans) ever emerged to monitor compliance. The only way the DOJ could find out whether the covered jurisdictions were complying with section 5 was when David Hunter, the chief of the DOJ lawyers in the voting section, received a telephone call from an unofficial monitor in a covered state.

Who were these monitors? Most were brave Black ministers in small towns in the Deep South and NAACP leaders in large Southern cities. Much less regularly, persons like me—academics studying the impact of the Voting Rights Act in Southern states—very cautiously called David to inform him that Indianola, Mississippi, or West Point, Mississippi, or Stone Mountain, Georgia, had implemented voting changes without adhering to the preclearance process.

MONITORING MISSISSIPPI FOR THE DOJ'S VOTING SECTION

The real heroes in the effort to monitor whether the preclearance section of the Voting Rights Act was being implemented were the Black ministers across Mississippi and the other Deep South states. These men, at the same time, were the political, social, and religious leaders of these small communities of Blacks in the small, very rural towns dotting the Mississippi landscape. It was a bleak, thankless, even dangerous task they took on (and the same kind of work today is often thankless as well). For in these towns, the local white power holders knew that the Black minister was in touch with the DOJ. As one of the local attorneys told me: "That fella [the Black minister] has got a direct line to the feds, an' he uses it like clockwork!"

Certainly, the voting section lawyers did not go out of their way to encourage these men of the cloth to pick up the telephone and report voting changes that had not been precleared by the DOJ. For the federals did not want to be seen as encouraging this type of behavior from locals in Mississippi. The DOJ was happy with the number of preclearance submissions they received from some of the local attorneys in the South.

The DOJ maintained that more than 90 percent of the covered jurisdictions were indeed voluntarily submitting voting changes for clearance by the federal agency. Furthermore, the federal agency pointed out, most of the voting changes were approved by the personnel in the DOJ's voting section. By 1980, with more than thirty-two thousand submissions reviewed by the voting section, the preclearance percentage was almost 98 percent. (During this time frame, 1965–80, of the DOJ's objections—which totaled less than six hundred—81 percent involved substantive issues: changed election methods, redistricting, and annexations.)

DOJ pronouncements, however, sadly diverged from assessments by others. The data collected and published by the Joint Center for Political Studies and the Voter Education Project, by lawyers, and by academics on implementation of the preclearance section of the act disagreed with the rosy compliance picture painted by the DOJ. Even the government's own watchdog agency, the General Accounting Office (GAO), found that almost four hundred general sessions bills passed by Southern state legislatures had never been precleared. And if these major statewide voting changes had not been precleared, the GAO concluded, thousands more voting changes, passed in small, rural, isolated towns and cities in the countryside, with nary a monitor, had never seen the light of preclearance.

And so, even after Chief Justice Warren's history lesson to Americans about the evil vitality of a century of vote denial, when I was in Mississippi, Black votes were now being diluted by the white power holders in small towns across the South. There were too many examples of blatant noncompliance by local white power holders—and their lawyers—to warrant the DOJ's positive assessment. In any town or city where

the Black population was in the range of 40–60 percent, where nondis-
crimination voting protocols and processes would lead to local Black
electoral victories and Black representation on the local board of select-
men, the researchers found either the maintenance of old discriminatory
voting processes or uncleared voting changes that strengthened white
voting power. And probably one-third of the towns that submitted voting changes for preclearance submitted them while simultaneously implementing the voting change!

The data generated by these nongovernmental organizations, published annually, clearly showed that a majority of covered jurisdictions
did not submit voting changes for preclearance by the DOJ. Even though,
as already noted, the Voting Rights Act included criminal penalties if a
local jurisdiction did not submit voting changes for preclearance, such
penalties were never used by the lawyers in the voting section of the
Civil Rights Division of the DOJ! To do so would go against the DOJ's
committed, and very public, philosophy of limited federal agency involvement in local affairs.

Under these circumstances, local government officials, including
the city or county attorney, simply instituted voting changes without
hesitation—and without following preclearance requirements. One of
the early centers of this deliberate noncompliance was Indianola, Mississippi. For years, the city leaders took whatever action they felt necessary to dilute Black voting strength and never once precleared any of
the changes. And the word spread, not only in Mississippi but across the
Deep South. "Let's do it the Indianola way" became the mantra for many
local communities as they sought ways to continue to dilute the Black
votes. I remember a local city attorney in Kosciusko, Mississippi, telling me, with a pensive expression, "It's easier to work with them [vot-
ing section paralegals and lawyers] than with the local electric power
company!"

My role in the monitoring process was quite limited. I traveled
across the state to visit towns and cities as part of my research on section 5 compliance in Mississippi. An important product of that research
was the 1982 publication of *Compromised Compliance: Implementation of*

the Voting Rights Act, which I wrote with Dale Krane, a colleague at Mississippi State, and Thomas P. Lauth, a professor of political science at the University of Georgia.[17] When during our research we found statutes or newspaper accounts of legislation that impacted voting procedures in the state but had not been precleared, we would call the DOJ in Washington, DC.[18]

Once the voting section lawyers were informed of noncompliance with section 5 by any locality, they could bring suit in federal district court in the state to which that locality belonged to enjoin further implementation of the voting change until preclearance was completed. However, the DOJ did not act until the information was verified. And so, after receiving the noncompliance information, the assistant attorney general for civil rights immediately requested FBI assistance to determine whether the information received by the monitors was accurate.

The DOJ used the FBI because it was the only federal law enforcement agency with field offices in most of the covered jurisdictions that was tolerated by white Southerners when I was in state. It was not overtly oppressive for a local community if one of the FBI agents attached to the Jackson, Mississippi, field office either checked the records in Jackson or visited the small town or city mentioned in the monitor's report to determine whether a voting change had taken place without preclearance.

Once the FBI agent reported back to the voting section lawyers that, for example, the city of Carthage, Mississippi, had not precleared a voting change, then the DOJ began interactive "negotiations" with the city attorney and other local officials. Given the small number of attorneys in the voting section (by 1982, there were about fourteen attorneys in the submission unit and an equal number of litigative staff) with this responsibility—for the over seven thousand jurisdictions in twenty-two states—the office's first response was a letter to the local town leaders informing them of their responsibilities under section 5 of the Voting Rights Act. This would be followed up by telephone calls from the DOJ attorney to the local attorney, inquiring about the status of the preclearance submission and offering the town attorney whatever assistance was needed to move the submission process along. When the locality continued to categorically reject the DOJ's "urgings" to file, it became necessary for a DOJ attorney to visit the town for person-to-person talks with the local town leaders. And if this failed, the DOJ would then go into the federal district court to enjoin the city from continuing to implement the uncleared voting change.

These efforts to dilute Black and other minority voting strength in local, county, and state elections are still a major problem for the DOJ's voting section attorneys, especially since the US Supreme Court handed down its controversial decision in *Shelby County, Alabama v. Holder* in 2013.[19] *Shelby* made ending vote dilution an impossibility and allowed state actions denying the right to vote to reappear in the Southland and beyond. Already when the Voting Rights Act was written, advocates faced a major political and legal dilemma, because in the law the DOJ was not given sufficient human resource funding to ensure that implementation would be effectively monitored. And more aggravating was the fact that from the creation of the radical act, it was accepted that federal agents implementing the act in the South should be "invisible." This hopeless situation, however, was mooted by *Shelby*, in which a five-person majority of the court invalidated section 4 and, consequently, section 5 of the Voting Rights Act. The "Indianola way" became the new voting rights standard.

INVALIDATION: *SHELBY COUNTY, ALABAMA V. HOLDER* (2013)

In *Shelby*, the US Supreme Court killed the Voting Rights Act. Unless Congress passes new legislation to reinstitute the Act and—unimaginably—President Donald Trump signs the new bill, playing taps is appropriate. In the 5–4 decision, Chief Justice Roberts and his conservative brethren overturned both lower court cases (one in the US District Court for the District of Columbia and another in the US Court of Appeals for the District of Columbia Circuit) that validated the constitutionality of the act's section 4. Roberts delivered the opinion, in which Justices Scalia, Kennedy, Thomas, and Alito joined. Justice Thomas filed a concurring opinion. Justice Ginsburg filed a dissenting opinion, in which the appointees of Democratic presidents—Justices Breyer, Sotomayor, and Kagan—joined.

The litigation involved two major sections of the Voting Rights Act. One was section 4, which "provides the 'coverage formula,' defining the 'covered jurisdictions' as States or political subdivisions that maintained tests or devices as prerequisites to voting and had low voter registration or turnout. . . . In those covered jurisdictions, Section 5 of the Act provides that no change in voting procedures can take effect until approved by specified federal authorities in Washington." The chief justice ruled that the section 4 formula for determining which states had to preclear was too broad and too dated. It was, he reasoned, "unconstitutional in light of current conditions." He didn't overturn section 5; he didn't need to: without a valid section 4 formula to use, the paralegals and lawyers would simply be unable to preclear! Finally, he blamed Congress for its inaction: "A fundamental problem remains. Congress did not use [its constitutional power] to fashion a coverage formula grounded in current conditions. It instead re-enacted a formula based on 40-year-old facts having no logical relation to the present day."

The very day the decision was announced, a number of Southern state legislators announced "that [vote discrimination] laws that had been on hold were going to be pushed forward": "Texas declared it would be moving forward with a strict photo ID law that had been blocked under Section 5. Then soon after, North Carolina lawmakers passed a strict photo ID law, along with other restrictions to early voting and voter registration. Alabama and Mississippi also moved forward on strict photo ID laws that had been passed before the ruling. The consequences of the Court's decision were immediate."[20] Reading the Roberts opinion reminded me of an epigram attributed to a nineteenth-century French writer: "The more things change, the more they remain the same!" Or, better, recalling the words of a Mississippi native, William Faulkner, who wrote that "the past is never dead. It's not even past."[21]

Still, I believe one must push the rock up the damn hill, regardless of its—and the pusher's—fate. The pusher, I know, still hopes for an end to the existential folderol. It is a forlorn hope!

A BIZARRE PRECLEARANCE REQUEST:
THE (WARM) BEER REFERENDUM

In the spring of 1980, I was involved in an off-the-wall voting-change filing in Starkville, Mississippi. Usually, voting changes are proposed to strengthen one political group's power at the expense of another—whether Democrats, Republicans, Hispanic voters, Black voters, or whomever. And in the Deep South, usually a proposed annexation or a redistricting will strengthen the power in local government of whites over the minority group, of Democrats over Republicans, or the like. In Starkville in 1980, a group led by Baptists and Methodists introduced voting changes primarily to defeat efforts of the students at Mississippi State—all eleven thousand plus—to vote on a beer referendum. A pre-clearance submission was promptly sent to the DOJ.

Beer sales were, in 1980, prohibited in Starkville. While one could go into a store and purchase wine or liquor, one had to travel outside Oktibbeha County for beer, usually at the "crossroads," an intersection about twelve miles due east of Starkville separating our county from Lowndes County (which allowed beer sales). Consequently, it was common for those in search of beer to travel a few dozen miles to get it, drink some at the crossroads, and—under the influence—take the rest back home. After many years of assorted car crashes and injuries and over a dozen deaths, however, the students and their Starkville supporters were able to get the issue on the ballot. A referendum was scheduled for the end of April, a time when all the students would still be on campus and could be relied on to vote for beer.

However, the city manager, working with the city attorney and with the support of the religious groups, came up with a strategy that would easily defeat the beer referendum. It was a very simple and perversely wicked idea: change the voting places, *file* a preclearance submission, and thereby delay the vote, because under the law, voting section researchers were automatically allowed sixty days to determine whether the change in voting places would adversely affect minority voters in Starkville!

On day 60, the voting section, according to the regulations in the CFR, had to inform a jurisdiction whether the voting section objected or whether the change was precleared. The city officers had no reason to expect an objection from the DOJ on day 60. Consequently, the vote would be pushed back to that date, a time when most students were not on campus and could not vote.

Clearly, this was a voting change to disfranchise the university students. There was no other way to delay the beer vote; if it were held as scheduled, beer would have been voted in—although the proposal, if passed, would allow only *warm* beer sales. The Baptists and their religious allies would have none of that nonsense. For them, although they could enjoy wine and bourbon, students drinking beer was just an invitation from the devil to drink Bud and engage in lustful behavior.

As soon as the voting change was submitted and then announced in the *Starkville Daily News*, the president of the MSU Student Council called me to see if anything could be done to keep the end-of-April vote date. I told him I would check and get back to him. After reading the bill, I phoned David Hunter, the voting section's supervising attorney and, by this time, 1980, a friend. I told David that the submission from Starkville was not going to dilute Black voting power in the county. The only persons aggrieved were the university students at State, who, if the voting preclearance process ran its typical course, would not be in Starkville to vote on what was simply a beer referendum.

Hunter guffawed. The city's strategy, he said between laughs, was a hoot, and it would quickly crash. I asked him to short-circuit the preclearance process and send Starkville a letter preclearing the voting changes immediately. He readily agreed and within four days the letter was received approving the changes. There was no need to cancel the end-of-April vote. A small story in the *Daily News* indicated that Dale Krane and I were responsible for the rapid preclearance. I received a very nice letter from the student body president. The Baptists ran a full-page ad in the *Daily News* the weekend before the vote, pleading with people to defeat the beer vote. Many Baptists signed the ad. To no avail. The students turned out en masse to vote for beer, as did others living in Starkville. Beer won by a 3-to-1 margin. Thanks to the quick work of the voting section, warm beer became available in Starkville stores. Although not a very regular beer drinker, I knew that warm beer is better—

and safer—than no beer. And so the two of us became folk heroes in the students' eyes. However, for the antibeer religious establishment in Starkville, I was, once again, that damned New York Jew!

TESTIFYING IN CONGRESS IN 1981: EXTEND THE
VOTING RIGHTS ACT!

My 1981 testimony before the House Judiciary Committee on the importance of extending the 1965 Voting Rights Act, like my involvement in the beer vote a year earlier, did not endear me to a great many Mississippians. Given the research I was doing with my colleagues in Mississippi and Georgia, there was some interest—and at the same time some bafflement—among the staff of the House Judiciary Committee about the argument I would make. Did the title of our forthcoming book, *Compromised Compliance*, suggest that the act was not working and should be scuttled—replaced by some other process to make sure that minorities would not have their votes diluted? Or did it suggest that, though many compromises had been made since the law passed, the act was the best of all possible solutions and should be extended and strengthened?

For the three of us the answer was clear: the Voting Rights Act had to be extended because white power holders in small towns across the South were still performing many actions that, if not enjoined or struck down, clearly diluted the votes of Blacks. We also maintained that the political and budgetary reality for any bureau, section, or department of government, displayed in its annual report to its oversight committee, had to show *success*! New budgetary decisions followed the past year's department activities. Presenting data that showed the agency was doing its work meant, minimally, no cuts. The voting section was in desperate straits. It needed new staff, but the funds were not coming. Compliance had to be shown to legislators. The "Indianola way" was not shown.

In late June 1981, I was invited by Congressman Peter Rodino (D-NJ), chairman of the House Judiciary Committee, to testify regarding the extension of the Voting Rights Act. I immediately accepted because our research had given us insights into the implementation problems facing the DOJ that needed to be brought to the attention of the national legislators. But also, we believed that the act had to be extended—and improved—because the problem of vote dilution needed to be confronted.

I flew to Washington, DC, on a late evening flight and arrived at the hotel after midnight. I unpacked and was ready to hit the hay when the phone rang. Two staff members of Democrats on the Judiciary Committee wanted to speak to me *now* about my testimony the following morning. They were in the hotel bar and asked me to come by as soon as possible. In five minutes I was having a cold beer with the two attorneys. Basically, they wanted to talk to me about my statement and whether I favored extending the act. I gave them a copy of my ten-page statement and told them I supported extension. They seemed happy enough and after an hour they left.

I went upstairs. It was about 1:30. As I opened the door the phone rang again—a call from staffers of Republican members of the Judiciary Committee. I joined them and had a very similar conversation. I gave them a copy of my statement and told them that, while we were concerned about the chronic problems facing the DOJ's voting section staff, I supported the extension of the Voting Rights Act. They informed me that I would be joined by a Black attorney from Columbus, Mississippi, and his view was that the act should not be extended. I thanked them for the information, wished them goodnight, and went up to my room. By now, it was around 2:30 and I was really tired.

I realized that these visits were examples of the hardball politics of the Voting Rights Act extension controversy that would embroil the Capitol—and those who were observing the mess—for more than a year.

Less than half year earlier, on January 20, 1981, the very conservative Republican president-elect Ronald Reagan took the oath of office. His initial position on extending the Voting Rights Act, expressed in a televised press conference, was that he did not support extending it. It was not needed. I was not at all surprised.

Rejection of civil rights legislation was in the Republicans' DNA. The first time the question of extending the act came before Congress,

President Richard M. Nixon became the first Republican president to try to derail such an extension, but in the end he signed the extension on June 17, 1970. Confronted by hundreds of DOJ lawyers and staff who supported extension, as well as by popular support in Congress and in society, he had to back down from his impulse to veto the extension.

The Voting Rights Act was extended in 1970 and 1975. Both times, the applicability of section 5 was extended: for five years in 1970 and for seven years in 1975. In 1982, it was extended again, this time for twenty-five years, and section 4 was also strengthened. In 2006 Congress extended the act for the last time. The *Shelby* decision dramatically changed the future of the Voting Rights Act.

Regarding the feelings of the "gipper" residing in the White House when I appeared before the Rodino committee, I could not fail to remember that candidate Reagan opened his 1980 national campaign for the presidency by giving a major speech at the Neshoba County fairgrounds in Mississippi. For the millions of Americans who knew the history—and the symbolism—of that bloodstained Mississippi locale, the Reagan announcement at that place was a scary portent of the kinds of actions he and his DOJ would take in the field of voting rights. After all, he told the supportive, shouting crowd of ten thousand white Mississippians, "I believe in states' rights!" However, like Presidents Nixon, Ford, and, after Reagan, Bush, Republicans all, Reagan reluctantly signed every extension of the Voting Rights Act.

The following morning, I walked over to the committee hearing room. Inside the room a modest crowd awaited the hearing. I met the attorney from Columbus. And then we both found ourselves observers as another hardball incident developed! The Democrats did not want the two of us to sit together and testify, whereas the Republicans did. Their battle over the matter lasted for over an hour before the Democrats won. However, the Columbus lawyer would testify first.

During the battle I sat down and had coffee with the Mississippi lawyer, a bright person whose argument had been discussed in law journals for years. Basically, because of the many problems with enforcement of section 5, he wanted to have the federal district court judges in all the covered jurisdictions hear complaints on a timely basis from the DOJ's voting section attorneys and, if the DOJ did not litigate, from individuals who claimed voter dilution. He was gravely concerned about the hazards of leaving implementation to a handful of lawyers and young paralegals hundreds of miles away from the vote dilution controversy. The difference between us was that although I was concerned—not gravely— about compromised compliance, I felt that the act could be fixed to address these problems. I was not willing to allow federal district judges serving in the covered states, some of them very hostile to civil rights petitioners, to make these determinations that would affect local politics in the South, possibly for decades.

Finally, it was my turn to testify. My statement contained many surprises for the committee members. I discussed the extremely pressed voting section staff and attorneys. They simply could not, with the personnel on hand (fewer than forty), adequately deal with the voting changes—submitted and not submitted—from attorneys in the seven thousand jurisdictions in twenty-two states that were covered by the Voting Rights Act. And so, they had to develop processes which gave a semblance of oversight but that led to a more than 98 percent preclearance rate.

I spoke about the untold hundreds of local covered jurisdictions who did not preclear but followed the "Indianola way." And I pointed out that the voting section attorneys had never used the criminal penalties found in the statute to deal with those white officials who refused to preclear voting changes. I said I believed that if the DOJ brought criminal indictments against a single local city attorney who intentionally refused to preclear a voting change with the DOJ, within a minute that message would be received all across the covered jurisdictions and preclearance submissions would immediately improve!

I urged extension of the act, with more funding for the DOJ's voting section so that section 5 would be better enforced. Finally, I told how disenchanted the Blacks I met in Mississippi were. In 1965, they had believed, they had finally been given the means to use the right to vote. However, as soon as they largely overcame vote denial, they saw new actions by the white power holders that effectively diluted their vote by, for example, changing voting district lines or making some positions appointive rather than elective. Votes by Blacks did not elect local Blacks to serve as select-persons on the county board—in spite of a strong majority Black vote in their town or county. This was, I said, the voting reality in the Deep South. This had to be fixed, and it was up to Congress.

In the questioning period, one clearly saw the two parties at work on me. The Democrats asked me to amplify a number of points that addressed the noncompliance problem. One Black legislator, Harold Washington, from the Chicago area (he became mayor of Chicago after serving in Congress), was clearly shocked, as he told me, about the "Indianola way" response to section 5. He said that my testimony was "shocking" and that it showed clear evidence of a "massive failure of compliance." Another legislator, a Republican from Illinois, Henry Hyde, responded to my testimony by saying that "the Justice Department [had] utterly failed to enforce the law." He was amazed that the DOJ had never used the criminal penalties in section 12, which provided for imposition of a maximum five thousand dollar fine and a five-year jail term for local officials who did not comply with section 5. He said: "If one or two people go to the slammer, they'd start to comply."

The chairman, Don Edwards, a Democrat from California, was also dismayed by the immense problems, mostly communications ones, that the voting section faced in implementing the act. "This Committee could be faulted, we're supposed to have oversight responsibility," he grumbled at one point. "Actually," he concluded, "I didn't know that thousands of submissions were not made. Somebody should have come to us." (In a letter to me sent the very day of my testimony, Congressman Edwards told me that I had presented "really first-class information that will be of great help.")[22]

The Republican staff and congresspersons focused on the alternative solution: placing responsibility for preclearances with the federal judiciary in the covered jurisdictions. I respectfully pointed out that when the act was drafted, the drafters in the White House and the DOJ placed responsibility for preclearance with the federal district court judges in the District of Columbia and with the DOJ. Why? Because they knew very well the history of judicial discrimination practiced by many of the federal district court judges serving in the South!

Testifying before the Committee was, for me, a very revealing experience. This was the first and only time I encountered "DC" politics up close. All I said to those who asked me about the experience was that "I was very happy that I did not live and work in Washington."

I returned to Mississippi to find that my testimony and that of the Columbus attorney were page-one stories in the *Columbus Commercial-Dispatch*, the *Starkville Daily News*,[23] and the *Jackson Clarion-Ledger*.[24] I urged extension of the act, with more funding for the DOJ's voting section so that there could be a more substantive response to the dilemma of vote dilution in the South. However, as I knew, my view was a distinct minority one in Mississippi, and I was greeted with disdain when I returned to Starkville. By this time, I was not surprised.

WRITING OP-ED PIECES ABOUT MISSISSIPPI'S VOTING "WRONGS"

Another activity that did not endear me to a great many Mississippians, especially my new friend, US senator John C. Stennis, was the op-ed pieces I wrote for the *New York Times* and *Washington Post* about the inequitable state of Black voting rights in Mississippi. These newspapers were very eager to print essays written by persons in the South who argued for the extension of the Voting Rights Act, and my essays fit their agenda. I was happy; the editors were happy. Native Mississippians were not happy.

The *Times* piece was written first and published in early July 1981. Entitled "Voting Rights," it laid out in general terms the continuing need for the Voting Rights Act. I encouraged enlargement of the voting section staff, "improved monitoring by the department [and] other federal agencies," and DOJ "use of civil and criminal sanctions [which] may convince people to obey the law."

In the *Post* piece, "Mississippi's Voting Wrongs," published in late January 1982, I wrote about the many ways in which white power holders in Mississippi had diluted Black votes so as to deny Blacks representation in local and county governing boards. I pointed out that in Tunica

County, with a 73 percent Black voting majority, all five county supervisors were white! Of the twenty-two majority-Black counties in Mississippi in 1982, eight had no Black elected officials and only two of the twenty-two, Claiborne County (75 percent Black) and Jefferson County (82 percent Black), had Black majorities on the boards of supervisors.

On the day my *Post* op-ed piece ran, the lead editorial, "Voting Rights: Be Strong," once again called for the extension of the act. "As Professor Howard Ball's article on the opposite page demonstrates," they wrote, "efforts are still being made to subvert the law and dilute the voting power of minorities. The Voting Rights Act is the most powerful weapon available to defeat these efforts."

I received some letters from readers. Most were extremely critical of my views, calling me a "n****r lover" and other epithets too vile to put down on paper. One stood out; it evidently was from an American lover of Adolf Hitler. The message consisted chiefly of a large photo of Hitler with a nineteenth-century Prussian, possibly Otto von Bismarck, pasted next to the Fuhrer. Above and below the picture, he wrote, "YOUR BOOK IS GARBAGE AND UN-AMERICAN," and at the bottom, A NATION THAT DOES NOT MAINTAIN IT'S [*sic*] RACIAL PURITY WILL PERISH.

A handful of thank-you notes came from others. W. S. McFeely, a historian who had written about Frederick Douglass and Ulysses S. Grant, thanked me for my "excellent op-ed piece." He knew well the consequences of the Compromise of 1877, where federal protection of Black voters ended in the South. "Apparently," he wrote, "we're about to do it again—unless good people like you prevail."

Another supportive letter came from Roscoe Saville of Arlington, Virginia, a faculty member and head of a department in the College of Agriculture and Life Sciences at Mississippi State from 1947–56. He was there at the height of Jim Crow higher education in Mississippi and was saddened to read that things had not changed much in the three decades since he left the state. "Your article is excellent," he concluded. "May it have the desired impact." Saville's letter mentioned a brief encounter he had with a former student of his at MSU. The young Black man was working in the US Department of Agriculture at the time. "I asked him," Saville wrote to me, "'Why don't you go back to Mississippi to help those folks out.' After all several of us [at MSU in the 1950s] had tried to help him get his education and into a good job. He gave me a look like I had never seen before and said calmly: 'I'll never go back to Mississippi to work.' So much as to say—I may be a Ph.D. but to them he's still just a 'n****r.'" (I ran into that perception of Mississippi when our department at MSU consciously tried to recruit Black students—both male and female—into our master of public administration program. I will discuss that effort in the next chapter.)

SENATOR JOHN STENNIS AND ME: GOOD MAN, BAD MAN

Later, I learned that on the day that my *Post* piece ran—January 26, 1982—US senator Ted Kennedy (D-MA) held up a copy of the *Post* and read from my essay and the editorial on the Senate floor. He then addressed Mississippi senator John C. Stennis: "Senator, this was written by someone from your own alma mater, Mississippi State University, calling for the extension of the Voting Rights Act because of the many successful efforts of whites in Mississippi to dilute Black votes!" (My source for the quote is Bill Collins, director of the Stennis Institute at State. He was told about the incident by one of the senator's staffers.)

Evidently the senator fumed and, minutes later after leaving the floor, called two top Mississippi State University officials to demand that the university's president, Dr. James McComas, fire me immediately for my comments. McComas, one of the few strong supporters of my efforts to provide support for Black students, casually rejected the senator's demand. Not satisfied, Senator Stennis then called Dr. Bill Collins, director of the John C. Stennis Institute of Government on campus. Collins, who by 1980 had become my mentor, reminded Stennis of the First Amendment's freedom of speech. Besides, he told Stennis, Ball was a tenured professor and could not be summarily dismissed.

That incident ended what had become a most unusual association between Senator Stennis and me. Early in 1978, the senator took a liking to me. I'd been the head of the Department of Political Science for little more than a year by then, and I had visited Washington, DC, several times to lobby for graduate student support for our master's students in the public administration program. Each time I was there I dropped by the senator's office to talk to him about our departmental efforts to provide public management training to young men and women so that they could take positions in local, rural government in Mississippi and Alabama.

Well, after he took a liking to me, he would call me up and invite me down to his home in DeKalb, Mississippi. He saw himself as a throwback to the eighteenth-century Jeffersonians. He knew that one of my areas was constitutional theory, and he and I spent time talking about the revolutionary and constitutional periods in American history. He enjoyed reading the Federalist Papers, and we often explored Madison's famous essay in the Papers, Federalist 10. On other occasions—unfortunately, Saturday *early* mornings—he would telephone me to discuss one of the founding fathers. Usually, I would talk to the senator from my bed, with Carol between me and the phone's base. He truly believed that he was part of a constitutional continuum that began in the summer of 1787 and continued in the 1980s. Try as I might, I could not get the senior senator to see the value of a contemporary piece of legislation, the Voting Rights Act.

If I was flying up to DC, he would on occasion join me on the plane. It was a very unusual relationship between a venerable Mississippian who believed in the concept of states' rights as he believed Jefferson understood that term and a New York Jew who spoke, wrote, and called for greater national protection against a local majority's successful efforts to deprive, dilute, or deny civil and voting rights to Blacks and other minorities. Our conversations were based on his understanding of the Constitution itself and on the Federalist Papers, and I could never get Stennis to talk about contemporary issues such as voting rights. Every time I brought the subject up, he would, as fast as a spotted leopard, move back to the eighteenth century's understanding of freedom.

The *Post* incident suddenly ended that very strange relationship. It went from very, very good to very, very bad overnight. At the least, I was able to sleep without too many disturbances on Saturday mornings for the rest of my stay in Mississippi.

CHAPTER 6

A Solitary Jew on Campus
and in the Field

I came down to Mississippi State University with the title of professor of political science. I was going to teach courses in my favorite area: constitutional law and civil rights and liberties. I would have many opportunities to continue my research into, understanding of, and writing about voting rights and wrongs. It was the kind of job description I had wished for over the past decade at Hofstra University. I thought I was ready for this new teaching environment.

I plunged right into the teaching and immediately knew that the move was going to be an intense learning experience not just for the students but for me. For the first time since I began teaching in 1965, I was discussing constitutional law and civil liberties and civil rights in an integrated student environment. And all my students were living in cities, towns, and a state that I knew only from news stories, books, and judicial opinions. I was now actually *in* Mississippi, where a fierce commitment to race discrimination and the belief in white supremacy was the dominant value.

In the nineteenth century, Mississippi was a part of America where hundreds of thousands of white sons, lovers, brothers, fathers, and husbands died defending the Confederacy's hallowed values. After the war, Mississippi was one of many defeated states that turned toward violence to maintain the "old values" of the South. And Carol and the girls and I were transplants to a place where, a century later, some of my students' parents did business with or were relatives of the men who lynched civil rights workers just a dozen years before we arrived in Starkville.

Before long, the incongruity of the move hit me in the head. In the civil rights course, I began discussing the 1964 Freedom Summer and then just leaned back against the blackboard. At least seven students from Neshoba County, including two Black students, self-started a discussion about conditions in that county based on their personal knowledge of some of the people involved—either as victims or as relatives of the perpetrators—in the cruelties that occurred.

Over the six years I was in the classroom, my students—some of them still connect with Carol and me now—taught me more about life in a place where the white political, religious, and economic leadership was fighting efforts by the federal government to ensure due process and equality for its African American citizens. Soon, though, our family found out about these southern "troubles." Inexorably, we all became participants in the struggle for equality.

MISSISSIPPI: MY PETRI DISH FOR INVESTIGATING THE ETIOLOGY OF RACISM

My research activities were more than I had hoped for while I was in New York. Mississippi, with respect to my research on the impact of the Voting Rights Act on its then mostly white politics and politicians, was a Petri dish! Local government leaders, whether town managers, mayors, or town attorneys, were always available to talk about their actions—or inactions—in the Voting Rights Act age. And they were comfortable telling me of their city's actions to avoid and evade following the voting rights law.

I never saw a hint of shame or embarrassment whenever a city attorney spoke with me about why the city or county did not file a preclearance request with the Department of Justice. "We're doing the prefiling the Indianola way," said another attorney. I soon found out that Indianola, Mississippi, simply, regularly, made changes in its local voting process and never precleared these changes!

Evidently, many local government leaders *knew* that the voting section had only about a dozen lawyers to oversee implementation of the Voting Rights Act. When I was doing my research, beginning in the 1970s, almost two dozen states were "covered" by the act! So doing it the "Indianola way" was a safe bet that the jurisdiction would not see a DOJ letter, and it was an even better bet that the local mayor would not meet a Justice lawyer in person!

Furthermore, regarding my often jaw-dropping voting rights work, I found two colleagues who were interested in researching and writing about the political dynamics surrounding the "putting into practice" of the Voting Rights Act. One of my new research partners, Dale Krane, was a colleague of mine in the department. He studied and wrote about intergovernmental relations: how well (or whether) local, county, state, and federal agency personnel worked together to carry out congressional legislation and federal regulations such as voting rights.

My second collaborator was Tom Lauth, my best friend and former colleague at Hofstra, who was living in Georgia and was on the faculty of Georgia State University's political science department. His teaching and research focus are on American budgetary politics. Tom is interested in the connection between, on the one hand, state lawmakers, agency heads, and county officials, and, on the other hand, in the private sector, the state's business leaders (and their lobbyists) and other interest groups in the putting together of the annual state budget. He also wants to understand how, when racial animosity is mixed in, racial discrimination comes out of the oven.

In the South, ever since the passage of national civil rights legislation beginning in the 1950s, majority-Black towns have continued to be treated unfairly in the allocation of state funds. It is a controversial issue, reflecting the meaning of politics: who gets what, where, and how much.

The Ball family, Bronx, New York, ca. 1954

Howard Ball, in
the annual brochure
"Welcoming New Faculty,"
1976

Howard Ball
Professor
Department of Political Science
Degrees Earned:
  B.A., Hunter College
  M.A., Rutgers University
  Ph.D., Rutgers University
Previous Position:
  Hofstra University
Achievements:
  Regional Mediator, AAUP
  Author of *The Vision and the Dream
    of Justice Hugo Black, The Warren
    Court and Democracy, Changing
    Perspectives in Contemporary
    Political Analysis,* and *No Pledge
    of Privacy: The Watergate Tapes
    Litigation*

Temple B'nai Israel,
Columbus, Mississippi, 1981

Temple B'nai Israel
100th Anniversary Service
May 11, 1980

Brochure marking the
one hundredth anniversary of
Temple B'nai Israel, 1980

History of "a church of the Hebrew persuasion"
in brochure, 1980

1879 - 1979
Columbus, Mississippi

CONGREGATIONAL HISTORY

Over one hundred years ago, on July 23, 1879, to be exact, Jewish leaders of the Columbus, Mississippi community met and organized as Congregation B'nai Israel. Four months later they secured the services of Rabbi Joseph Herz at $300 a year and Howard Tisdale as musical director at $150 per annum. Rabbi Herz's salary was increased to $500 in 1891 and to further show its appreciation, the congregation voted $50 to cover the Rabbi's trip to a meeting in Baltimore. Rabbi Herz continued to serve as religious leader of the group until his death in 1909.

Among the first Jewish settlers in Columbus in 1840 were the Hoffmans, Crusmans, Nathans, Grosses, Lorschs, Schwartzes, Rautchs, and Wolffs. The congregation was swelled by more than 200 Jews who settled in Columbus. Among them were the Kaufmans, Simon Loebs and Albert Loebs. A secretary of the congregation and one of its mainstays was Isidor Rubel. Others were the Weitzenhofers, Friedmans, Finesteins, and Rosenzweigs. The present congregation is composed of members from Aberdeen, Columbus, and Starkville.

In 1879 a Sunday School was begun and the first confirmation class was in 1895. Services were held in the Odd Fellows Hall until 1906 when the congregation accepted an invitation to meet in the Christian Church of Columbus. The Sisterhood ladies were very active and served on numerous committees. Through their efforts congregation obligations were met. In 1896 a note in the minutes read "the ladies of the Temple were asked to hold a strawberry festival to raise funds."

The first Temple in Columbus was built for the Methodist Church in 1844 and was similar in design but much smaller than the present Methodist structure. When the Methodist congregation outgrew the building on North Second Street, the building served as a private military school, a city gymnasium and a community place for musical concerts. In 1907 following a series of meetings, Congregation B'nai Israel bought the building known as Concert Hall. Thus the building constructed for the worship of God in 1844 returned to the purpose for which it was built 63 years later.

The building continued to serve the congregation until 1960 when the old building was torn down and the present structure was erected using the old bricks. During the time the Temple was being built services were held in the Episcopal Church. Members of B'nai Israel will forever be grateful to the Christian and Episcopal Churches for their kindness during the development and building periods.

Dr. Louis Kuppin served as the Rabbi in the new Temple, after many years as leader in the old Temple. In 1962 the Congregation subscribed to the Student Rabbi Program offered by the Hebrew Union College in Cincinnati, Ohio.

In 1961 the first confirmation class in the new Temple consisted of David Smith, Rachael Bergman and Michael Kleban. The first wedding in the new Temple was in August of 1961 when Marjorie Meyer became the bride of Norman Goldner.

Serving as president during the building of the new Temple was Bernard Lasky. Other presidents were Raymond Goodman, Henry Meyer, Ralph Katz, Joe M. Kleban, Hymie Schur, Norman Mitlin, Mrs. William H. Smith, Dr. Howard Ball, and Henry Leveck, who is also the present president.

MISS SUSAN GABRIELLE BALL became bat mitzvah on Saturday, April 19, at Temple Israel in Columbus. She is the daughter of Dr. and Mrs. Howard Ball of Starkville.

Society - Clubs - Locals

MRS. VIRGINIA McCAIN
Phone 323-1643 Before 3 p.m.

Susan Gabrielle Ball Becomes Bat-Mitzvah

On Saturday morning, April 19, Susan Gabrielle Ball, daughter of Dr. and Mrs. Howard Ball, Starkville, became a bat mitzvah at Temple B'nai Israel in Columbus. Rabbie David Straus, Cincinnati, Ohio, officiated at this traditional religious ceremony.

The Bat Mitzvah is the ceremony commemorating the entry into the Jewish religious community of those young women who have reached the age of 13 years. In this traditional religious ceremony, the young person reads a portion of the Torah Five Books of Moses in Hebrew, and can thereafter participate in all religious services of the Hebrew faith. The Bat Mitzvah, translated, is "Woman of the Commandments."

Susan Gabrielle read, in the traditional hebrew words, from Leviticus Chapter XIX, verses 3-20, and then spoke about the meaning of holiness. At the conclusion of this portion of the religious service, Susan became a bat mitzvah and was given a scroll by the Rabbi to so indicate.

Attending the ceremony were 100 celebrants, including her sisters, Sheryl Lisa and Melissa Paige. Visitors from out of state were: Susan's paternal grandparents, Mr. and Mrs. Abe Ball, Monticello, New York; Susan's maternal grandfather, Sidney Neidell, East Hampton, New York, her aunts and uncles in attendance were: Dr. and Mrs. Lester Neidell, Syosset, New York; Carol Teplin, Hicksville, New York; and Dorothy Rabin, Mineola, New York.

Susan's cousins visiting for the religious occasion were: Jeanette Teplin, Hicksville, New York; Shara, David and Jason Neidell, Tulsa, Oklahoma. Very close family friends from out of state who visited were: Gail Weinstein, Stony Brook, New York; Ellen Handler, Centereach, New York; and Dr. and Mrs. Thomas Lauth and sons, David and John, Stone Mountain, Georgia. Also in attendance were Mr. and Mrs. Alfred

Cohen and son, Jonathan, Tupelo, Mississippi.

Susan's friends from Starkville who attended this traditional Jewish ritual were: Mary Steele Arnold, Nice Monterim, Tonya Lee, Suzy Callison, Julia Housley, Courtney Couvillion, Michelle Amos, Leslie Mayo, Sabrina Vise, Carolyn Lynch, Diane Boyd, Gia Eubanks, Jamie Hill, Amy Hidgen, David Wallace, Larry Graves, Jay Reed, Tray Batson and Al Treadway.

The service was concluded with the Kiddush, the traditional ceremonial blessings over wine and bread.

At 1:00 p.m. Dr. and Mrs. Ball entertained over 100 guests at a dinner buffet in their home at 622 Sherwood Road in honor of their bat mitzvah, Susan Gabrielle.

Bat Mitzvah Ceremony Honors Sheryl L. Ball

Sheryl Lisa Ball, 13, daughter of Mr. and Mrs. Howard Ball of Starkville, became a Bat Mitzvah on Saturday, May 9, at Temple B'nai Israel in Columbus, Mississippi.

Sheryl was called by Rabbi David Straus to the Torah, where she read from the Torah scroll Chapter 19 of Leviticus. Sheryl's sisters, Susan and Melissa, assisted her in the service. Afterwards, she commented on her Bible portion saying, in part, "If God is holy, then we should imitate God's holiness by following the commandments. What you should do is treat all men equal, give to the poor, honor thy mother and father, and worship the Sabbath. Even if we make mistakes, God understands and we still are holy because we are trying to be holy."

Attending the Bat Mitzvah

from out of town were: her grandfather, Sidney Neidell, East Hampton, New York; grandmother, Fay Ball, Monticello, New York; her aunt, Dorothy Robin, Mineola, New York; her uncle, Stephen Neidell, Stony Brook, New York; and friends of the family, Thomas and Jean Lauth and son, Bob, of Stone Mountain, Georgia. Sheryl's friends also from Starkville were: Rhonda Phelps, Michelle Merner, Alan Bonner, Chris Loyd, Stephen Cuoetto, Tim Hunt, Melia Jefferson, Amanda Owens, Laura Vasek, Mali Williams, Cheri Hovet and Todd Childers.

On Saturday afternoon Sheryl was honored by her family and friends at a dinner buffet in home of her parents on Sherwood Road, in Starkville.

BAT MITZVAH - Sheryl Lisa Ball, daughter of Mr. and Mrs. Howard Ball of Starkville, became a Bat Mitzvah at services on Saturday, May 9, at Temple B'nai Israel in Columbus. Later she was honored at a buffet dinner at the home of her parents on Sherwood Road, Starkville.

Announcements in the *Starkville Daily News* about Susan's and Sheryl's Bat Mitzvahs, 1980 and 1981

FUN FOR THE SMALL FRY and of much interest to grown-ups was last week's doll show at the Starkville Public Library. Ms. Debra Wade, children's librarian and director of the exhibit, reported that 55 entries were registered for the show, held throughout the week and open to the general public. Children entering the show ranged in ages from four to nine. In the picture are the show winners with their prized dolls and stuffed animals as follows (reading from left): Shelley Flurry, Most Unique Doll; Brandie McVey, Judges' Favorite Doll; Melissa Ball, Most Unique Stuffed Animal; Linda Barker, Judges' Favorite Stuffed Animal. Children's Librarian Debra Wade, sponsor for the show, is standing in the background.

(Staff photo—Virginia McCain)

Picture in the *Starkville Daily News* of Melissa's win, ca. 1981

Student rabbi David Straus, 1980–81

(opposite-top)
Sheryl and Rabbi Straus after Bat Mitzvah service, 1981

(opposite-bottom)
Hortense and Henry Leveck, leaders of Temple B'nai Israel, 1981

NINETY-SEVENTH CONGRESS

PETER W. RODINO, JR. (N.J.), CHAIRMAN

JACK BROOKS, TEX.
ROBERT W. KASTENMEIER, WIS.
DON EDWARDS, CALIF.
JOHN CONYERS, JR., MICH.
JOHN F. SEIBERLING, OHIO
GEORGE E. DANIELSON, CALIF.
ROMANO L. MAZZOLI, KY.
WILLIAM J. HUGHES, N.J.
SAM B. HALL, JR., TEX.
MIKE SYNAR, OKLA.
PATRICIA SCHROEDER, COLO.
BILLY LEE EVANS, GA.
DAN GLICKMAN, KANS.
HAROLD WASHINGTON, ILL.
BARNEY FRANK, MASS.

ROBERT MC CLORY, ILL.
TOM RAILSBACK, ILL.
HAMILTON FISH, JR., N.Y.
M. CALDWELL BUTLER, VA.
CARLOS J. MOORHEAD, CALIF.
JOHN M. ASHBROOK, OHIO
HENRY J. HYDE, ILL.
THOMAS N. KINDNESS, OHIO
HAROLD S. SAWYER, MICH.
DAN LUNGREN, CALIF.
F. JAMES SENSENBRENNER, JR., WIS.
BILL MC COLLUM, FLA.

GENERAL COUNSEL:
ALAN A. PARKER

STAFF DIRECTOR:
GARNER J. CLINE

ASSOCIATE COUNSEL
FRANKLIN G. POL

Congress of the United States
Committee on the Judiciary
House of Representatives
Washington, D.C.   20515
Telephone: 202-225-3951

June 22, 1981

Howard Ball
Professor and Head
Department of Political Science
Mississippi State University
Mississippi State, Mississippi 39762

Dear Professor Ball:

The Subcommittee on Civil and Constitutional Rights of the House
Committee on the Judiciary is planning to hold a number of hearings on the extension of the Voting Rights Act of 1965.

I am writing to invite you to appear and testify before the Subcommittee on Thursday, June 25, 1981 at 9:30 a.m. in room 2237
of the Rayburn House Office Building.

Enclosed you will find a notice which sets forth the Committee's
requirement that prepared statements be filed at least 48 hours
prior to your scheduled appearance. Each witness is asked to
prepare a condensed version of their prepared statement for their
oral testimony - not to exceed 5 typed written pages, doubled-spaced.
Accordingly, copies of your prepared statement should be submitted
by Tuesday, June 23, 1981.

Your earliest acceptance of this invitation would be appreciated.

With warmest regards,

Sincerely,

PETER W. RODINO, Jr.
Chairman

PWRj:hgd

Enclosure

Letter from Congressman Peter Rodino to Howard Ball, inviting Ball to testify,
June 1981

Starkville Daily News

SERVING THE STARKVILLE TRADE AREA AND MISSISSIPPI STATE UNIVERSITY

eha County   Starkville, Mississippi, Thursday Morning, June 25, 1981   Associated Press News and Pi

Ball Testifying Today
On Voting Act Extension

A Mississippi State University political science professor is in Washington, D.C. today to testify in House hearings on the extension of the 1965 Voting Rights Act.

Dr. Howard Ball, professor and head of the political science department, will present a 10-minute prepared statement before the Judiciary Committee subcommittee on civil and constitutional rights which has been conducting the hearings for over a month. The 1965 Act will terminate in August of 1982. The subcommittee is expected to prepare a bill calling for a 10-year extension of the act. If the House passes the bill, it will then go to the Senate for consideration.

Ball was invited to testify by Rep. Peter Rodino of New Jersey, chairman of the House Judiciary Committee. Ball, along with Dr. Dale Krane of MSU and Dr. Tom Lauth of the University of Georgia, has been involved in research on the administration of the Voting Act. Their research will be published sometime this year by Greenwood Press in a book called "Compromise Compliance."

Ball favors a 10-year extension of the act "whether as it stands or with some improvements in Section V, the pre-clearance mechanism governing voting changes by local governments."

Columbus attorney Wilbur Colon is also expected to testify today.

Story in the *Starkville Daily News*, "Ball Testifying," June 25, 1981

NINETY-SEVENTH CONGRESS

PETER W. RODINO, JR. (N.J.), CHAIRMAN

JACK BROOKS, TEX.
ROBERT W. KASTENMEIER, WIS.
DON EDWARDS, CALIF.
JOHN CONYERS, JR., MICH.
JOHN F. SEIBERLING, OHIO
GEORGE E. DANIELSON, CALIF.
ROMANO L. MAZZOLI, KY.
WILLIAM J. HUGHES, N.J.
SAM B. HALL, JR., TEX.
MIKE SYNAR, OKLA.
PATRICIA SCHROEDER, COLO.
BILLY LEE EVANS, GA.
DAN GLICKMAN, KANS.
HAROLD WASHINGTON, ILL.
BARNEY FRANK, MASS.

ROBERT McCLORY, ILL.
TOM RAILSBACK, ILL.
HAMILTON FISH, JR., N.Y.
M. CALDWELL BUTLER, VA.
CARLOS J. MOORHEAD, CALIF.
JOHN M. ASHBROOK, OHIO
HENRY J. HYDE, ILL.
THOMAS N. KINDNESS, OHIO
HAROLD S. SAWYER, MICH.
DAN LUNGREN, CALIF.
F. JAMES SENSENBRENNER, JR., WIS.
BILL McCOLLUM, FLA.

GENERAL COUNSEL:
ALAN A. PARKER

STAFF DIRECTOR:
GARNER J. CLINE

ASSOCIATE COUNSEL:
FRANKLIN G. POLK

Congress of the United States

Committee on the Judiciary

House of Representatives

Washington, D.C. 20515

Telephone: 202-225-3951

June 25, 1981

Howard Ball
Professor and Head
Department of Political Science
Mississippi State University
Mississippi State, Mississippi 39762

Dear Professor Ball:

Thank you very much for testifying at our Subcommittee's hearing on Thursday, June 25, 1981.

Your testimony on the Extension of the Voting Rights Act was very valuable to the deliberations of the Subcommittee, and we are most grateful for your contribution.

Sincerely,

Don Edwards
Chairman
Subcommittee on Civil and
Constitutional Rights

DE:idd

Really first class information that will be of great help. D.

Letter from California congressman Don Edwards, chair of the Subcommittee on Civil and Constitutional Rights, to Howard Ball, June 25, 1981

The Voting Rights Act

SPEAKING in Washington to the subcommittee on Civil and Constitutional Rights in support of an extension of the 1965 Voting Rights Act, Mississippi State University Professor Howard Ball said: "I believe it is imperative that the 1965 Voting Rights Act be extended for as long as it takes to educate the affected publics, black and white, to the meaning and the responsibility of representative government in a free society."

There is no need to dredge up the horror stories of why this act was so badly needed in the years before 1965.

It is a fact that the South — the region to which the act's provisions applied — was the scene of brutal violence visited upon blacks attempting to vote. When violence became too risky for those employing it and triggered criticism of the South from the rest of the nation, legalistic tactics, such as gerrymandering, were used.

It is likewise a fact that since the act's passage voting rights for Southern blacks have improved — tremendously.

In Mississippi, for instance, only 6.7 percent of blacks in 1964 were registered to vote, yet blacks totaled 36 percent of the population. Today, 70 percent of black Mississippians have registered to vote.

Not only Southern blacks have benefited from the Voting Rights Act of 1965. Hispanics, too, especially in the Southwest, are registered to vote in larger numbers than ever.

Under these circumstances why the rhetoric about changing the law, of which vital parts are due to expire in 1982? The cry for repeal is heard most often from Sens. Jesse Helms and Strom Thurmond, the two veteran cheerleaders of the anti-civil rights movement. Both argue that the act has overstayed its effectiveness. Vigorously attacking Section 5 of the act — which calls for preclearance through the Justice Department by states which want to tamper with their existing voting laws — the two federal lawmakers say that the states should no longer be subjected to this "penalty box." Because of successful efforts to thwart minority voting power, Alabama, Georgia, Louisiana, Texas, Virginia, Mississippi, and Arizona are being scrutinized by the federal government, whose duty it is to enforce the Voting Rights Act.

The latter was adopted to reverse a constitutional wrong: the disenfranchisement of blacks. It is much too early for the act to be scragged. Blacks weren't permitted the vote for 65 years. More years are required to assure that what happened at the end of the 19th century to black voters isn't repeated. If Congress repeals or tampers with the Voting Rights Act, it will strike a blow against both minority Americans and every American who believes in universally applied equal justice.

Editorial in the *Charleston (WV) Gazette,* July 1, 1981

Critical letter with photo from an anonymous writer to Howard Ball, July 1981

The New York Times

Founded in 1851

ADOLPH S OCHS, *Publisher 1896-1935*
ARTHUR HAYS SULZBERGER, *Publisher 1935-1961*
ORVIL E. DRYFOOS, *Publisher 1961-1963*

Voting Rights

By Howard Ball

STARKVILLE, Miss. — The 1965 Voting Rights Act is due to expire next year and already loud voices are heard calling for burial of this major civil rights law.

The legislation, enacted in response to bloodshed in Selma, Ala., represented a strong national effort to end racial discrimination in voting. The act was triggered in any state if less than 50 percent of its voting-age citizens were registered or voted in the 1964 Presidential election. Because nine states of the old Confederacy — Virginia, North Carolina, South Carolina, Georgia, Florida, Alabama, Mississippi, Louisiana, and Texas — fall under the act's coverage, Southern senators have strongly urged scuttling it. Strom Thurmond of South Carolina and Jesse Helms of North Carolina call the law unfair and biased against one region. They and other Southern politicians recommend outright burial or "nationwide coverage" — their shorthand term for removal of the triggering mechanism, which would have the effect of requiring that every voting law enacted in America be approved by the Justice Department, making enforcement impossible.

Supporters of the act, including all civil rights groups and such legislators as Senators Edward M. Kennedy, Daniel Patrick Moynihan and Barry Goldwater, as well as Don Edwards, chairman of the House Subcommittee on Civil and Constitutional Rights, are fighting hard to extend the existing law through 1992. They believe that the task of ensuring voter equality, especially in the South, has not yet been completed and that the Justice Department should continue the eradication of racial discrimination in voting.

President Reagan's position on extending the act appears unclear. On Sunday, he said he would support only nationwide coverage of it, but on Monday, at the convention of the National Association for the Advancement of Colored People, in Denver, he refused to comment on the Administration's position, saying that he needed additional time and information to study the issue. It is easy to understand his pained uncertainty. Administratively and politically, the law is complex; in its major sections, it calls for interdependent changes in local registration and voting processes, supervised by Federal officials.

Since 1965, more than 1.5 million Southern blacks have registered to vote. In Mississippi, where blacks constitute about 36 percent of the population, in 1964, 6.7 percent were registered; in 1981, nearly 70 percent were registered. A section of the act that suspends various tests and devices that frustrate registration, among them literacy tests and poll taxes, has been moderately successful. It is Section 5, the "preclearance" section, that is anathema to white office-holders. This section, put in because of Southern whites' horrid record in delaying implementation of integration orders, calls for preclearance of all voting changes by the Justice Department, or by the Federal District Court in Washington, D.C.

Section 5 gets to the heart of the problem. The objective of the law is defeated if 70 percent of the blacks in Mississippi are registered but if Indianola, Miss., can successfully annex, without preclearance, white subdivisions in order to ensure continuation of the city's white power base, as it did in 1966. It is defeated if, though many blacks in Jackson are registered, on the night before the 1978 election for a United States Senator, the all-white elections commission can successfully order the voting machines moved from one set of locations in black districts to others without informing the voters, much less clearing the change with the Justice Department.

Studies of implementation of the act indicate that Southern communities have flouted it with regularity by not reporting voting changes. Since there are, in the Justice Department, only about 15 staff members to implement it, the chances are good that a municipality, faced with an increase in the number of black citizens to the point where the blacks may win a mayoral race, will redistrict, or annex white subdivisions, or change from ward to at-large elections, or call for reregistration of voters, to prevent blacks from winning.

Many Southern communities ignore the preclearance requirement. If there are 7,000 preclearances in a given year reported to the Justice Department, as there were in fiscal 1980, there are hundreds of substantive voting changes, not monitored by the department, that dilute blacks' votes in the South.

The act should not only not be junked, but implementation of it should be improved. An enlarged and better trained Justice Department staff is essential. Improved monitoring by the department, by other Federal agencies, by state agencies, and by civil rights groups is necessary. Justice Department use of civil and criminal sanctions, authorized by the Voting Rights Act, may convince people to obey the law.

In coming months, Congress and the public must examine the reality of voting-rights enforcement in the South. Southern rhetoric should be ignored. The facts in such municipalities as Indianola and Jackson should be examined. Litigation in Federal courts challenging voting changes and elections in the South should be made known. A lot has changed in the South, but the job of ensuring voting equality is not yet finished.

Howard Ball, professor of political science and chairman of that department at Mississippi State University, co-authored, with Dale Krane and Thomas Lauth, the forthcoming book "Compromised Compliance: Implementation of the 1965 Voting Rights Act."

Op-ed by Howard Ball in the *New York Times,* "Voting Rights," June 1981

Mississippi State Senate

JACKSON

COMMITTEE ASSIGNMENTS:
Fees and Salaries, Chairman
Appropriations
Corrections
Highways and Transportation
Interstate and Federal Cooperation
Investigate State Offices
Judiciary "A"
Public Utilities
Rules

SENATOR ROBERT L. CROOK

11th District

Bolivar - Sunflower Counties

P. O. Box 85, Ruleville 38771

December 12, 1980

Member
Joint Committee on
Performance Evaluation and
Expenditure Review

Chairman
Appropriations Subcommittees:
Corrections
Public Works
Social Welfare

Honorable Howard Ball
Department of Political Science
MS State University
MS State, MS

Dear Howard:

    This is to acknowledge your note and newspaper article on the intern bill. I am indeed pleased that this is receiving national publicity. I think you have done a good job on this important matter.

    Pursuant to your instructions, when I visited the University in November, I enclose herewith a statement reflecting the cost of my room at the Holiday Inn Motel. I charged this account on my American Express which was subsequently paid.

    With highest personal regards, I am

Sincerely,

ROBERT L. CROOK

RLC/cb

Letter from Mississippi state senator Robert Crook to Howard Ball, December 12, 1980

. . . *On the way to the forum*

John C. Stennis (center), Mississippi's senior senator and a 1923 Mississippi State graduate, returned to campus during February to spend a day lecturing to American government classes, visiting friends and answering questions from area reporters. As he sets a fast pace up Hardy Road to meet class, the 80-year-old lawmaker makes conversation with Dr. Morris W. Collins Jr. (left), director of the Stennis Institute of Government, and Dr. Howard Ball (right), political science department head. Also pictured are William Giles and Douglas Feig, both of political science.

Senator John C. Stennis on campus, February 1981

THE ROBERT F. KENNEDY
SCHOLARS IN RURAL
MANAGEMENT PROGRAM

DEPARTMENT OF
POLITICAL SCIENCE
Mississippi State University

Brochure announcing the Robert F. Kennedy Scholars in Rural Management
Program at Mississippi State University for political science graduate students,
1979. University Archives Collection, Special Collections, Mississippi State
University Libraries.

—THE ROBERT F. KENNEDY MEMORIAL

Created by the late Senator's family and friends, the R. F. Kennedy Memorial, located in Washington, D.C., challenges America's young men and women to affect the world they live in, to shape a better life for themselves and others, and to illustrate that one person can have an impact on his or her community. The Memorial sponsors four basic programs: 1) The Fellows Program (financial support to over 250 individuals with creative solutions to societal problems); 2) The Youth Policy Institute (operated by college students, it helps young people understand and act upon public policy that affects them); 3) The Journalism Awards Programs (established in 1968, they recognize and encourage outstanding media coverage of the disadvantaged in America); and 4) The Book Awards (awarded to the author of a book that "most faithfully and forcefully reflects Robert Kennedy's concern for the poor and the powerless and his conviction that a decent society must assure all young people an equal opportunity.") The Memorial has set in motion a variety of practical solutions—but the goal is to encourage and pay recognition to what young people are saying and doing about ending inequity and unfairness in America. The Memorial is a tax-exempt, public organization.

ADDITIONAL INFORMATION

Students interested in additional information on the Kennedy Scholars in Rural Management Program, please contact: Head, Department of Political Science, P. O. Box PC, Mississippi State University, Mississippi State, MS 39762; (601) 325-2711.

FACULTY

DEPARTMENT OF POLITICAL SCIENCE
MISSISSIPPI STATE UNIVERSITY

HOWARD BALL, Ph.D., Rutgers University; constitutional law, civil liberties, and administrative law, Head, Department of Political Science

TIP H. ALLEN, Ph.D., University of Alabama; political theory and American government

KRISH G. BHANSALI, Ph.D., American University; international relations, international law and organizations, and South Asia

EDWARD CLYNCH, Ph.D., Purdue University, American University; American politics and budgeting

MORRIS W. H. COLLINS, Ph.D., Harvard University; public administration, state and local government; John C. Stennis Professor and Director of John C. Stennis Institute of Government

DOUGLAS G. FEIG, Ph.D., University of Minnesota; American politics, judicial process, research methods and applied statistics

GERALD T. GABRIS, Ph.D., University of Missouri; public administration and public policy

KATHIE S. GILBERT, Ph.D., Louisiana State University; economics, public finance

WILLIAM A. GILES, Ph.D., University of Georgia; public administration, public personnel management

THOMAS H. HANDY, Ph.D., University of Texas; state and local government, southern politics

DALE A. KRANE, Ph.D., University of Minnesota; public policy and intergovernmental relations

LAWRENCE LUTON, Ph.D., The Claremont Graduate School; public policy, political theory, American government

DAVID MASON, Ph.D., University of Georgia; comparative politics

KENNETH MITCHELL, Ph.D., Florida State University; public administration and financial management

STEPHEN D. SHAFFER, Ph.D., Ohio State University; American national politics, electoral behavior

FINANCIAL SUPPORT

Mississippi State University, the Kennedy Memorial, and the National Conference of Black Mayors, gratefully acknowledge the support of the Joseph Beirne Memorial Foundation, Washington, D.C., the Ronald McDonald Corporation, Oakbrook, Illinois, the Gulf Oil Corporation, Houston, Texas, and the Phil Hardin Foundation, Meridian, Mississippi. For those wishing additional information about supporting the Kennedy Scholars program, please contact: Head, Department of Political Science, P. O. Box PC, Mississippi State University, Mississippi State, MS 39762; (601) 325-2711.

PURPOSE OF THE KENNEDY SCHOLARS PROGRAM

The Master's in Public Policy and Administration (MPPA) degree program at Mississippi State University is committed to providing Mississippi and the Midsouth with a cadre of young men and women professionally trained to meet the critical management needs of rural small town and county government. The Kennedy Scholars in Rural Management are graduate students, black and white, male and female, preparing for a public management career in a small town or city in the South. Selected on the basis of outstanding undergraduate grades and because they exhibit those leadership traits and motivation necessary to assume a position of responsibility in small town government, the Scholars take their coursework at Mississippi State University (and at George Washington University while they are in Washington, D.C.), and do at least two internships—at the Kennedy Memorial in the District of Columbia and in a small town in Mississippi or Alabama. At the conclusion of their academic and internship program, the Scholars receive the MPPA Degree from Mississippi State University and are placed in management positions in the rural, small towns of the South.

Senator Robert F. Kennedy

THE MPPA PROGRAM AT MISSISSIPPI STATE UNIVERSITY

The MPPA Program offered by the Department of Political Science is a twenty-four month program involving theoretical and applied work in the general area of public management. It consists of 42 credit hours in the following three segments.

Mississippi State University

I. COMMON CORE (27 Hours)

    PS 8703 Government Organization and Administration Theory
    PS 8713 Public Personnel Management
    PS 8723 Public Budgeting and Financial Management
    PS 8803 Research Methods for Public Affairs
    PS 8813 Quantitative Methods for Public Affairs
    PS 8903 Public Policy Analysis
    PS 6743 Administrative Law
    PS 6413 Public Finance
    PS 7001 Communication Skills Module
    PS 7002 Public Affairs Practicum

II. ADVANCED SPECIALTY AREAS (12 Hours)

    —City and County Management (Kennedy Scholars)
    —State Government Administration
    —Program Implementation and Evaluation
    —General Public Administration
    —Open-Ended

III. PUBLIC ADMINISTRATION INTERNSHIP (3 Hours)

Admission to the MPPA Program (and consideration for a Kennedy Scholarship) is open to students who have earned at least a "B" in a relevant undergraduate major, or by special permission of the graduate faculty of the Department of Political Science. Submission of GRE scores on verbal and quantitative sections and two letters of recommendation are also required for admission. (Students with less than a "B" undergraduate average must score 1000 on the GRE for admission into the MPPA Program.)

THE COOPERATING AGENCIES

—MISSISSIPPI STATE UNIVERSITY

Mississippi State University, located in the Northeast quadrant of Mississippi, 35 miles west of the Alabama state line, is a major land-grant University with an enrollment of approximately 12,000 students. It is the largest of eight public colleges and universities in the State. The Political Science Department's MPPA Program was created in 1975 to meet the needs of the people throughout Mississippi for trained government management personnel, particularly the people in rural and small town areas. The MPPA Program is complemented by the Center for Government Technology, the John C. Stennis Institute of Government, and the wide range of professional and academic resources available in the various colleges (Agriculture, Architecture, Education, Engineering, Arts and Sciences, Forest Resources, Business and Industry, Veterinary Medicine) at this public land-grant institution. The faculty in the MPPA Program are committed to the attainment of its goals and objectives. Most have published in scholarly journals and numerous books have been published. All are involved in counseling students, most are involved in consultative services in the field of Public Administration, and all are imbued with the notion of serving all the "people" of the State and region.

—NATIONAL CONFERENCE OF BLACK MAYORS

In 1974, a group of southern black mayors agreed that real progress for the almost 200 mayors of small predominantly black rural communities required a mechanism for sharing information and a base for advocacy. Out of this agreement, the National Conference of Black Mayors, Inc. (NCBM) emerged. NCBM, headquartered in Atlanta, Georgia, conducts a number of different programs in its effort to improve the quality of life of the citizens in these communities, including an annual development conference, a National Demonstration (12 towns in six states) Water Project, University Year in Action program involving undergraduate internships in these small towns, and the development of grant programs to help local governments meet the costs of new equipment and rennovations related to energy efficiency. NCBM is a private, non-profit, non-partisan service organization.

Mississippi State University

National Conference of Black Mayors

Howard and Carol Ball at the signing of the intern bill in Governor William Winter's office, May 1980

Judge Marcus Gordon speaking with defendant Edgar Ray Killen, Neshoba County Courthouse, January 6, 2005 (Kyle Carter/Neshoba Democrat, via AP, File). AP Images.

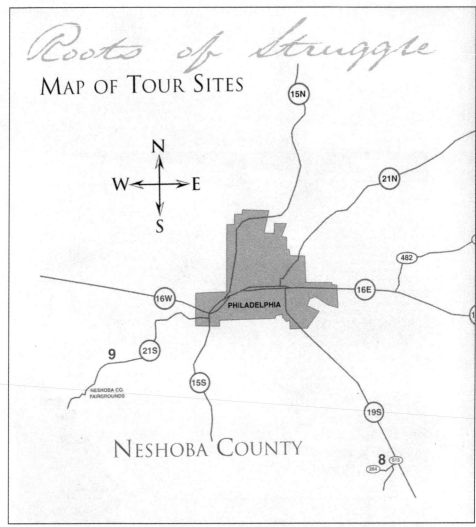

MAP OF TOUR SITES

Roots of Struggle

N
W ← → E
S

NESHOBA COUNTY

15N

21N

482

16W

16E

PHILADELPHIA

9

21S

15S

19S

NESHOBA CO.
FAIRGROUNDS

8 515
264

Map from the Neshoba County Tour Agency, 1990, "African American Heritage Driving Tour, Philadelphi, Mississippi," highlighting the sites in Neshoba County where the three CORE civil rights workers were stopped, arrested, jailed, released in the evening, murdered, and buried by Klansmen on the night of June 22, 1964

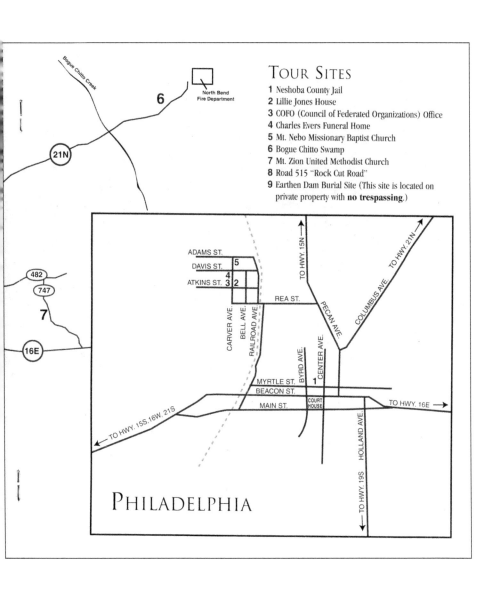

Tour Sites

1 Neshoba County Jail
2 Lillie Jones House
3 COFO (Council of Federated Organizations) Office
4 Charles Evers Funeral Home
5 Mt. Nebo Missionary Baptist Church
6 Bogue Chitto Swamp
7 Mt. Zion United Methodist Church
8 Road 515 "Rock Cut Road"
9 Earthen Dam Burial Site (This site is located on private property with **no trespassing**.)

PHILADELPHIA

The Ball family, May 1982

With new legislation—particularly the Civil Rights Act of 1964, the Voting Rights Act of 1965, and the Civil Rights Act of 1968—the federal government, including the federal courts, with the imprimatur of the US Supreme Court, began to act as the sword and the shield for groups that had experienced discrimination and inequality for generations. Nevertheless, the discrimination has continued to this day.

This new energy of the national government, embodied in the civil rights legislation of the 1960s, directly threatened the long-embedded racial discrimination policy reflected in Mississippi's folkways and "state ways." This renewed clash between federal and state laws clearly appeared in the blatant discrimination of state lawmakers in their annual disbursement of public funds. Every year, overwhelming numbers of lawmakers in Georgia, Alabama, Mississippi, and all the other Southern states openly provided less funding to towns and cities in which the majority of the population belonged to minorities, refusing to supply equitable resources for educational needs (school buses, new textbooks, new roofs, teacher salaries, etc.), health needs (medical equipment, clinics, building conditions, etc.), and infrastructure needs (roads, street lighting, sewers, etc.). Tom was very aware of these basic racially discriminatory budgetary decisions, and he agreed to participate in our two-state analysis of the impact of section 5 of the Voting Rights Act on local communities in Mississippi and Georgia.

Both colleagues had been doing research in their areas for years before I came, and during their field trips around their states they met with local government lawyers, mayors, and county supervisors; on the basis of these previous contacts, they were able to reach many of them again when the three of us began our voting rights research. Sadly, I fulfilled my hopes of better understanding the political impact of intentional inequality in this region. My research plans were taking shape. I worked with Dale and Tom on the project throughout my years at State.

In the summer of 1977, I was given a small research award by the College of Arts and Sciences to finish a book focusing on overturns of Supreme Court precedent by subsequent court majorities. The grant enabled our family to spend more than three months in a wonderful campground on the banks of a wonderful class-A trout creek, Rock Creek, twenty-five miles from Missoula, Montana. The head of the Department of Political Science expected me to do my research at the University of Mississippi Law School. That was not our family's plan. Summers in Mississippi are simply brutal, and so we hitched our RV to our blue Chevrolet station wagon and took off for Montana and the Rock Creek campground. From there I drove thirty minutes into Missoula to research and write at the University of Montana's law school library. And three times a week, heading "home," I picked up excellent firewood at a lumberyard for our evening campfires.

By summer's end I finished the manuscript that would become *Judicial Craftsmanship or Fiat? Direct Overturn by the United States Supreme Court.*[1] On the dedication page I acknowledged the beauty of Rock Creek and the gentleness of the denizens of the forest (beavers and deer) who, at twilight, came down to drink the waters oblivious to me and my golden retriever.

Every member of the family was thrilled with this summer trip, which afforded me a fulfilling time of research and writing and gave Carol and the girls exciting opportunities to ride horses, swim, and go to rodeos—mostly ride horses. (The girls worked out a great deal with the owner's three sons: bicycles for ponies.) On returning from the law library, I would head for Rock Creek with my golden retriever and fish till dark, nearly three hours. It was an idyllic time for all of us. We returned to Mississippi in late August, in time for the 1977–78 academic year.

BECOMING DEPARTMENT HEAD AND LEARNING ABOUT PUBLIC ADMINISTRATION

In December 1977, however, less than four months later, I was asked to take over as head of the political science department, which had been in a tumult since August and whose head had stepped down in December. The fourteen-person department had only two full professors: Tip Allen and me. Tip absolutely refused administrative responsibilities; he had done it once earlier and did not like the work at all. So, by default, I was asked to become the acting head (chairperson), and I accepted and assumed duties in January.

By June 1978, after MSU conducted a national search for the position, I was recommended by the search committee and the department faculty to become permanent head of the department. The dean of arts and sciences, Lyle Behr, formally offered me the position, which I accepted. I remained head until I left MSU in June 1982 for my new position at the University of Utah.

My new administrative responsibility challenged me, primarily because the great strength of the department lay in a field of political science I was totally unfamiliar with: public administration. This area (many argue that public administration is a separate discipline altogether) focuses on the varied responsibilities of public service, primarily government employees and managers. The general goal of a master of public administration (MPA) program is to train future government managers so they can act effectively, ethically, and efficiently when they translate public policy into specific actions, regulations, and practices that benefit the people living in their jurisdiction. The public administration curriculum focuses on developing budgetary skills, understanding the characteristics of personnel administration, formulating and implementing policy, and understanding the essential limitations of a government organization by studying constitutional and administrative law and the ethical administration of public policy.

Frankly, these topics, except for constitutional law, were unknown to me. Graduate work leading to the PhD is essentially scholarly labor along narrow corridors of knowledge. My education and my teaching experience at Hofstra University did not touch the field of public administration. I literally needed a crash course of study in this area, and I needed it yesterday. The expertise of more than half of the MSU political science faculty was in either public policy or public administration.

Two colleagues came to my rescue: Tom Lauth, my Hofstra colleague for nine years, and Bill Giles, the director of our MPA program. Tom began teaching me about public administration while we were attending a Southern Political Science Association meeting in New Orleans. (With Dale Krane, we were to present to our colleagues our initial research findings about implementation of the Voting Rights Act.) The first night, scribbling on dozens of cocktail napkins as we sat at the hotel bar, Tom began my tutorial. For several nights my classroom was the hotel bar and my teacher a sober Professor Lauth.

By the time I returned to Starkville, bar napkins in briefcase, I had an overview of the new discipline and of the exciting possibilities awaiting students who did graduate work in public administration. Tom had converted me into one who recognized the importance of public administration, both as an educational experience that provided government operations with trained young people eager to enter public service and as a genuine area for academic research about its problems and solutions (which is what we did in our voting rights implementation work). And as a reborn convert, I instantly continued my studies, joining public administration organizations and developing a graduate course in public administration focusing on administrative law. I totally bought into the value of a public administration education.

Bill Giles—my good friend Billy—received his PhD from the University of Georgia in the field of public administration. As befits a native of New Orleans, he was and remains the epitome of the laid-back personality. However, he has always looked at the field of public administration and, truthfully, at life itself, through strong ethical lenses.

On a trip from Starkville to Jackson to visit colleagues at Jackson State University (JSU), he outlined Abraham Maslow's theory of self-actualization and argued it had to be incorporated into our MPA students' ethical core as they prepared for careers in public administration. Maslow developed a theory of human motivation known as Maslow's hierarchy of needs. As a psychologist, Maslow noted that some human needs were more powerful than others. He divided needs into five general categories, from most urgent to most advanced: physiological, safety, belonging/love, esteem, and self-actualization. For Maslow, self-actualized people (1) are problem focused, (2) incorporate an ongoing freshness of appreciation of life, (3) are concerned about personal growth, and (4) can have peak experiences. Bill argued that in addition to budgeting, public finance courses, and personnel classes, the MSU political science department had to provide a learning environment that enabled our students to reach self-actualization. If we could do that, we would really be preparing our students for life itself. Bill's lectures on

Maslow, combined with Tom's instructions about public administration, provided me with an important foundation—ethical and practical—that enabled me to lead the MSU department into some very exciting endeavors in the effort to provide a first-class, integrated education in public administration. And that, of course, led me to the buzz saw of racism, even on a university campus.

ESTABLISHING NEW EDUCATIONAL VENTURES IN PUBLIC ADMINISTRATION

When I became head of the political science department, only a few students were enrolled in the master of public policy and administration program (MPPA)—as it was formally known. The public administration faculty and I wasted no time establishing new parameters for enhancing the program and for developing a plan to recruit Black students, especially women. Eventually, through our recruitment efforts the program grew significantly. As we visited schools where we wanted to recruit, however, we learned that before trying to get our message across, we had to listen to a message from them.

In one of our first planning meetings, my colleagues and I looked at the demographics of the program. Most of our less-than-two-dozen students were white males, most had recently completed undergraduate programs, and almost all were preservice. We also discussed what sort of curriculum and student population would characterize an outstanding MPPA program. We concluded that, given our location and demographics, our curriculum should concentrate on educating students for positions in *rural* government service, and we had to recruit more women and more Blacks. We would then need to find grants and scholarships for the students we hoped to recruit into our redesigned program.

After presenting these ideas to the dean of the college, I requested authorization to purchase a van the department would use in pursuing our recruitment goals. We had targeted ten predominantly Black undergraduate colleges in Mississippi and the four surrounding states,[2] and we needed transportation to visit them. To my happy surprise, the dean, a gentle, reserved chemistry professor, agreed, and before long we had our own wheels. (When not using the van, we added to our departmental one-time cash funds by renting it out to other departments.)

When we began, we had no idea how difficult our task would be. As it turned out, recruiting out-of-state Blacks to attend *any* university in Mississippi, much less one of the predominantly white ones, was a tough, unimaginably thorny task. We found very few Black students who were unafraid of going to graduate school in Mississippi! (And even in the case of these, their parents were afraid on their children's behalf.) For Blacks and also other minorities, the reputation of the state was a huge obstacle in the way of our effort to make our program look attractive.

Actually, before we ever made our first trip to appeal to the students themselves, we spent two years arranging and holding campus get-togethers with academic administrators and senior faculty at the schools in our five-state network.[3] We would first visit the campus leadership—for example, its president and academic vice president and the dean of the college—then talk with faculty teaching political science. We wanted to discuss our goals and begin to generate trust in us and our graduate program.

Two of us made each of these visits, and all my public administration colleagues participated. The initial visit was always an eye-opener, as when Bill Giles and I went to Little Rock to talk with representatives of the University of Arkansas at Pine Bluff. We entered a conference room in the administration building and met with the top academic administrators: the president, the provost, and the dean of the college—all of them Black. "Why in hell's name should we send our graduates to Mississippi?" was the opening greeting of the provost! He told us that when as a young man he once traveled through Mississippi on the way from Arkansas to Georgia, he was pulled over by a police car. The officer said he was speeding and instructed him to follow him to town. After a "terrible, frightening ride" into a small town, he parked as instructed and was taken to a small park adjacent to the courthouse. In an outdoor courtroom composed of a table and chairs under an immense tree he was charged with speeding, and the judge fined him on the spot. The terrified young man paid and left and never traveled east through Mississippi again.

"I always travel to Atlanta by going up and around your damn state," he said.

And then came the question, again: "And why should we encourage our young graduates to step foot into that damned racist place much less send them to Starksville [sic]?"

Then the other two Black administrators chimed in with their own Mississippi horror stories. For most of an hour we just listened. Although we had expected to hear concerns about Blacks living and learning in Mississippi, we were not prepared for these soulful recollections of un-forgettable past hurts and humiliations triggered by tough, often violent, racial incidents. But it was very important that we heard them.

Having prepared a rather scripted response back in Starkville, we of-fered it, along with literature about the graduate program. We talked about changes in the state, from the influx of faculty (like the two of us) from across the country into Mississippi to the MPPA scholarship sup-port we were generating from organizations and groups inside and out-side Mississippi. We assured the administrators of our commitment to diversity in our graduate student population and of the importance of placing our MPPA graduates into positions of responsibility in small towns and cities across the Deep South. Above all, Bill and I assured the administrators we understood the critical importance of creating a trust relationship with them and, through them, with their students. And we knew that trust in a person or a program took time to develop. "We do not want to meet with your students now," I said. "We wanted to meet with you in order for all of us in the room to talk frankly about race and discrimination, fear about the state, and about the quality of our graduate program." Our visits had to serve as stepping-stones toward trust in our commitment to an integrated and diverse MPPA student population and to a very safe and secure learning environment at MSU.

This experience Bill and I had in Little Rock was replicated by our other department colleagues when they visited campuses outside the state. Racial discrimination was the big elephant in every conference room we sat in for the next year or so. Every administrator had person-ally experienced discrimination and fear in Mississippi or knew friends or family who had. And every one, concerned about the impact of such discrimination on their students when they left the safe haven of their undergraduate school, wanted to hear from us about the present state of race relations in Mississippi.

Over the next year we built on our initial contacts with these administrators. We invited them to the MSU campus and sent them information about financial and other social supports for students in the MPPA program. We spoke with them on the phone. We met some of them at regional conferences. We then visited the campuses again, this time to meet with students to discuss the importance and the value of a career in rural public administration.

Just before I left in 1982, and after five years of recruitment work, our program awarded more than sixty MPPA degrees and placed 97 percent of our students in local and state government management positions in Mississippi and across the Deep South. In that year the National Association of Schools of Public Affairs and Administration (NASPAA) ranked our program thirty-third-best in the nation and sixth-best in the Southeast. Only Duke University, the University of Virginia, the University of North Carolina–Chapel Hill, Virginia Polytechnic Institute, and the University of Georgia ranked ahead of us. And in the 1981–82 academic year, over sixty students were studying in our career and precareer MPPA programs.

THE ROBERT F. KENNEDY SCHOLARSHIP IN
RURAL PUBLIC ADMINISTRATION

While cultivating our associations with the administrators and then the students in this academic network, we were also finding new sources of financial support for incoming students. By the end of the first year, I was able to establish a highly unusual scholarship for incoming students of color: the Robert F. Kennedy Scholarship in Rural Public Administration. It was a multiparticipant, integrated creation that enabled the department—with the help of the Robert F. Kennedy Foundation in Washington, DC (working with David Hackett), the National Conference of Black Mayors in Atlanta (with the assistance of Michelle Khorouma), and a grant from a baking company in Meridian, Mississippi—to provide funds for minority students. To receive the scholarship, the student had to commit to a four-month internship in a predominantly Black town or city in either Mississippi or Alabama.

To have such a named scholarship in the land of powerful conservative US senators James Eastland and John C. Stennis caused consternation for many Mississippians, including some high-level administrators on the MSU campus. Perhaps the brochure about this new scholarship, with pictures of Robert Kennedy's visit to the Delta but no picture or mention of Senator John C. Stennis, set off the sparklers. But we were recruiting young Black women and men, and this small pamphlet was a message to them about the political science department at Mississippi State.

OTHER MPPA PROGRAM INITIATIVES

In addition to finding funding for preservice, entry-level MPA students, we also addressed the lack of experienced, in-service managers in the MPA program. Having preservice students interacting with in-service students would benefit everybody. Indeed, NASPAA's accreditation standards required such a mix of students, and of faculty as well—in-service practitioners teaching some MPPA courses alongside academically trained faculty.

To attract these practitioner-students, we adopted a fairly new idea. Given that they lacked time during the week to travel to Starkville from the state's largest cities (Jackson and Hattiesburg), we developed a three-weekends-a-semester intensive MPPA program. At the beginning of the semester they would receive the required books and a syllabus. They would meet on the Starkville campus three weekends a semester: the third, sixth, and ninth weekends of the fourteen-week term. Each weekend "class" consisted of twenty-five hours of scheduled instruction from Friday evening through Sunday afternoon. The syllabus assigned them pages to read and problems to solve for each session. They would hand in their written solutions as homework assignments, and the class would discuss them. The students also had to prepare term papers and mail them in during the week of final examinations. The paper had to incorporate their real-time work experiences as managers with the subject matter of the course.

The program proved popular with many practitioners: police chiefs, office managers, military personnel (officers from the Meridian Naval Air Base, including one officer who flew a small plane to class), and other practitioners from across the state enrolled and eventually received their MPPA degrees. It was also an exciting—sometimes daunting—teaching challenge for our public policy and administration faculty, most of whom had not had the unique experience of teaching in-service practitioners.

However, all of us, including Bill Collins, the respected John C. Stennis Professor and director of the John C. Stennis Institute of Government (hereafter "the Stennis Institute"), participated in this special program. And we, too, benefited from this cross-fertilization of ideas and energies. After a few years, we added visiting professors to the intensive semester, including outstanding professors such as Phil Cooper, then a professor at Georgia State University, who drove over to Starkville from his Atlanta home to teach administrative law in the program.

Many students drove RVs or motor homes to campus, parked, and plugged in for the weekend. Others stayed at local motels. Besides benefiting students academically, the program enabled them to develop personal professional networks that helped them on the job.

WONDERFUL NEWS FROM THE FEDERAL GOVERNMENT ABOUT SCHOLARSHIPS

With encouragement from Bill Collins (one of the founders of NASPAA when he was at the University of Georgia) and our contacts in Washington, DC, especially our helpful don, Senator Stennis, our MPPA program annually applied for the coveted Patricia Roberts Harris Graduate Professional Opportunities Program (G*POP) scholarship for our incoming preservice students.

The program was named in honor of Patricia Roberts Harris, the first African American woman to serve as an ambassador, representing the US in Luxembourg under President Lyndon Johnson. When Jimmy Carter was elected president in 1976, he appointed her secretary of the Department of Housing and Urban Development (HUD), a position she served in from 1977 to 1979, and in 1979 she served as secretary of the Department of Health, Education, and Welfare.

Because our program closely paralleled the parameters for receipt of the scholarships—which paid the recipient's tuition and provided a decent monthly stipend (as well as generating indirect costs, for which our departmental account was reimbursed)—from 1977 through my departure in 1982, we received between six and ten such G*POP scholarships annually—the most per year received by any university in the nation during this time.

And so, by the time we held a three-day program on the campus for students and faculty from our minority college network (now six schools) in spring 1979, we had generated Kennedy scholarships and G*POP scholarships and, with funds generated by the federal scholarships and the general funds, were able to support a decent number of graduate assistantships. Using these funds very frugally, we were able to support annually, fully or in part, more than two dozen students.

Although some students in the network still hesitated to apply to the program out of concern about racism, by year three we were receiving applications from the network. I will never forget the day in late August 1980 when one of my colleagues came into my office to get me. It seemed one of our new students, a bright young Black female student from Xavier College in New Orleans, was sitting in a car outside our building. Her father would not let her out until he met and spoke to the head of the department. I went out to meet the dad. His daughter seemed to be beside herself with embarrassment. He continued to sit in the car while we talked for about a half hour. Seemingly put at ease, he turned to his daughter and said she could get out and get to her business. He thanked me; I gave him my card and told him to call me if he had any concerns, any questions. Then he headed south to Louisiana. His daughter was an excellent student and left us with an MPPA degree in hand and a job in local government in Louisiana waiting for her.

MY INVITATION TO WORK WITH A CROOK

When seeking to complete the support package for students in our MPPA programs, I was fortunate enough to meet a very influential state senator, Robert Crook. He was the powerful chairman of the Mississippi Senate's Fees, Salaries, and Administration Committee—and his political mentor was a fellow Democratic politician from one of the state's "very troublesome" counties, Sunflower County. It was the home of one of the most outspoken opponents of all federal executive, legislative, and judicial activities in support of due process and equality for all persons residing in America, US senator "Big" Jim Eastland.

Carol and I met Senator Crook—where else but in the White House. During the administration of Democratic president Jimmy Carter, 1977–81, the president invited groups of visitors from various states to attend national security briefings conducted by Carter and his national security advisor, Zbigniew Brzezinski. Carol and I were part of a delegation of about fifty Mississippians, including Senator Crook, at a conference in February 1980. Our group was joined by a caucus from Illinois.

After the hour-long slide-show presentation and a nice little-sandwich stand-up lunch in the White House, with the US Marine band, resplendent in their scarlet uniforms, playing for us, we left for the airport and the flight home. On the flight we bumped into Senator Crook again. He was sitting in our row, and while Carol rested in the middle seat, he and I spoke about Mississippi "things." Early in our conversation he started complaining about the laziness of faculty in his alma mater, the University of Mississippi ("Ole Miss"). He told me he wanted to pass legislation to create an internship program for public management graduate students to serve as legislative interns. As he went on, my eyes almost popped out of their sockets with excitement.

"I've tried to light a fire under the asses of the Ole Miss faculty to draft me a bill creating such a program, but they've farted around and have never given me anything," he said.

Instantly I said: "I'll get you a bill in two weeks!"

He laughed and said, "That'll be the day!"

It was: The day after I returned, I met with Tom Lynch, our budgeting professor in the department, and told him about the break we had been given by Crook to craft an internship bill. He and I worked for about a week and produced draft legislation that looked really good! Two weeks from "That'll be the day!," I lightheartedly hand-delivered the draft bill to Senator Crook in his Jackson legislative office. He was shocked that I had actually delivered. He scanned the draft and said he liked it very much. He promised to move it quickly through committees and get it to the governor by the end of the regular session of the Mississippi legislature. I kept my promise; Crook kept his promise. Senate Bill No. 2313, An Act to Establish the Mississippi Public Management Graduate Intern Program, sped through the legislative process and passed as written. Carol and I, along with Bill Collins, a representative from the Mississippi Board of Higher Education, and faculty from Jackson State University and the University of Southern Mississippi, witnessed Governor William Winter signing the bill in his office. It became law in late May 1980.

The bill came about through a largely serendipitous moment—because Senator Crook and I sat in the same row on a plane and I jumped upon a golden opportunity to create legislation that would spectacularly assist our preservice MPPA students.

The end of this story was just as positive as the beginning. As drafted by us, enacted by the legislators, and signed by Governor Winter, the internship bill provided funds for thirty-six students annually to work in Jackson. They would assist state agencies and legislative committees with needed research and writing of draft regulations and laws. Eighteen would be selected each academic semester and would live and work in the state capital. The law provided $750 a month for each intern, a very generous stipend at the time.

The legislation created a committee of representatives from the three universities that had graduate programs specified in the legislation. I was selected to chair this group, whose task was to select the students to serve as interns in the state capital.

The new law provided for the appropriation of more than a quarter million dollars a year—a huge sum. It was used to the best advantage for Mississippians. Worthy students and legislators and all the people of Mississippi benefited from the law. I was absolutely thrilled when I stood in the governor's office, looking over the shoulders of Governor Winter when he signed the legislation. It was a notable day of my life.

One stipulation that we wrote in the draft and that was still in the final bill stated that only students attending NASPAA-accredited graduate programs could apply for an internship. This limitation meant that only three state universities could participate in the graduate internship program: Mississippi State (MPPA program), Jackson State (MPA program), and Southern Mississippi (criminal justice administration program). Sadly, because Senator Crook's alma mater, Ole Miss, did not yet have an accredited MPA program, their students were ineligible and could not apply for the internships. I was quietly delighted with the end result. I am not sure how Senator Crook felt about his alma mater's situation. I did not want to get close to the oddity because I did not want to create any problems with Crook that might jeopardize any new initiatives that required state funds. (Several years later, prodded by Crook and Ole Miss administrators, Ole Miss's political science department was accredited by NASPAA.)

One minor problem arose in the implementation of the internship law. Given our success in recruiting Black students into our MPPA program and given the reality of Jackson State's MPA student population (near totally Black), most of the interns selected during the early life of the program were minority men and women. (Southern Mississippi's CJA program had not yet graduated any students, and its participation while I was in Mississippi was minimal.) Senator Crook and others were eager to publicize this new program but were concerned about the public's reception if the stories ran with photographs of the interns.

He solved that problem quickly, with no complaints from the beneficiaries of the legislation: the schools and the interns. He simply had the publicists write juicy stories about the bill and send them off to the media—without including any photos of the graduate interns. For many years no photographs of our students appeared in the legislative newsletter or in news stories in the state's papers. But our students received their stipends and the invaluable experiences the internships afforded them.

A NEW YORKER ON CAMPUS, A.K.A. "JEW N****R-LOVER"

While we were absolutely thrilled at the good fortune we realized over my first four years as head, I found out early on about the resentment about me—racial and religious—that our successes generated on the MSU campus. Simply put, some administrators and faculty were offended by our successful efforts at diversity and were not too embarrassed to call me that "damned Jew n****r-lover." In the beginning of our department's efforts to diversify our programs, some said things like, "Don't you think you have enough *Negras* in your program?" By the time I left, their comments were much more hostile and hateful.

For the most part, I did not hear directly from the angry crowd. Although some snide remarks were directed at me about our MPPA program, most of the criticism came by mail. And most of the mail was addressed not to me but to President Jim McComas.

EXCHANGE PROGRAM WITH JACKSON STATE UNIVERSITY

While developing opportunities in our own department, we also were improving our special relationship with the political science faculty at Jackson State University, the predominantly Black institution in the state capital. We developed an exchange program between the two departments in order to expand and enhance the political science and public administration offerings in both departments. Initially we exchanged faculty. Jackson State would send a faculty member once a week to the Starkville campus to teach a course, for example, in urban politics. We would at the same time send a faculty member to Jackson to teach a course, say, in international relations.

When I became acting head of the department in January 1978, one of the first things I did was to drive down to Jackson with Bill Giles to meet with the chair of the political science department, Leslie McLemore. We hit it off immediately. Les and I worked together to improve the relationship between our two departments and between our competing public administration programs. These interactions were very positive ones. Why? Essentially because of the substantive differences in our MPA programs. The Jackson State graduate program's focus was on urban administration. Our program's emphasis was on rural, small town governing.

In the Mississippi educational wars that continued before, during, and after my tenure in the state, Les and I generally worked cooperatively to foster greater awareness of the value of strong focused public policy and administration programs in Mississippi. We cooperated on the implementation of the internship program and tried, not always succeeding, to broaden the exchange program to include students as well as faculty.

The bitter wars regarding the status of the eight Black and white colleges and universities were waged "above us," in the federal courts, in the legislature, and in the corridors of the Mississippi State Board of Higher Education Institutions. Throughout most of my tenure in Mississippi, hordes of outside evaluators were visiting the eight institutions trying to determine, for example, which political science department was the best one in the state. That premier department was then designated as the state's "flagship" department in political science. And there were efforts to determine which one of the universities was to be designated as the "flagship" for the state after we left for Salt Lake City in 1982.

Through it all, we in the political science department at MSU continued to interact very positively with our colleagues at Jackson State. In the end our relationship with that predominantly Black institution was infinitely better than our association with the University of Mississippi.

The only close rapport I had with a member—just one—of the political science faculty at Ole Miss was based on our mutual love of football officiating! The head of the department at Ole Miss had once been a football official, and every time we met, at meetings in Jackson or at professional political science conferences, he and I would talk animatedly, but only about football. We never spoke about curricular matters, nor did we ever speak about substantive issues such as civil rights or state politics.

Given the worldview of many of the faculty at Ole Miss, the scene of bloody rioting in 1962 because a Black student, James Meredith, was admitted to Ole Miss pursuant to a Supreme Court Justice's order, it seemed pointless to try to pry open closed academic doors. Whether it was the institution's very recent history of palpable opposition to integration or the playing of "Dixie" and the waving of Confederate banners at all sporting events or whatever, while I was in Mississippi, there was a wall of separation between Ole Miss and the other universities in the state.

In the years since I left MSU, Les McLemore has continued to be a good colleague and friend. I've had him visit the University of Vermont (UVM) as a University Lecturer. He has spoken to our students and faculty about civil rights and voting rights problems in the South. I also invited him to assist me in lobbying the UVM faculty to approve the creation of a required set of courses on race and ethnicity in America. And after fourteen months of engagement, lobbying the faculty, I was able to get the Vermont curriculum change approved by a large majority. Another African American colleague, Ronald Coleman, a history professor at the University of Utah, also visited Vermont as a consultant on curricular changes that addressed the kinds of programs being introduced at many colleges and universities. While at Utah, the two of us annually taught a large freshman interdisciplinary course on American racism.

JIM MCCOMAS: A GREAT UNIVERSITY PRESIDENT; A *MENSCH*

Dr. James McComas and his family and our family arrived in Mississippi at the same time. I quickly found out who he was, and when I was head of the department, I came to view him both as an ardent supporter of our department's efforts to recruit minorities and women into our graduate public administration program and, after working closely with him on a number of projects over our first three years, as a good friend and mentor.

For a long time, he had been a faculty member and then an academic administrator at the University of Tennessee. His field of expertise was education, and he was the dean of the College of Education at Tennessee before coming to MSU.

I think I had my first extended conversation with him on the Starkville High School football field in August 1976. I was refereeing a preseason football scrimmage, and McComas's son was a kicker for Starkville. Jim and his lovely wife, Adele, who was a nurse but was unable to work in a hospital because of her responsibilities as the university's first lady, were walking to their seats when he spotted me in my zebra uniform.

"What the heck are you doin' in that outfit," he asked. I told him and we began talking about football and campus goings-on. Adele drifted off to the seats. Having started my research on voting rights, I told him of the research three of us would be doing in Mississippi and Georgia on the impact of the Voting Rights Act in the South. He was extremely interested in the subject and asked me to send him research findings from time to time. Then he joined his wife to watch the scrimmage.

When I became acting head of the department in January 1978, I began to meet McComas more regularly. He was very excited about our department's plans to develop a more innovative and more focused graduate program in public administration. He supported our plans for the minority college network as well as our effort to attract in-service practitioners to our intensive semester graduate program. When we had our three-day conference for the students and faculty in our network, he graciously supported the program by hosting a number of events and speaking to our Black guests at the opening event.

From the beginning of our relationship, McComas's discretionary funds were seemingly available to the department whenever the need arose for "emergency" research or travel support. So when, early in 1980,

President Carter invited him to attend a national security briefing, he phoned me to see if Carol and I were interested in attending in his place. We were, we went, and on the way back we sat next to Senator Crook on the plane from Washington, DC. Funny how fate works its mysterious ways! I told Jim about my contact with Senator Crook, and he encouraged me to work with him as cooperatively as possible. "He's a very powerful man in the legislature, and anything you can do to help him out will, in the long run, benefit the university at budget time."

After the bill Tom Lynch and I wrote was enacted into law, McComas was as thrilled about that event as we were, perhaps more so if that was possible. And he was as surprised as we were that the bill went through the political process like a hot knife through butter. He sent me a very brief "thanks" note after the legislature finally passed the new year's budget package. It surprisingly allocated more-than-expected general funds for the state's eight institutions of higher learning. After all, Jim suggested when we had a farewell meeting in his office in 1982, Senator Crook was pleased with the communications and joint planning he saw between Jackson State, an urban, predominantly Black campus, and Mississippi State, a rural, predominantly white "cow" college. And after all, McComas noted, Crook's pleasure was reflected in the better budgetary treatment all eight of the state universities received that year.

And when the department, the following year, made Senator Crook an honorary member of Pi Alpha Alpha, our discipline's honor society, McComas was thrilled. Crook visited the campus a number of times to speak with our public administration students, and once to receive the PAA certificate. Each time he visited MSU, the president was there to greet, wine, and dine this important legislator. These events, in some enigmatic way, led to increased funding by the state to the institutions of higher learning that year. I still have a handwritten note, written to me by McComas in February 1981: "Howard, your efforts to recognize Senator Crook have benefited the University this year! Thanks, Jim."

McComas also was aware of some of the difficulties we faced within our small Jewish community as well as the nasty and cruel criticisms of my efforts to diversify our graduate programs. In one of my last meetings with him in his presidential office, we chatted about Mississippi and about my move to the University of Utah, in Salt Lake City. I told him about the fanatical KKK phone calls we had been receiving for some time. I told him how surprised I was that we had not received many more crazy and cruel letters from the racists in the state. He burst out laughing. "Let me tell you why you didn't receive those hate letters," he said as he walked to his desk. "Come here." From one of the file drawers he pulled out a voluminous "Ball file." "They sent their hate mail to me instead of you. All the letter writers insisted that I fire you for your behavior. I've been collecting these notes for about four years!" I didn't even look inside the file (and I never asked him if I could). I was floored at the way he responded to these condemnations of my academic behavior: he did nothing!

He never called to tell me about the volume of mail he was receiving about our departmental efforts to change the character of the state, at least insofar as graduate programs in public administration were concerned. (And he never told me about the phone call he received from an irate senior US senator Stennis demanding that I be fired because of my support for extending the Voting Rights Act. It was Bill Collins who told me of Stennis's two phone calls.)

I asked him why he never spoke to me of these letters. McComas simply said: "It was none of your business. You were doing things I wish others on campus would do to enhance the quality of graduate education at State. The last thing you needed was my sending you copies of these evil notes."

The qualities he possessed have, collectively, a name in Yiddish: *mensch*.[4] I always thought of Jim as a Maslow-type self-actualized leader. This last conversation sealed it for me. Forget Maslow, I told myself, McComas is a *mensch*. We continued our friendship after I left State. When I became Dean of the College of Social and Behavioral Sciences a few years later, he sent me a congratulatory letter with at least two pages of advice on "deaning." And when he was installed as the president of the University of Toledo, I was one of his invited guests. McComas then moved to Blacksburg, Virginia, to become president of Virginia Tech.

Sadly, much too soon, McComas died of pancreatic cancer a few years later, in the mid-1990s. Months before his death, he wrote tender farewell notes to those of us who were close to him. I cherish that letter. He was a very shrewd academic leader; more important, he was a good man. Jim McComas was an unforgettable *mensch*.

THE SHADOW OF POWER LOOMING OVER THE CAMPUS

Power is the coin of every realm ever established by sentient human beings. It is axiomatic. For some, power is an aphrodisiac. For others, most of us, it is the instrument used by someone to persuade, to bribe, to control, or to coerce another person to do something he does not want to do.

In certain complex and controversial realms the consequences of power brandished by any number of actors—for example, xenophobic political zealots—are horrendous. They perpetrate assassinations: of Archduke Franz Ferdinand in Sarajevo in June 1914; of Democratic party leader and presidential candidate Bobby Kennedy in California in June 1968; of Martin Luther King Jr. in Memphis in April 1968. They order the bombing of cities, killing millions of noncombatants: Madrid, 1937; London, 1940; Pearl Harbor, 1941; Berlin, 1944; Tokyo, 1945; Hiroshima, 1945.

And then there are the more banal uses of power, such as in higher education. Its use is known in every college or university: denominational schools, private elite universities, public colleges, professional schools, community colleges—all of them. In every university I taught in—no, in every college I attended as an undergraduate and as a PhD candidate and every campus I taught at, power was at work.

As dean of the College of Arts and Sciences at the University of Vermont, I had to probe and reach a decision on a tenure case where the power wielders were faculty who disagreed about the quantity and qualitative value of the candidate's research, and therefore recommended that the candidate be denied tenure. When it came to my desk, I reviewed the file, examined the controversial tomes in light of written departmental guidelines for tenure, and concluded that the deny recommendation was wrong. I then passed on my recommendation in favor of tenure to the provost, who overturned it. The package of divergent recommendations was then sent to the president's desk for a final judgment.

President Tom Salmon read the conflicting tenure recommendations and, in what I believe was a positive use of his power, convened a meeting of all the judging faculty and administrators to learn about this conflict firsthand, eyeball to eyeball. This was Tom's first controversial tenure case, and as a former Democratic governor of Vermont, he needed more data and needed to hear the arguments before making his decision (which, in the end, aligned with my recommendation).

The use of power by administrative leaders at Mississippi State University was, for me, more disturbing. I vividly recall one example, most probably because I was personally offended by language the vice president for academic affairs (VPAA) used in a memo to us. The issue arose toward the end of what seemed to be an ordinary hiring case in July 1980: the offer of a faculty position to one of two out-of-state finalists. It turned into something more disconcerting because of how the VPAA, Dr. Wolverton, voiced his views and then acted, basing his reasoning on noneducational, political issues. Wolverton rendered his decision in a way that would have befitted a slave master on his antebellum Mississippi plantation—without meeting with any of the search committee members to get additional information or simply to tell them of his concerns. He conveyed the decision to us impersonally, via a memorandum from his office, which concluded by unilaterally "suggesting" who should be appointed to the position. It is the kind of decision making that I saw only in Mississippi. I've saved the letter because of the nakedness of his abuse of power in a very ordinary decision-making situation. He rejected both candidates. The note began cavalierly, "Although I do not wish to *seem presumptuous*, I do wish to convey to you my reactions to the two candidates recently interviewed" (emphasis added, here and in the following quotation).

In honesty, I think that neither of them fits our needs: the first candidate has had little experience and would have some problems in dealing with the general public and the Senator's [Stennis's] staff. *The second candidate, while more affable and aggressive, would not serve as a representative of MSU well; he comes across as just what he is—a transplanted New Yorker. While he has had some better experiences, he too, I believe, would be negatively received by the public and by the Senator's staff.*

Wolverton's note contained a diktat: "Conduct another search for someone who is more experienced and would meet the public in a more credible manner." Ending, he recommended his own candidate. "Mrs. Farley, for example, would be much better than either of the men we had in."

I have saved this communication because it is unlike any other personnel decision I was involved in as a chairman or as a dean at either Utah or Vermont. Make no mistake, everywhere I worked, power was employed, wisely and unwisely, for a host of good and terrible, discriminatory reasons.

The power that loomed and brooded over the whole campus, of course—with the exception of a few administrators including President McComas, who avoided the *undue* corruption of their integrity by shortening the shadow—was my former good friend Senator John C. Stennis. Wolverton's decision, like most campus decisions that had even the remotest nexus to the "senator's staff," and to the man from DeKalb himself, had to be measured by the academic decision maker. An example of the plantation model? I couldn't answer that question, but his letter was written proof of the presence of the plantation master's powerful shadow.

MY FIRST LOVE: TEACHING AND LEARNING

Although many of my administrative activities, especially travels with colleagues to predominantly Black colleges across the Deep South, afforded out-of-body experiences, and although I learned much about living in a very different culture, I loved the classroom. Wherever I taught I made lasting friendships with my students; I'm still connected with some from the 1960s. They pop up everywhere. I was having dinner with my sister Carol in a lovely waterfront restaurant in Montego Bay, Jamaica, when I saw one of my former Vermont Law School students rushing over. She was the manager, and we had a wonderful time and dinner with wine and with her company. She was getting married in September and reminded me that she hadn't received the little confirmation card yet. We were planning to attend, but I had forgotten to return it. Unfortunately, all of us missed the wedding. Her flight back to the mainland was canceled. It had been scheduled for September 11, 2001.

My first love has always been the classroom. Teaching my students is learning from my students at the same time. In Mississippi, I learned a hell of a lot from them about everything. I learned to eat fried cucumbers and fried green tomatoes. And I learned about the terrible pains brought on by racial humiliation. And how some of them grew up in small towns like Philadelphia, Mississippi, where one of my students, while a small girl, had a broken watch fixed by "nice" Cecil Price, the Klansman responsible for masterminding the killing of three civil rights workers in the town in June 1964.

I also learned a lot from Sid Salter, another resident of that infamous little town, who was a distant kin to another Klansman involved in the killings. (I first met him when I refereed a football game between Philadelphia and Neshoba County. He reminded me of that game when he arrived on campus a few years later.)

Most of all, I learned about courage from my students, the courage it takes for a young Black person to confront the slurs, the epithets, and worse and to stay focused on the goals—and the dreams—she fashioned in her mind's eye while growing up in the Deep South in a less than hospitable environment. For these learning experiences alone, I am happy our family decided to go down to Mississippi. We all graduated from a very different school.

CHAPTER 7

Leaving the Magnolia State

By the sixth year at State, I was ready to leave for another job. By then, 1982, many good things had happened in the political science department. However, by then, our already-strained relations with the Jewish community had become more painful; we wanted to move to a city where we could attend a conservative synagogue with an identifiable, visible, and young Jewish community with a full-time rabbi.

Also, the irregular late-night telephone calls from the Klan-types continued unabated—with the same ugly messages, even after we changed our number. Carol and I felt tension generated by our activities in school, in the religious community, and in the community generally. Although we had been involved in some rewarding professional and personal activities, the negatives began to tire us out.

SIX YEARS OF LIVING FRETFULLY

When we came to Starkville and MSU in 1976, we had no idea what kind of life, personal and professional, we would experience. (Recall that, knowing the uncertainty that we would face, I had taken a two-year general leave of absence from Hofstra University.) However, within the first eighteen months, given our activities and our commitment to some kind of fair, social justice, we began to realize the actuality of life in Mississippi for a family of Jewish outsiders. In public school, our daughters, especially Sue, had to deal with some insensitive teachers and with the pervasive religious commitment of the Protestants—especially, for us, their commitment to the daily intrusion of religion into the public schools.

Additionally, from the very first months of living in Mississippi, Carol and I had to continually confront the reality of Southern Judaism's religious customs and patterns of social behavior, customs that were very uncomfortable and led us to decisions that offended many congregants. Our decision to attend High Holy Days services in the synagogue in Tupelo, after the great unease and discomfort we experienced attending our first and only Holy Days services in Temple B'nai Israel, is just one example of our mutual differences.

Although the temple's service was led by our student rabbi whereas the families of the Tupelo congregation hired a conservative Jewish lay reader to lead their services, we felt very comfortable in this *haimish* group.[1] We shared similar experiences before coming to Mississippi and very quickly made lifelong friendships with Al and Marilyn Cohen, fellow Jewish wanderers—from New Jersey!

As for me, my actions as a voting rights advocate, as a board member of the Mississippi ACLU, and as a visible supporter of extending the 1965 Voting Rights Act led the local Jews to distance themselves from us. It was a sort of social ostracism from our coreligionists, as well as from many faculty and administrators on the MSU campus and from townspeople we thought we had befriended.

Added to the consequences of that combination of out-of-the-ordinary activities (for most Mississippians, regardless of religion) were my generally successful efforts—with my colleagues in the department—to create a truly diverse, first-rate graduate program in public administration.

After a few years of reacting to slights and general resentments from some of the persons we came into contact within the public schools, in the high school, and so on, we didn't throw in the towel. We were, however, just very weary because of all the roiling around us, much of it caused by the two of us. I knew that things would not get any better and might get worse. We were now loath to move any closer to the by-now-unpleasant Southern way of life.

Getting out of Starkville during the monthlong Christmas break between semesters in the public schools and at the university was like a furlough for us from an increasingly edgy environment. And we relished those six annual holiday vacations. Every year we made the nearly twenty-hour trip across Alabama and then, in Florida, south down the very long Interstate 95 freeway to an America Outdoors campground on the west side of Key Largo, Florida, fronting the Bay of Florida. There each year we met the same friends with their kids, their Hobie Cats, their dogs, and their cats. It was really a big family reunion. We found simple ways to really relax. Our favorite time was sunset. Carol and I, with the girls, and with glasses of wine in our hands and soda pop in theirs, would leisurely walk on the beach to our favorite tree. We would lean against it and watch the sun set over the water. Needless to say, I took hundreds of photographs from that spot.

During the summer months, every summer we were in Mississippi, we would always travel to the cool Western states to get away from the steamy South and meet up with camping friends and family in Montana, Colorado, Oregon, Washington State, and camping sites in western Canada. After living only a few years in Mississippi, we began to grumble about having to return to Mississippi and the woes, old and new, awaiting us.

SOME VERY HEARTFELT SUCCESSES

One satisfaction of living in Mississippi while developing new educational programs was that we saw the results of the political science department's labors fairly quickly. Although it took us almost two years to create an atmosphere of trust between us and the students, faculty, and administrators of the schools we visited, in the third year our work yielded results, and they were quite positive. Many students, most of them Black graduate students, applied, were accepted, and were provided with financial supports we were able to cobble together from government scholarships, private scholarships, and the frugal use of departmental general funds set aside for support of graduate assistants.

And the students' feedback to their faculty mentors and friends back home was very positive; and we saw a few of their friends apply for admission into our MPPA program. In five years, our graduate MPPA enrollment went from about a dozen full-time students to nearly fifty full-time, pre-service students. (Our intensive semester programs were also positively received by our more senior, in-service students. By 1982, we had developed two separate intensive semester cohorts.)

The creation of the graduate internship program was a prime example of seeing results quickly. It was also an enormously successful program, which continued for many years after I left. We had an "instant gratification" sugar rush when Governor Winter signed the internship bill into law at the end of May 1980. From the beginning to that end, from the idea discussed on a plane to the finished and signed bill, took a total of about one hundred days!

Finally, during the 1979–80 academic year, we hosted NASPAA site visitors on campus. They were visiting because we had applied for an accreditation review and, in addition to reading a two-volume self-study report prepared by the department, NASPAA representatives visited our campus to see if the department MPPA program followed the guidelines established by the organization. These site visitors, all faculty and administrators in public administration at other universities, attended classes, interviewed our graduate MPPA students, and spoke with administrators to gauge the support the MPPA program received from the department, the college, and the university. They also looked at library resources, computer and other supports for the students, and office spaces dedicated to graduate student use. They carefully investigated the program to see whether the MPPA program was an autonomous one in the political science department. Did the MPPA faculty make decisions about curricular matters, admissions, and the hiring of new faculty without hindrance from the rest of the department's faculty?

At some schools evaluated by NASPAA, intradepartmental turbulence was so great—largely due to a lack of MPA faculty autonomy— that public administration faculty were removed from political science departments, were placed in a separate department of public administration, or taught business administration in another college. All accreditation site visits are always intensive and stressful times for the MPA faculty. And after the site visitors leave, the school must wait many months for the news.

In our case, good news came in the spring of 1980. The reviewers and the accreditation board of NASPAA were extremely pleased with our program and granted us accreditation. Our program and Jackson State's MPA program were the first graduate public administration programs accredited in the state. The MSU program was also one of a handful of accredited MPA programs in the South; nationally, we fell into a select group of universities, for while there were more than 250 MPA programs across America, only about 60 were accredited!

For me in my guise as the "rabbi," football officiating was an important and heartfelt blessing. For about one dozen Friday nights every fall, I could leave other tensions aside for about six to seven hours while I galloped around a football field and, afterwards, joined the other crews at the Starkville Shoney's. (And, then, after every game, for at least three days, I could often be found gulping aspirin to ease the pain in my limbs, especially my knees.)

In Mississippi, high school football was played, for the most part, at a much higher level than in both New York and Utah. And I never experienced the slightest hint of religious intolerance from any of the close to one hundred other football officials during our hours together before and at our regular dinner rendezvous at Shoney's. But, as with the feeling our family always had when returning to Mississippi from camping trips, I knew that after I recuperated from refereeing, some new churning knotty issues that needed to be addressed would await me when, Monday morning, I became the head of the Department of Political Science—again.

THE DECISION TO LEAVE

Although my family and I experienced some significant successes and joyous events, we constantly worried about religion, school, campus, social life, and the continuing specter of racial discrimination. The problems we encountered when we first moved into Mississippi were still there when we left six years later. It also remained uncomfortable for us in the Jewish community given our clear discomfort with Reform Judaism, Southern version. As the years passed, we understood more and more clearly how the Starkville Jews felt about us loud, fast-talking New York Jews. In six years, we were never invited to dinner with any of them, including Henry and Hortense Leveck, the leaders of the small community.

Nor was it easy for us, in the last two years of our stay in Mississippi, to receive the frightening late-night hate calls from angry racists. They woke us up early in the morning, but that was not the hard part. Merely waiting for the calls ruined many a night of sleep for the two of us. And, in my case, my mind began creating horrific scenarios: people fire-bombing our house, killing our pets, burning crosses, killing us! Although we never experienced anything other than the calls, the imaginings were terrifying. And although we got an unlisted number, soon the calls began again—and again. Somehow, they found the new number.

Carol's quasi-ostracism (with the three "other" teachers) in Starkville High School grew uncomfortable—from early on, she bore the stigma of "white liberal"—and after a few years it led her to leave her position. She was able to get a job at MSU in the Department of Mathematics teaching algebra to undergraduates. And for the last two years in Starkville, Carol enjoyed that position immensely.

FROM THE FRYING PAN INTO THE FIRE:
MOVING TO SALT LAKE CITY

I started looking for a job when the Klan's telephone calls began toward the end of our fourth year in Mississippi. I felt sure that something would open up. My résumé seemed quite good. Administratively, I had led the department in the process of successfully reconstructing an excellent graduate public administration program. I had also continued my scholarly research and writing and, by 1982, had a number of refereed articles published in political science, law, and public administration journals. And I had authored or coauthored almost a dozen scholarly books and had op-ed essays published in national newspapers.

During what turned out to be my last year at MSU, I pursued two very different kinds of jobs. The first was a Distinguished Chair in Civil Rights at a small private college, Lafayette College, in eastern Pennsylvania. That position would have enabled me to continue my research, writing, and teaching in constitutional law, civil rights, and international human rights. The second was as chairman of the political science department at the University of Utah. The department was larger than the MSU department: twenty-one faculty members, seven more than my department in Starkville. Unlike MSU, Utah had a modest PhD program as well as a small graduate program in public administration. (Utah's MPA program was unaccredited when I arrived, but when I left in 1989, it had been accredited by NASPAA.)

With nearly twenty-five thousand students, Utah was a large public university in a beautiful mountainous state. And the state of Utah was the home base of the Church of Jesus Christ of Latter-day Saints (Mormons). The campus was on a small peak—part of the Wasatch mountain range—that overlooked Salt Lake City, the state capital.

The city itself, with more than 160,000 residents, was quite attractive. It is in a valley between the Great Salt Lake and the beautiful Wasatch Mountains and at an elevation of about 4,500 feet, almost a mile high. Unlike in Mississippi, the air is thin and dry and the humidity low. Although the temperature occasionally reaches into the 90s during the height of the summer, it is a dry mountain heat. The state's population was 70 percent Mormon, but Salt Lake City was evenly divided between Mormons and "No-Mo's" (non-Mormons).

And—happy days—the city had a large *conservative* synagogue, Kol Ami, with over three hundred member families. It had everything we did not have in Mississippi: a full-time rabbi, a full-time cantor, a full-time educational administrator (for the many, many youngsters attending Hebrew school), and many, many Jewish families like us—in their late thirties to late forties, with teenage children, and with many of us holding professional jobs in the hospitals, the clinics, and the university.

However, my first choice was the Lafayette position. It would have brought our family to within about two hours' driving time from many of our family living in New York State. The trip from Easton, Pennsylvania, to Long Island was a very manageable one made in less than a day. My mother lived in the Catskills at that time, and that too would have been an easy ride. And, as I love teaching and writing about constitutional law and civil rights and would have liked to enter the field of international human rights to do research, teach, and write, Lafayette was quite attractive. As a matter of fact, more than a decade later, while teaching at the University of Vermont (UVM), I did move into the field of international humanitarian law (also called the laws of war or the law of armed conflict [LOAC]).

I developed and then taught an international law course at UVM that focused on war crimes and genocide and how the world community has responded to these evils. (As a Distinguished Fulbright Professor, I taught that same course at the law school in Sofia, Bulgaria.) And I've published a number of books in this general area of international politics as well, including *War Crimes and Justice* (ABC-CLIO, 2002), *Prosecuting War Crimes and Genocide: The Twentieth Century Experience* (University Press of Kansas, 2000), and *Working in Bosnia's Killing Fields* (University of Nebraska Press, 2015).

However, serendipity popped up once more. The University of Utah invited me to visit the campus before I received an invitation to visit the Pennsylvania school for the job interview. (Ironically, although I never taught at Lafayette, my daughter Sheryl studied there and graduated in 1990, the year we moved to Vermont.) And so, I flew off in late January 1982 to visit with the faculty and students in Utah's political science department. (While I was there, my op-ed piece in the *Washington Post* was published. I found that out because one of the Utah faculty, working in DC, excitedly called the department to tell them about my voting rights piece.) Things went well on my first visit, and a month later

I was offered the job. Carol and I flew to Salt Lake to visit with important cohorts: the rabbi and members of the Jewish community, high school administrators (for a mathematics job for Carol), and real estate agents.

Looking for a new home was daunting. We were encouraged to find a residence in one of the "mixed" neighborhoods, that is, a neighborhood that had non-Mormons scattered among the Mormons. The University of Utah had very few Black students: many, many fewer than MSU; and it had fewer minority students than Hofstra University had almost two decades earlier.

When we moved to Utah in 1982, only about six thousand Blacks lived in the state. Most Black families lived in the region of Ogden, a small city about fifteen miles north of Salt Lake City that is the home of Utah State University. However, they were not Mormons coming home. Rather, most were Southern Baptists and Methodists; nearly all of them came from the South in order to find work during World War II in the war munitions industry—and to escape from the Jim Crow Southlands. Most stayed in Utah after 1945.

In moving to Utah, we would be exchanging fundamentalist Protestant territory for the Latter-day Saints' holy ground. (When Brigham Young, the leader of the mid-nineteenth-century Mormon wagon train, saw the Salt Lake valley for the first time, he said: "This is the place!") We knew the environment we were leaving, but we had no clue about what to expect in Utah territory. We New York outsiders were leaving one strange land for, as it turned out, another equally bizarre region. And we found out that in Utah (and wherever Mormons live) the natives refer to all non-Mormons, including Jews, as "gentiles." (I remember calling my mother before we moved, to sadly tell her that we were now gentiles, *goyim*! "My son, my son, what have you done *now*?" she cried out on the telephone. Her painful screams immediately brought to mind similar shrieks when I told her of our move to Mississippi. I quickly explained the situation to her before she had a faux attack.)

Carol visited Salt Lake City a few more times in the spring of 1982 to search for a house for our family. On one trip, she took one of the girls, Sheryl, with her to check out available housing and the public school system. (Although Jim Crow never existed in the state, the Utah school

system, like most other public institutions located in heavily popu-
lated Mormon districts, had a symbiotic relationship with the Mormon
Church. Built next to every public school in the state was a Mormon
seminary building. Once a week, Mormon children were released from
afternoon regular classes to attend seminary. "No Mo" children either
had home room or study hall or were allowed to visit their churches or
the synagogue for religious classes.)

After several visits Carol finally found a house in a mixed neighborhood in the foothills of Mount Olympus, a major Wasatch range mountain. (Our dining room had a magnificent view of the Great Salt Lake,
especially beautiful every sunset.) A Jewish family affiliated with the Kol
Ami Synagogue lived on the same block. (We found out after our move
that there were many more hundreds of unaffiliated, secular Jewish families than there were synagogue members.)

And so in early July 1982 we set out for our new home in Salt Lake
City. For our girls the move was sad because they had made some very
good friends in Mississippi. Carol and I were both sad and relieved. After
all, we saw it, we had worked hard and contributed our time and energy
to improve life in Mississippi—for the Girl Scouts, on the MSU campus,
and for minority graduate students—through our personal and professional activities.

At the same time, we both felt a huge feeling of relief from the terrible phone calls and from the disdain shown us by members of the
Jewish community. Those calls made us afraid like never before. We
were once again wandering Jews searching for a more convivial
community—a place we could call home!

WANDERING JEWS CONFRONTING WRONGS IN THE
MOUNTAIN WEST: SNIPPETS

In July 1982 we arrived in Salt Lake City. Utah and Mississippi were
similar in one obvious way: religious proselytizing. The organization,
strategy, and tactics Mormons used to persuade persons to join their
church differed sharply from those used by the Christians in Mississippi.

However, both states had very energetic salespersons. More than 60 percent of young Mormon males went on a two-year mission in an American city or abroad; their destination could be anywhere from European cities to South Pacific Islands to many locations in between. After graduating from high school and being trained for several months at Brigham Young University by their church, the young men were assigned a territory and paired up, and after saying their goodbyes to family, friends, and sweethearts, each duo would travel to begin proselytizing. While we were living in Utah, less than 50 percent of young Mormon women volunteered to serve as missionaries. Their preparatory regimen paralleled that of the young men. However, women served eighteen months as missionaries.

Irregularly, in Mississippi, we were visited by these young Mormons, immaculately dressed in black shoes and pants, white shirt, and black tie, with a two-inch-by-three-inch black badge pinned on their chests. The young missionaries were as aggressive as their proselytizing elders. Their skill had not yet matured, though we were sure they were the future core of Mormon pulpiteers. Not waiting for them, the church continued to confront gentiles like us with the religious wisdom of the elder speakers. When one went too far in their conversion spiels, I had to object.

One humorous event occurred because I complained about a speaker at a large campus ceremony. She was an official with the Mormon Church, and her speech was a very long disquisition on a Mormon theme. After the ceremony I spoke with the university president, Dr. Chase Peterson, about the speaker's insensitivity, for many gentile graduates, their gentile families, and gentile faculty were in the audience. He listened and nodded politely, and then, just as we were separating, I invited him and his wife to attend our Passover seder for a different religious experience. It was a spur-of-the-moment invite, but he quickly accepted. I then told Carol to expect some new guests at our seder. Knowing my inclination to do such things without informing her, she thanked me for at least telling her about the additions before they arrived!

Months later we had our seder. We had invited some friends to attend: my cardiologist and hiking buddy Frank Yanowitz and his wife, Betty, a high school principal, along with their son Peter, a "close" friend of our oldest daughter, Sue. With the Petersons, we had a group of ten: eight gentiles (Jews) and two Mormons. Aware of Mormonism's dietary customs, we had grape juice for the Petersons and wine for the rest of us to use during the service, which tells the story of the exodus of the Jewish community from slavery in Egypt. Carol prepared a wonderful dinner with the traditional holiday offerings, especially our favorite, *charoset*. It is a delicious apple-walnut spread made by mixing chopped-up Fuji apples, walnuts or other nuts, brown sugar, raisins, cinnamon, and Manischewitz sweet wine, with honey to bind the ingredients into a delightful fusion that is smeared on a matzo or just eaten naked. It is part of the seder plate and symbolically represents the mortar the Jews worked with while enslaved in Egypt. We read in the Passover prayer book, the Haggadah, that the Egyptians "embittered the Jews' lives with hard labor in brick and mortar." We eat the *charoset* to remember the suffering of the ancient Jews enslaved in Egypt. It is the most enjoyable of the seder plate symbols of our years in slavery.

The Petersons absolutely loved the sweet mortar. They ate it on matzo and they put dollops of it on their dinner plates. And Mrs. Peterson asked Carol for the recipe. And then it dawned on Carol why it was such gastronomic delight for our guests. She used Manischewitz sweet wine in the *charoset*!

The presidential couple was enjoying a symbol of enslavement, not knowing of the presence in the spread of a century-old venerable liquor staple: Concord grape wine. We did not tell them of our unintended error. The recipe Carol gave to Mrs. Peterson listed grape juice; and they took home a portion of the *charoset* when they left our house.

Although we did not receive phone calls from Klansmen while living in Utah (1982–89), we quickly came to understand the enormous power of the Mormon Church in every segment of life in Utah. Politically, economically, socially, in education, and in providing social services—the Mormon Church wielded great influence in all these areas. Its power and influence even extended to officiating football games. I had to leave my refereeing avocation after only one year because of an incident I had with my team of football refs (all garment-wearing Mormons). It was one of the first games I officiated in the state. When I arrived at the site to suit up and talk football, I noted the garments on all of them and, still unaware of their religious significance, I asked them where I could get a set because, unlike in Mississippi, games in Utah in September were played in bone-chilling weather and I needed long johns under my official's garb. They were put off by what they thought was a gentile's joke about garments. Of course, they didn't tell me where I could purchase a pair. However, they reported my slight to the secretary of the association. My schedule was altered, and I immediately found myself traveling fifty to seventy-five miles one way to officiate a high school football game. Every weekend! Coalville, only fifty-five miles away, was a very short drive!

At one point I was so frustrated I was ready to bring a case into the federal court, arguing that I was discriminated against because I was a gentile! A friend, the chief lawyer in the ACLU office, suggested that I just hang up the cleats and the yellow flag and retire. After another trek across the state, I took her advice. As I noted earlier, somewhere in the recesses of my Vermont home lies a bag full of my refereeing gear. Carol has often suggested that I get rid of the outfit I wore after my last game, nearly four decades ago, in 1983! It's still there, but without the long-john garments! Small victory?

Unlike MSU, where the ever-present specter of Senator John Stennis (and his staff) hovered over all university decision making, the University of Utah had no powerful individual exerting undue influence over its academic leaders. In fact, my first boss, the dean of social sciences, Irwin Altman, was a brilliant psychologist who was also Jewish, grew up in the Bronx, and graduated some years before me from my high school, Taft High! Within a year of my arrival he took over as academic vice president, and after a national search I became dean of the College of Social Sciences. With only a few rebukes from my detractors (and from a staff person who was uncomfortable with the takeover of the "Lions of Judah"), in July 1978, I became an administrator! Now I had to figure out how to act like one!

However, Carol had more uncomfortable situations as a mathematics teacher in one of the many public high schools in the Salt Lake City area. She faced excessive and humiliating words from the chairperson of her high school's mathematics department. He was a very religious

Mormon (who tithed, did not smoke or drink coffee and alcoholic beverages, and wore religious garments under his clothing) and was a Marine Corps veteran; he was also probably a misogynist to boot. He was, evidently, an authoritarian chairperson who was not very receptive to any debate over departmental policies he would announce in departmental meetings.

By this time Carol, who had taught mathematics for nearly two decades and had a master's degree in mathematics education, became increasingly concerned about the total lack of discussion about changes the chair was announcing, especially curricular changes. Every time she tried to open a discussion, he instructed her to stop in a clear dulcet Marine tone of voice. He knew she was a female and a New Yorker, and he probably knew she was Jewish as well: three strikes against her! Finally, after months of verbal abuse, in another typical meeting, Carol spoke out in her own tone. Calling him a Hitler-type person who was ignorant of the correct ways to teach math to high schoolers, she stormed out of the room.

Surprisingly, she was not fired; but she no longer taught college-prep math and calculus. Her students were now largely the "sweat hogs" of 1970s television fame.[2] However, by the end of the first semester in her new role, these students loved her! She did some things in the classroom that her students had not experienced: she listened to their problems with math and developed a problem-solving curriculum to use in these classes. The students took to her ways of teaching math very quickly, and she became a very popular sweat-hog teacher. When classes ended in June, some of her students would surprise Carol with thank-you cards, and many parents told her how much they appreciated her listening to and working with their kids. One young man gave Carol a gift that is still hanging in our house in Vermont: a stained-glass Star of David!

Teaching in that high school on the west side of Salt Lake City led Carol, for her very first time, to tackle a very different, higher-order problem. It was—and still is decades later—a terrible issue, but it was not talked about openly by administrators and health providers then. The issue is teen-age suicides, especially among those young, mostly female, students living in a polygamous family environment. At the time, more than one hundred thousand fundamentalist Mormons lived in the state. A traveler in the city knew when she passed such a community: high walls surrounded the enclave. (On the southwest side a fairly large community of such Mormons still practiced polygamy more than a century after the church prohibited the practice in the 1890s—in part, to enter the federal union.) Because Carol is a listening teacher, she began to be visited by these unhappy fifteen- to eighteen-year-old women. They felt comfortable speaking with her. Their faces, red-eyed, teary-eyed, showed their pain and distress as they sat forlornly in class. When one of these girls approached her after class, Carol would quietly speak with her for a moment and then begin a series of private conversations to hear the problem and try to figure out a way to resolve it. (After a few years Carol saw the anguish on a young lady's face and did not wait for the student to talk to her.)

Generally, the youngster's suffering was caused by sexual harassment from her father in a large family (three or more wives and many children). The girl was trapped in a brutal environment: she could not complain to the polygamous community's religious leaders, nor could she seek help from the establishment Mormon Church. And Carol observed that when she went—with the youngster's OK—to the school administrators to report the sexual attacks, inevitably the father would move the entire family to another school district or to another state. Carol experienced this scenario annually; she was saddened but not surprised when she learned that another high schooler had committed suicide. Every year she taught at the high school, there was at least one female high schooler who committed suicide.

My experience with the excessive efforts by Mormon leaders to keep illegal Mormon actions out of the public eye was different. By the time I had sat through that tedious speech at the graduation ceremony and hosted the Petersons for a Passover dinner, I had been a member of the board of directors of the Utah affiliate of the ACLU for over a year. In Utah civil liberties work never put us in the same fear-producing danger as in Mississippi. The legal staple of the ACLU in the state was applying the Establishment Clause of the First Amendment. Invariably, like clock-work, there would appear another legal situation involving a small Utah public institution of higher education—for example, Utah State in Ogden—that totally ignored federal guidelines for hiring staff, faculty, and, especially, high administrative positions. Their hires, in case after case, were generally unilateral decisions of the president and the provost that favored coreligionists. Challenges were filed by qualified applicants who were overlooked in favor of the selected Mormon brother or sister. For the ACLU, winning these federal district court cases, year after year, paid all expenses for the organization.

While I was on the board, the only legal issue that led to a lengthy, serious debate in the organization was whether we would provide coun-sel for two sisters whose older sister died of cancer, leaving them her five children (ages seven to fifteen, all daughters) to raise. The dilemma came about because the dead sister had been a wife in a polygamous family and had gradually changed her view of that way of living. Her husband was an abusive person whom she had successfully kept away from her girls. However, when her cancer grew worse and she was dying, she be-came unable to protect her children from her predator husband. After speaking to her sisters, both Mormons living in Oregon but not polyga-mists, she obtained their agreement to raise her children. She engaged a lawyer to document her wishes, and when she died, the sisters sought assistance from state adoption officials in Utah to remove the five children.

Further compounding the tragedy, the mother alleged that her two oldest daughters had already been sexually assaulted by their father, whereas he denied the accusation and fought the effort to take his chil-dren away from the only religious community they had known since birth. His challenge brought to a stop any Utah court action to resolve the controversy. At this point, the two sisters appealed to the Utah ACLU to take their case and, to protect the children, move them out of the closed environment.

Their request triggered a dilemma within the Utah ACLU board of directors that the Mississippi affiliate had experienced when the KKK asked for legal representation: in both states, the request for assistance led to a split within the board and the membership. In Utah, as in Mississippi, the question was very contentious: (1) Did the case provide the ACLU with an opportunity to defend the father's arguments on the grounds that a polygamous Mormon group had a First Amendment right to freedom of religion; that all five children were minors, under the father's control until they reached majority; and that if he wanted them to remain within the community, then the five must stay until majority? Or, (2) Did the case encourage the ACLU to defend the two sisters' position that the mother sought removal of the five youngsters from the community because of the danger they faced from a predatory adult, their own father?

The Utah affiliate ruptured irrevocably: the board majority and many members saw the issue as a freedom of religion case and were prepared to defend the father's right to practice a very fundamentalist Mormonism with his children; the minority wanted the ACLU to defend the dead mother's plea to remove her children to a safe, open haven. In this clash, I was in the minority. There was data that showed that in a closed and secretive religious community, sexual assaults were not unusual. Indeed, Carol's experiences with sexually harassed female students who succumbed to the terrible consequences of such attacks bolstered my unwillingness to defend the dad who was alleged to have attacked his daughters.

Not surprisingly, and probably because the case was a potential hornet's nest of trouble, to avoid the stings, the state courts continuously delayed hearing the case on the merits until most of the children reached majority! Then the legal issue was moot. When the kids were able to leave, they did and sought refuge with their mother's sisters. However, unlike the ACLU members who quit the Mississippi affiliate over the KKK, the minority in the Utah group remained, and the typical business—Establishment Clause issues—of the ACLU returned.

In short, our life in Utah, while the state is a curious place and the home base of a powerful worldwide religious force, did not reprise the experiences our Jewish family of five had living in the Magnolia State.

CODA

In my life I have lived in five states: New York, New Jersey, Mississippi, Utah, and, since 1989, Vermont. To only one of these have I repeatedly, albeit briefly, returned for research or to renew close friendships and make a few new—and young—friends: Mississippi. I know how crazy, how paradoxical, this sounds, for, as I've already said probably too many times, we grew to long for the move *out* of Mississippi in 1982. While I did not promise, like General MacArthur when he was ordered out of the Philippines in 1942, that "I shall return," I did return to Mississippi many times after our family exodus—seven times, to be exact.

Usually I traveled to Jackson to do research in the Mississippi State Archives on the Mississippi State Sovereignty Commission when the commission's documents were made available to the public. While in Jackson, I have always found time to spend with my former students Donna Ladd, the editor in chief of that crackerjack weekly she created, the *Jackson Free Press*, and Sid Salter, who in the 1980s and 1990s was one of the leading columnists for the *Jackson Clarion-Ledger*. Both grew up in Philadelphia, Mississippi, both became my friends when they took classes with me at Mississippi State University, and afterwards both have continued to be my friends and mentors in my continuing effort to understand the people and the events in Neshoba County and in Mississippi in the mid-1960s.

I was in Jackson in 2002 when Donna began to realize her goal of putting together a weekly newspaper that tore into the soft underbelly of racial politics in the state. It was an exciting, exhilarating week with Donna and the gang. I remember the break we took during that seemingly chaotic week to attend the third annual celebration of Medgar Evers's life (called the Third Gospel Celebration), held at the Anderson United Methodist Church in Jackson. What a night that was. It was such an appropriate climax to Donna's plans and preparations for an alternative newspaper. These plans quickly came to fruition. Within the year, the *Jackson Free Press* became a reality. And it has had, from the very first issue, a genuineness that I've not seen in any other paper, daily or weekly, inside Mississippi.

I also spent time in Mississippi to do research on the 1964 murders of civil rights activists Schwerner, Goodman, and Chaney[3] for my book *Murder in Mississippi*, published in 2004, and then, one year later, I was in Philadelphia to cover the 2005 trial of "Preacher" Killen, the mastermind behind those crimes.

And of course, whenever in Mississippi I've visited Starkville. In 1998 I served as the Distinguished John C. Stennis Lecturer at MSU. Ironically, I spoke about US Supreme Court justice Thurgood Marshall's lifelong fight against racism as NAACP legal director and as a Supreme Court justice. On other occasions, I would come up from Jackson to do additional research in the archives of MSU's library. And every time I visited, I renewed my friendships with wonderful people, especially Charles and Suzie Lowery, Bill Giles, Doug Feig, and some of my other faculty friends in the MSU political science department.

Since moving to Vermont in 1989–90, Carol and I have sometimes taken our Class C motor home to Starkville with our two horses and our two dogs. (We would be traveling on our way from our home in Vermont to our winter stay in Tucson, Arizona.) Our friendships with a small group of Mississippians, including our undergraduate students, have lasted for decades, ever since we left for Utah in the summer of 1982.

Just what is it that draws me—a liberal Jewish kid raised in a tenement in the Bronx—back again and again to Mississippi? I keep trying to understand my permanent attraction to the state and its people. There are a great many unforgettable people, more that I've known personally than in any of my other "home" states. Some are among the noblest people I have ever met; a few are pure evil. All are indelibly impressed in my mind. I will never forget them and their actions.

The noble included courageous people like Edwin "Ed" King, Dick Molpus, Florence Mars, Stanley Dearman, Medgar and Myrlie Evers, Aaron Henry, Judge Marcus Gordon, and former governor William Winter. Noble also were those anonymous yet courageous people living in small Mississippi towns who stood up (like my friends the Lowerys), when it was very dangerous to do so, to speak out against the racial violence and the unequal opportunities for the Blacks living in their towns.

They, like Ed King, also condemned the segregation of the Mississippi churches. And how can I forget the many brave Black clergy—most NAACP members and DOJ monitors—whom I've met while traveling across the state doing my work.

But Mississippi also has its share of wicked men, cold-blooded killers like Byron De La Beckwith and Edgar Ray "Preacher" Killen. They and their cohort engaged in objective murder. Their insistent claim was that the persons murdered by the KKK were all "anti-Christs, Communists, Negras, and/or Jews." And they had to be killed in order to save the Aryan race from "mongrelization." No passion prodded them; they were stone-cold executioners. These men were totally unlike other bad persons I've known. Killen and the other "in cold blood" executioners are unforgettable Mississippi natives.

Whenever people learn that I lived in Mississippi, they ask me to characterize the state and its people. And I tell them about the unforgettable people I've known. But I also talk about the complexity of what seems to be a bucolic society. Under a thin veneer of easygoingness lies intricacy. Other than religion, friendships, and sport, nothing is as simple as it seems for Mississippians. Certainly not the disdain for the "others" coming into the state. (The state needed educators, doctors, dentists, veterinarians, and other professionals to come into the state. When they arrived, most faced problems similar to the ones we faced. We were the transient others, here today, gone tomorrow.) Certainly, the politics of race was not uncomplicated! (The challenge for the white politician, after the Blacks were registered to vote, was how to dilute their votes while at the same time working to maintain the superior-inferior relationship between the races.) I've witnessed hardball, cutthroat politics in Washington, DC, and I can attest that politics in Mississippi has been more multifarious and bitter and, of course, more violent and murderous than national politics. As former speaker of the House of Representatives Tip O'Neill said again and again: "All politics is local." And this is especially true in states such as Mississippi.

Nor can I forget the darkest nights I've ever witnessed and the brightest lights in the distance, which led us unerringly, like evening bugs, to them. And the football wars fought on Mississippi earth are unlike football games in all the other states I've lived in and refereed in. I have not seen the human passions displayed at these events in any other state. Even the high school rivalries between the county team and the city team were passion plays acted out for almost three hours on Friday's nights in the fall.

Attending an Ole Miss–MSU football game or, for that matter, any Southeastern Conference (SEC) game, is akin to attending a shootout between the Hatfields and the McCoys. When I moved to Utah, people told me of the rivalry between Brigham Young University and the University of Utah. I went to my first game expecting bloody fights in the stands, with acrimony heavy in the air. Not at all: the fans behaved as if they were attending high tea or some similar refined event.

And how can I *not* love the efforts of the Neshoba County NAACP, the Philadelphia Coalition, Philadelphia–Neshoba County Tourism, and the Community Development Partnership to attract tourists to Neshoba County, Mississippi, to visit the local sites where the three civil rights men's lives were snuffed and where they were buried in 1964. These organizations, with the assistance of the Neshoba County Chamber of Commerce, produced a very attractive ten-page brochure entitled *The Heritage Driving Tour of Philadelphia: The Roots of Struggle; The Rewards of Sacrifice*. At times I wonder about the chamber of commerce's pushing the idea of taking a vacation in the lovely (murderous) Klan town of Philadelphia. Should the chamber's marketers receive the national Ad Council's annual award for chutzpah? Is it chutzpah or is it a sincere effort to educate people in and out of Mississippi about the terrible events that took place in the state a half century ago? Probably both, but that is exactly my point about life in Mississippi.

And there is the story of how the Starkville High School senior prom was integrated once and for all, *maybe*. Until that unforgettable event, although the school was integrated, it held separate proms for whites and for Blacks. The whites-only prom was held in the Starkville Country Club. (I really do not know where the Blacks had their senior prom.) One fateful year Tom Lowery (the oldest of three sons of my dear friends), the starting guard on the Starkville basketball team—the only white starter—decided to invite his fellow, Black, basketball friends to the white prom at the country club. They accepted and, with their dates and with Tom and his date, walked into the Starkville Country Club. Starkville senior proms were integrated after Tom's action; however, the Starkville Country Club was no longer the venue.

In my studies of section 5 implementation, I'm embarrassed to say that I came to admire the cleverness and inventiveness of Mississippians as they focused their energies on creating devices and tactics to restrict and delay, or, at best, just dilute the Black vote in the state. I was amazed at the relative ease with which they came up with creative annexations or redistricting plans to keep themselves in power and, at the same time, to deny the "others" a fair share of power. I always wondered what the state would look like if these nefarious though knowledgeable skills had been directed toward the really substantive problems Mississippi faces, troubles like high levels of poverty, poor health care, the need for educational improvements, and the like. My hope has always been that Mississippians will stop fighting the lost cause of racism and use their intelligence, their skills, and their good will to deal with these very critical issues. Given the lunacy that passes for policy making today in America, I hope for the best but will not hold my breath until the nation returns to the cacophonous normalcy of a democratic Republic.

I have seen changes in the state that have improved conditions for the people. I hope they will continue to occur, sometimes too slowly, so long as, in the words of an old Mississippi saying, "the good Lord's willin' an' the creek don't rise."

CHAPTER 8

Conclusion

The Yin/Yang of Life in Mississippi, and
Two Men from Union Collide

When Klan leader Edgar "Preacher" Killen was indicted for murder in early January 2005, I begged (successfully) the managing editor of the *Burlington (VT) Free Press* to give me the cachet of "special correspondent" so I could go down to Mississippi again, this time to cover the trial that most people thought would never happen. I wanted to see and hear about the changes in the state that had finally led to Killen's indictment. I wanted to see and write about the "Preacher." (The following account of the trial is based on my contemporaneous notes taken there and on my stories published in the *Free Press* on June 23 ["When Past Becomes Present"] and June 24 ["60 Years for Miss. Killings"], 2005.)

The news assignment turned out to be very different and much more dramatic than I had expected. The trial became much more than a capital case in a state court. In essence, it was a stark drama about two men from the same small town, Union, Mississippi, who were neighbors and knew each other growing up. Each man, however, emphasized one of two opposite, core ways of thinking that all humans display in their lives: goodness and evilness.

Judge Marcus Gordon, who presided over the trial, had been a trial judge for more than twenty-five years; it was his ninth capital case. During his nearly four-decade career, Gordon had "earned a reputation for being a no-nonsense, firm and fair judge with a steady hand of control over the proceedings."[1] Like Killen, the judge was a big man, over six feet tall, broad shouldered, with thick white hair. Like so many Mississippians, he grew up in farm country and loved hunting and fishing and horse riding. To escape the tensions inherent in a trial court, he often returned to his farm in Union, less than a mile from his birthplace, where he saddled his horse and just rode. (Horse lovers know how much good "just riding" does for lowering the rider's blood pressure and renewing good thoughts. Just ask my wife, Carol, my Jewish horse whisperer.) The judge, unlike Killen, served six years in the US Air Force, including service in Korea, and then went to Ole Miss as a mature first-year undergraduate. After earning a degree in business, Gordon attended Ole Miss's law school. For most of his legal career he served as an elected district attorney and as a county court judge. Gordon was elected district attorney of the 8th Judicial District in the 1970s and served in that role from 1971 to 1977; a few years later he ran for judge in the same district. When he retired in March 2016, Gordon was the longest-serving circuit judge (thirty-seven years) in Mississippi's history. He died three months later, age eighty-four.

For the judge, the Killen trial "hit close to home." Marcus Gordon and "Preacher" Killen lived next to each other on the same road in Union. Killen ran a sawmill in town and was a part-time Baptist minister. He "preached at the church that Judge Gordon's parents attended and presided over their combined funerals [they died within a day of each other] just a year after the murders [of the three civil rights workers]." Gordon, as district attorney, also knew Killen professionally: "He once prosecuted Mr. Killen for making a threatening phone call."[2]

More than forty years after the 1964 killings, not one of the nineteen Klansmen involved in the murders had faced homicide charges until Killen's trial in 2005. The majority were never convicted of the murders in both federal and state trial courts. They all had church services and burial in Philadelphia's cemetery. But in the 8th District Circuit Courthouse in Philadelphia in late June 2005, Killen was charged with masterminding the murders of the trio of young CORE workers.

It wasn't a long, drawn-out litigation battle. Testimony was presented by a few witnesses on both sides. It was televised by Court TV to viewers in the United States and abroad. The prosecutors and defense attorneys presented their arguments about Killen's guilt or innocence and proffered closing arguments. At a dramatic point during the state's presentation, the photographs of the dead civil rights workers in situ were shown to the jurors. Speaking to them, Mississippi attorney general Jim Hood pointed to the defendant and said, "He is a murderer and we have shown you the central role he played as the Klan organizer."

Killen, sitting directly in front of me, sneered at the attorney general and said, in a way-above-a-whisper threat to Hood, "You'll get yours, you son of a bitch!" I heard those words clearly. They were said in the seconds after Hood's closing. The courtroom was very quiet. Most of those in the courtroom, including the judge, heard the threat. The judge, however, was impervious; he had heard such attacks before from defendants in capital trials in his courtroom.

After the attorneys concluded closing arguments, Gordon discussed the relevant state laws that the jury had to understand in order to correctly apply the law to the case facts presented during the trial. Finally, Gordon sent them back into the jury room to reach a verdict. They were armed with the laws and the facts they had gleaned listening to witnesses and reviewing documents and photographs. Later that day, Gordon sternly charged the temporarily deadlocked jury (nine white and three Black jurors). "Continue talking," he said, "until a unanimous verdict is reached." The jurors were quickly escorted to the jury room to find unanimity.

The following day they found it. They formed a semicircle before the judge, and the foreperson read their verdict: guilty of three counts of manslaughter. Ironically, they announced it on the forty-first anniversary of the crime. As soon as Killen heard the first guilty verdict, his face turned ashen and he slumped in his wheelchair. His white-haired wife, dying from an unchecked form of cancer, was sitting in the first row near me and my friend and former student Sid Salter;[3] she began to sob hysterically and rushed to Killen to comfort him. His face color had already changed from ashen to beet red. He was livid. In the row behind me, all his friends were angry, some apoplectic, seemingly ready to charge the bench and destroy some thing or somebody.

Gordon immediately committed Killen into the custody of the sheriffs. Killen was wheeled to his cell; as he passed the television setups outside the courthouse, cursing, he knocked down two booms and pushed a cameraman down. He remained in the jail until the sentencing phase of the trial, a few days later.

The large crowd was impatient. While we waited to hear the sentence, I could not stop thinking about the now-convicted killer. I could not forget my eyeball-to-eyeball staring matches with Killen during his trial. He was slowly swiveling in his wheelchair at the side of the defense table. I was in the first row of the courtroom. We were not more than ten feet apart, and when he looked at me, I felt fear so close to me. And I could not imagine the three murdered young men's astonishment and terror when the horde of Klansmen, including the deputy sheriff who had just released the trio from the jail, took turns killing each one of them. Behind his thick-lens glasses, Killen had cold steel-hardened eyes. Although he was eighty years old, I could see, comparing photographs of him taken at his first trial in 1967 with the live sight of him sitting at his second trial, his still undeniable power, and his wickedness.

The first trial for the murder of the three young civil rights workers, in district court in 1965, ended in dismissals for all seventeen Klansmen. In a 1967 federal court trial, they were indicted for the crime of conspiracy to deny a person's constitutional right to life. Seven were convicted and served three to ten years in a federal penitentiary. Killen was not one of them. His jury deadlocked, eleven to one. The holdout, a middle-aged churchgoing woman, told her fellow jurors that she "could never convict a preacher." The federal district court judge presiding, avowed segregationist Judge William Harold Cox, when sentencing the convicted Klansmen, said in December 1967: "They killed one n****r, one Jew, and a white man. [sic] I gave them all what I thought they deserved."

I had no trouble imagining Killen easily, casually, and coldly intimidating and harming people. I also could imagine how parishioners shrank when he was preaching and how civil rights workers and residents of Black towns must have trembled when he led his Klansmen on arson raids and killing sprees across Neshoba County. Though in a wheelchair, with two broken legs and hooked up to oxygen, he frightened me! Never have I felt so petrified in the presence of an old man sitting in a wheelchair and sucking oxygen as I did while sitting near Edgar Killen in an open courtroom surrounded by two dozen sheriffs and their deputies! The fear the early morning "Get out o' town, n****r Jew" phone calls left with the two of us was not even close to the sinister feeling I experienced sitting about ten feet from an old cripple in a wheelchair. Staring at him produced sweat-inducing dread because I knew that I was in the presence of pure malevolence. Although I am old enough to know that evil people reside in the world, it is only in Mississippi that I personally encountered such evil.

And only in Mississippi were dozens of reporters from all over the world offered a variety of delicious snacks, cakes, and sandwiches while we awaited sentencing day. These goodies were available in the large room set aside for the media two blocks from the courthouse, with the good wishes of the Philadelphia Chamber of Commerce and a newspaper in Tupelo. The room was air-conditioned, had phones available for the correspondents, and had a large-screen television for us to use when the trial was "live" and it was close to lunchtime. Bottled water was also provided. The bottles, from a nearby Sam's Club, all had labels pasted over the Wal-Mart logo: "Compliments of the First Baptist Church, John 4:13."[4] All the while we were covering the trial in Philadelphia, we drank the water, and we were never thirsty.

Finally the day of sentencing came. Judge Gordon shared with the more than two hundred in the court the difficulty he always had before sentencing a person. Unless you're a trial judge, he told all of us, "you do not know the difficulties a judge faces. . . . You're not taught how to do it; you do the best you can based on the facts and the law." He addressed the criticisms uttered by many when they heard a verdict of manslaughter— that is, that Killen was not guilty of murder. Then, in the voice of a man of the cloth, he reminded us of what the core issue was in all such trials: "While there are distinctions between manslaughter and murder, a conviction for committing either felony means that homicide has occurred." Someone or some people lost life at the hands of someone else. Gordon then asked the courtroom audience two rhetorical questions: "Is sixty years an excessive sentence for this convicted killer? Should age and health be factors in determining the length of the sentence?" Quickly he answered both in the negative. "Each life has value. Each life is equally as valuable as the other life, and I have taken that into consideration. The three lives should absolutely be respected and treated equally.

"I have made a decision," he announced. After Killen was wheeled around the defense table in order to directly face Gordon, the judge passed judgment on the convicted killer. He said, softly but sternly, "Three men's deaths and missing lives have been taken into consideration and have beared [sic] most directly on the sentence I now pronounce: Count one, twenty years; count two, twenty years; count three, twenty years. Sentences to run consecutively." Gordon had just given Killen the maximum sentence: sixty years. It surprised me and most of the audience, whether they were friends of the Preacher or friends and family of the three murdered CORE men. Neither cohort expected the maximum. Killen's friends and family wanted the minimum: the three twenty-year sentences to run concurrently. The family and friends of the three murdered men didn't want leniency but struggled with how much the visible age and infirmity of both Killen and his dying wife would impact Gordon's decision.

Ruth Schwerner Bender, Mickey Schwerner's widow, was surprised, happily, with Judge Gordon's sentencing judgment. She smiled for the first time at the trial, kissed her husband, and then turned and began hugging the many friends, including her Neshoba County friends she made over the past four decades while waiting for justice to arrive. Ben Chaney, the younger brother of the murdered victim from Mississippi, James Chaney, told the assembled reporters, "I want to thank God today."

Later that day, I met with the judge in his chambers. His coat was off, a hot cup of coffee had just been poured, and his hands were removing his tie. "It's going to be a pleasure to pull off this tie," he said, smiling broadly. We talked a bit about the trial, and then I asked him what led him to the "consecutive" judgment. He paused, then said: "My good parents taught me to recognize the difference between right and wrong. The more you put into practice the values associated with judging—guilt, facts, the law, religious factors—the easier it is to make these sentencing judgments." Another pause, and then Gordon said, "Killen got what he deserved." I didn't ask how difficult it was to reach judgment in this case, because he had answered that question weeks earlier when he told a Neshoba County news reporter, "I have never found a way not to take the cases home with me. I am not the kind of person that can leave it at court. The cases haunt me, and I have spent many a sleepless night because I couldn't leave it behind."[5] He then admitted that the sentencing part of any trial was hardest. "I just don't know how to sentence a person, I never learned. I just try to do what's right."

I felt miserable when I found out that the judge had passed on. He was a man from Union, Mississippi, who was blessed with loving parents who conveyed fundamentally good values to him as he was growing up. Gordon served his country for six years with honor in the US Air Force. Then in his mid-twenties he became a very mature college freshman. Law school, private law practice, election and service as a prosecutor, and then election and decades of service as a judge preceded his presiding over the trial of his neighbor from Union, Mississippi, Preacher Killen.

No parsing of words is necessary: in a windowless courtroom in Neshoba County, good encountered evil, in the form of two men separated by more than just a picket fence separating their homes in Union. Good won on that day.

Where else could this clash take place? Only, my dear friends, in Mississippi, the Magnolia State.

Appendix

The Memory of Our Community

For over two years, my coeditor, Marilyn Coe, and I put together a modest newsletter, the *Light,* for our small Jewish community in Columbus, Mississippi. It was generally six to eight pages long and consisted of a few articles touching on Jewish cooking, Jewish humor from our very own Henny Youngman, announcements about the next visit by our student rabbi, a note "from the editor's vantage point," some observations in "Rich's Corner," written by our president, Adelaide Rich Smith, and an essay by our rabbi. Putting together the newsletter was a challenge. We did all we could to wheedle out a recipe or a few jokes from our members, but after a few years Marilyn and I ended our version of the *Light* because we ran out of volunteers to contribute to it. (There was a newsletter years before we took over the job; in 2020, there is a new version put out by the temple. Reflecting changes in the Jewish community since I left, it is a vibrant many-page monthly sent to a much larger, younger community of Jews in northeast Mississippi and northwest Alabama.)

The issue of the *Light* excerpted below came out after our young rabbi was summarily fired by the board during the Oneg[1] immediately following the Friday night Shabbat service in December 1976. The rabbi's inclusion of Judaism's founding matriarchs into the opening prayer and his Lilith sermon shocked the members. He was modifying the service by adding the names of the matriarchs to the traditional prayer honoring only the founding Jewish patriarchs. He also spoke about Lilith and other Jewish women who were unknown to a traditional, reform temple in the 1970s. And he was praying in this manner before some two dozen Christian visitors attending their first Jewish Sabbath! The extract below includes a short essay by the editors, a brief "Rich's Corner" note, and a draft of parts of the rabbi's last sermon prior to his abrupt departure from our temple. Ironically, it was not the sermon that triggered the decision to send the rabbi back to Cincinnati.

EXCERPT FROM THE FEBRUARY–MARCH 1977 ISSUE OF THE *LIGHT*, A PUBLICATION OF TEMPLE B'NAI ISRAEL, COLUMBUS, MISSISSIPPI

FROM THE EDITOR'S VANTAGE POINT. The departure of our student rabbi underscores the importance and the necessity of traditional Jewish customs and values in our lives. Reverence of tradition is important for all Jews; it is especially important for us Jews living in Mississippi (which has about 4,000 Jews). For us, surrounded by a phalanx of Churches, tradition and traditional Judaism is our bedrock. It is the keeping of the sanctified traditions and customs of Judaism—especially the traditional Sabbath service—that enable us to function in the deepest part of the so-called Bible Belt. Without traditions and the coming together of the Jews as a community to share these values with each other, the benign oppressiveness of the forty-odd churches becomes a possibility. We have to struggle to retain our identity; tradition and cherished values help us to save and pass on our heritage. We are too fragile to become "fiddlers on the rooftops of the 'Golden Triangle' towns."[2] Besides, some of us are too old to climb up! So, everyone, let us celebrate our heritage and traditions. L'chaim! Come to services conducted by members of the community for the remainder of the year. Partake in the joyfulness of Judaism. Shalom.

RICH'S CORNER. Some good and bad news for the community. I am sad to say that Meyer Bergman, a strength in our Temple for many years, has resigned as treasurer due to ill health. We wish him well and thank him for his fine work over the years. The good news is that Hortense Leveck is recovering very well from her recent surgery and we expect her cheerful face at services soon. Until I see you all this Friday evening, be well. Please, do come to services!

RABBI'S NOTES FOR THE SERMON. Last month when I was in Columbus we had a discussion group on myths and facts concerning Hanukah, which this year falls on December 25th, a day when, for some reason, all the banks and schools are closed. That discussion started me thinking, and I decided to re-think and re-state some of these things.

You see, Hanukah used to be a minor holiday, but no more. We've emphasized it, perhaps in imitation, perhaps in response to, our neighbors. But on Hanukah we actually feel rather uncomfortable about being Jewish. We are forced, like it or not, into comparing Hanukah with Christmas, Judaism and Christianity.

One thing we know for sure: Hanukah is not "the Jewish Christmas." It also turns out that the old story about brave Judah Maccabee fighting off the evil Greeks is not so accurate either. If we are to deal with our yearly identity crisis, we should know what, historically, we are celebrating. Actually, I think, [Hanukah] is more like Bastille Day.

Notes

PREFACE

1. Eli N. Evans, *The Provincials: A Personal History of Jews in the South* (Chapel Hill: University of North Carolina Press, 1973, 1977, 2005; in this volume I cite the 1977 ed.), 38.

2. Fred Lewis, "We Are All Jew-ish Now," Perspectives from the President, *Voices of B'Nai Shalom*, January 2018, https://religiondocbox.com/Judaism /94414362-T-he-tagline-of-the-conservative-a-sked-what-makes-them-jewish -many-reflections.html.

3. Devorah Baum, "We Are All Jew-ish Now," *New York Times*, September 29, 2017, https://www.nytimes.com/2017/09/29/opinion/sunday/we -are-all-jewish.html?searchResultPosition=1.

4. Ibid.

5. Albert Einstein, "Prof. Einstein Discusses Judaism," *Daily Bulletin* [published by the Jewish Telegraphic Agency], September 30, 1934.

6. Jill Jacobs, "The History of 'Tikkun Olam,'" *Zeek*, June 2007, http: //www.zeek.net/706tohu/.

7. Rabbi Hillel, Pirkei Avot (usually called "Ethics of the Fathers"), chap. 1, sec. 14.

8. bimah: "A raised platform in a synagogue from which the Torah is read." *Merriam-Webster's Collegiate Dictionary*, 11th ed.

9. More commonly referred to as Sabbath or Shabbat.

10. *bochrim*: the plural of "young unmarried male, especially a yeshiva student." Chaim M. Weiser, *Frumspeak: The First Dictionary of Yeshivish* (Northvale, NJ: Aronson, 1995).

11. *parsha*: a section of the Torah read on Shabbos (Sabbath).

12. Tzvi Freeman, "Are Jews a 'Race'?," *Chabad*, March 2019, www.chabad .org/library/article_cdo/498027.

13. A klavern was a local unit or chapter of the Ku Klux Klan. The word could also refer to a Klan meeting place. It was coined as a combination of the words *klan* and *cavern*.

14. Sarah Mitchell Parsons, *From Southern Wrongs to Civil Rights: The Memoir of a White Civil Rights Activist* (Tuscaloosa: University of Alabama Press, 2009), 2.

15. "Few communities in America are as easily recognizable by name as Levittown, New York. . . . Levittown is the model on which scores of post World War II suburban communities were based—a place that started out as an experiment in low-cost, mass-produced housing and became, perhaps, the most famous suburban development in the world." "Levitt Houses," Research History, August 4, 2012, http://www.researchhistory.org/2012/08/04/levitt-houses/.

16. See note 1, above.

17. Evans, *Provincials*, 140.

18. Ibid., 189. Evans is quoting Gertrude J. Selznick and Stephen Steinberg, *The Tenacity of Prejudice: Anti-Semitism in Contemporary America* (Westport, CT: Greenwood Press, 1979).

19. W. J. Cash, *The Mind of the South* (New York: Vintage, 1941). In the book, Cash noted that, although "contact with other peoples is often represented as making inevitably for tolerance, that is true only for those who have already been greatly educated to tolerance. *The simple man everywhere is apt to see whatever differs from himself as an affront, a challenge, and a menace*" (emphasis added).

ACKNOWLEDGMENTS

1. There was one exception. It was a very tough, lengthy—more than seven years long—Mormon polygamy case involving five children, their dead mother's dying request to have her two conventional Mormon sisters take the five kids out of the compound and adopt them because, she said, the girls were sexually molested by the father, the polygamist widower who fought to keep his children, and the many county and state prosecutors and judges who studiously refrained from *any* substantive ruling in this moral conundrum.

2. Once I did have an agent, my next-door lawyer-neighbor in Stony Brook, New York. The association went nowhere for we were living on different planets.

3. According to dictionary.com, a memoir is "a record of events written by a person having intimate knowledge of them and based on personal observation."

4. The second RV was owned by Bob and Gail Weinstein, friends of mine from Stony Brook. Two weeks before, four Jewish couples had a farewell party for us, the *meshugenahs* going into the desert. Bob and Gail did not believe us. But once they realized we were serious, they decided to join us all the way down, since they had already been planning to start their summer RVing with their three boys soon. So in early 1976 two RVs with New York plates pulled into Starkville. He still shakes his head when we meet.

5. See www.donnaladd.com.

6. Now Herbert Lehman College of the City University of New York.

7. In 1981, Senator John C. Stennis demanded that McComas fire me for writing critiques of Mississippi's voting rights record that were published in the *New York Times* and the *Washington Post*.

CHAPTER 1.   Going Down to Mississippi

1. *meshugenah*: crazy person.

2. *trafe*: nonkosher food.

3. The shipyard filed a Chapter 11 bankruptcy in 1987. However, Todd came out of it in 1991, emerging as a considerably smaller company trying to rebuild its lost commercial business. Ultimately, because of the state of shipbuilding, lawsuits, and other issues, it was sold to Vigor Shipyards in 2011. It now provides the Navy with repair services at its West Coast yards.

4. *momzer*: bastard.

5. *mishpucha*: Jewish family, with very close friends included.

6. *kolkhoz*: collective farm in the former Union of Soviet Socialist Republics (USSR).

7. *schvartze*: Black person (derogatory).

8. Hereafter I will sometimes refer to the Ku Klux Klan as simply the Klan.

9. *goniff*: thief, swindler, crook, or rascal.

10. The name Sid Biddulph is a pseudonym.

11. The public school system of Soucier, Mississippi, was among the last to implement an integration plan—in 1980, twenty-five years after *Brown*.

CHAPTER 2.   The Jewish Community in Starkville, Mississippi,
and We "Fast-Talkin' New York Jews"

1. *latkes*: potato pancake, enjoyed during the Hanukkah holiday.
2. *hamantaschen*: three-cornered pastry filled with poppy seeds and jam, used by Jews when celebrating the holiday of Purim.
3. *matzohs*: piece of unleavened bread, used during the Passover holiday.
4. The name Helen is a pseudonym.
5. Evans, *Provincials*, 90.
6. The name Marilou is a pseudonym.
7. *shiksa*: gentile woman.
8. Kol Nidre is the prayer that begins the holiest day of the year for Jews, Yom Kippur. A haunting, sacred chant recited three times by all congregants as they stand together, it seeks the annulment of all vows made before God: "All vows we are likely to make, all oaths and pledges we are likely to take between this Yom Kippur and the next Yom Kippur, we publicly renounce. Let them all be relinquished and abandoned, null and void, neither firm nor established. Let our vows, pledges and oaths be considered neither vows nor pledges nor oaths." Cantor Deborrah Cannizzaro, "A Brief History of the Kol Nidrei Prayer," ReformJudaism.org, September 17, 2018, www.reformjudaism.org.
9. *Encyclopedia of Southern Jewish Communities*, Goldring/Woldenberg Institute of Southern Jewish Life, last updated 2019, www.isjl.org/mississippi-columbus-encyclopedia.html.
10. See Nicholas Lemann, *The Promised Land: The Great Black Migration and How It Changed America* (New York: Viking, 1992).
11. *mensch*: person of honor and integrity. For another example of a *mensch*, see the section on James McComas in chapter 6.
12. See https://bnaiisraelcolumbusms.wordpress.com/map/contact-page/.
13. *Everson v. Board of Education*, 330 U.S. 1, 15–16.
14. *gansa mishpucha*: the whole big family.
15. Evans, *Provincials*, 275.
16. *landsman*: fellow Jew who comes from the same district or town, especially in Eastern Europe through the 1930s. Now, a fellow Jewish member of the tribe.
17. Evans, *Provincials*, 275.

CHAPTER 3.   "Hey, Rabbi"

1. Congress of Racial Equality (CORE) was a civil rights organization founded in 1942. It was one of the organizations that sponsored the 1964 Mississippi Freedom Summer project. CORE and a few other civil rights groups recruited, trained, and mentored nearly a thousand college students, both white and black, and sent them into towns in Mississippi to prepare local black residents for the byzantine voter registration process and provide, through Freedom Schools, summer courses for young high school students.

2. Mississippi has sometimes been called "Redeemer country" because after the Civil War ended in 1865, white Mississippians strongly supported the efforts of white racists, members of the Southern Democratic Party known as the Redeemers, to effectively nullify the civil rights amendments through political and legal actions.

3. Bob Herbert, "Righting Reagan's Wrongs?," *New York Times*, November 13, 2007, https://www.nytimes.com/2007/11/13/opinion/13herbert .html ?searchResultPosition=1.

4. Howard Ball, *Murder in Mississippi: United States v. Price and the Struggle for Civil Rights* (Lawrence: University Press of Kansas, 2004), 3.

5. For the story of the trial see Howard Ball, *Justice in Mississippi: The Murder Trial of Edgar Ray Killen* (Lawrence: University Press of Kansas, 2006).

6. Willie Morris, a highly regarded writer who grew up in Mississippi, wrote a wonderful book about Dupree: *The Courting of Marcus Dupree* (New York: Doubleday, 1983; repr., 1992).

CHAPTER 4.   Confronting Racism While Serving the ACLU in Mississippi

1. W. E. B. Du Bois made these remarks, replying to Joel Spingarn (a white founding member of the NAACP), who had just criticized Du Bois's management of *The Crisis* during a July 1914 meeting of the NAACP Board (emphasis added). As the sole Black member of the board and editor of *The Crisis*, Du Bois believed that the monthly journal had to take a more radical stance regarding the status of the Black community in America at that time. See David L. Lewis, *W. E. B. Du Bois: Biography of a Race, 1868–1919* (New York: Holt, 1993), esp. 490–96.

2. For an examination of the Skokie litigation, see, generally, Philippa Strum, *When the Nazis Came to Skokie: Freedom for Speech We Hate* (Lawrence: University Press of Kansas, 1999); Donald A. Downs, *Nazis in Skokie: Freedom, Community and the First Amendment* (Notre Dame, IN: University of Notre Dame Press, 1985).

3. See "Methodist Minister Bears Witness, Scars from Voting Rights Crusades," *Jackson (MS) Clarion-Ledger*, April 18, 2018.

4. To read many of Moses's speeches, see Eric R. Burner, *And He Shall Lead Them: Robert Parris Moses and Civil Rights in Mississippi* (New York: New York University Press, 1994).

5. *Coen and Page v. Harrison County School Board*, United States Court of Appeals for the Fifth Circuit, 1981.

6. Ed King and Trent Watts, *Ed King's Mississippi: Behind the Scenes of Freedom Summer* (Jackson: University Press of Mississippi, 2014). The book contains photographs of the times.

CHAPTER 5.   Defending the 1965 Voting Rights Act

1. The National Youth Administration was a federal agency that was created by President Franklin D. Roosevelt in 1935 and operated until 1943. It provided work training to youth.

2. The Radical Republicans were members of the Republican Party who, "during and after the . . . Civil War, . . . committed to emancipation of the slaves and later to the equal treatment and enfranchisement of the freed blacks." "Radical Republican," *Encyclopedia Britannica*, last updated August 21, 2019, https://www.britannica.com/topic/Radical-Republican.

3. Lyndon Baines Johnson, "Transcript of Johnson's Address on Voting Rights to Joint Session of Congress," *New York Times*, March 16, 1965, www.nyt .com/johnson-rightsadd.html.

4. Jim Rutenberg, "The Speech That Defined the Fight for Voting Rights in Congress," *New York Times Magazine*, August 6, 2015.

5. Lyndon Baines Johnson, "August 6, 1965: Remarks on the Signing of the Voting Rights Act," Miller Center, University of Virginia, https://millercenter .org/the-presidency/presidential-speeches/august-6-1965-remarks-signing -voting-rights-act.

6. Joseph McAuley, "When LBJ Went All the Way to Voting Right(s)," *America: The Jesuit Review*, August 6, 2015, https://www.americamagazine.org /content/all-things/when-lbj-went-all-way-voting-rights.

7. McAuley, "When LBJ Went All the Way" (emphasis added).

8. John Adams, "Letter to the Officers of the First Brigade of the Third Division of the Militia of Massachusetts, October 11, 1798," in *The Works of John Adams, Second President of the United States* (Freeport, NY: Books for Libraries Press, 1969; first published 1850–56), 9:228–29.

9. "Benjamin Franklin's Last Great Quote and the Constitution," *Constitution Daily*, November 13, 2019, https://constitutioncenter.org/blog/benjamin-franklins-last-great-quote-and-the-constitution.

10. South Carolina v. Katzenbach, 383 U.S. 301 (1966).

11. Ibid.

12. Ibid.

13. Ibid. (emphasis added).

14. Regarding CORE, chapter 3, note 1.

15. "The Council of Federated Organizations (COFO) was a coalition of national and regional organizations engaged in civil rights activities in Mississippi . . . established in 1962. . . . The organization focused on voter registration and education." "Council of Federated Organizations (COFO)," Martin Luther King, Jr. Research and Education Institute, Stanford University.

16. *Extension of the Voting Rights Act: Hearings before the Subcommittee on Civil and Constitutional Rights of the Committee on the Judiciary House of Representatives, Ninety-Seventh Congress*, 2084, https://books.google.com/books?id=56MnAAAAMAAJ&ppis=_e&printsec=frontcover#v=onepage&q&f=false.

17. Howard Ball, Dale Krane, and Thomas P. Lauth, *Compromised Compliance: Implementation of the 1965 Voting Rights Act* (Westport, CT: Greenwood, 1982).

18. Howard Ball, Dale Krane, and Thomas P. Lauth, "The View from Georgia and Mississippi: Local Attorneys' Appraisal of the 1965 Voting Rights Act," in *Minority Vote Dilution*, ed. Chandler Davidson (Washington, DC: Howard University Press, 1984), chapter 9 (181–202).

19. Shelby County v. Holder, 570 U.S. 529 (2013). The name Holder refers to Eric Holder, who was the US attorney general at the time the case was filed.

20. Myrna Perez, "Voting Rights Five Years after the Supreme Court's Shelby County Decision," *Brennan Center for Justice Newsletter*, June 25, 2018.

21. According to Wikipedia, Jean-Baptiste Alphonse Karr wrote in 1848, "Plus ça change, plus c'est la même chose"—literally, "the more it changes, the more it's the same thing." The quote from Faulkner is from *Requiem for a Nun* (New York: Random House, 1951).

22. The 1982 extension bill did not reflect any concerns and suggestions voiced by the many who testified for and against extension.

23. "Ball Testifying Today on Voting Act Extension," was the headline in the *Starkville Daily News* in its edition of June 25, 1981.

24. The *Clarion-Ledger*'s page 1 headline on June 26, 1981, read: "Courts Should Handle Voting Rights Act, Lawyer Says."

CHAPTER 6.   A Solitary Jew on Campus and in the Field

1. Howard Ball, *Judicial Craftsmanship or Fiat? Direct Overturn by the United States Supreme Court* (Westport, CT: Greenwood, 1978).

2. Alabama: Alabama State and Tuskegee Colleges; Louisiana: Grambling State University and Xavier College of New Orleans; Arkansas: University of Arkansas at Pine Bluff; Tennessee: Tennessee State College; and Mississippi: Alcorn A&M University, Tougaloo College, Mississippi Valley State College, and Mississippi University for Women. (Jackson State University had its own MPA program, and we worked out other interactions with that predominantly Black university, including a joint MPA program involving exchanges of students and faculty.)

3. We had to reduce our network because we were simply unable to visit all of the schools because of our other responsibilities, like teaching, and advising our students on campus, and visiting with our wives and kids. We did not have the free time that was necessary for each visit.

4. Regarding the word *mensch*, see chapter 2, note 11.

CHAPTER 7.   Leaving the Magnolia State

1. *Haimish* is a Yiddish word that suggests that a "home" (*heim* in German), whether a private dwelling or a place of business—e.g., a bakery, a bookstore, a hotel—is sensed by the observer to be a cozy, warm, unpretentious place where no one stands on ceremony or puts on airs.

2. *Welcome Back, Kotter*, was an ABC-TV half-hour sitcom that was a surprise hit and ran for four seasons, from September 1975 to May 1979. Gabe Kaplan and John Travolta played central characters. Kaplan played a teacher, Mr. Kotter, who graduated from the same Brooklyn high school where he was now assigned to teach. He was selected because he had been a remedial misfit who

actually graduated and went to college. He was welcomed back because his students, like Kotter himself, were the "sweat hogs," a group of unruly, racially and ethnically diverse misfits labeled remedial students, led by Travolta's character, Vinnie Barbarino.

3. See the latter part of chapter 3.

CHAPTER 8.   Conclusion

1. Kenneth Billings, "A No-Nonsense Judge for Killen Trial," *Neshoba Democrat,* June 1, 2005.

2. Sam Roberts, "Marcus D. Gordon, Judge in 'Mississippi Burning' Case, Dies at 84," *New York Times,* May 27, 2016.

3. For more about Sid, see chapter 3, under "The Jewish Referee, Wearing Glasses"; the end of chapter 6; and chapter 7 under "Coda."

4. John 4:13 (NRSV) says: "Jesus said to her, 'Everyone who drinks of this water will be thirsty again.'"

5. Billings, "A No-Nonsense Judge for Killen Trial."

APPENDIX

1. Oneg: The celebratory event immediately following the Shabbos service. When there is a Bat Mitzvah, the Oneg's fare is prepared by the parents. Generally, a variety of foods are available, from bagels, lox, and tomatoes to salads, cheeses, desserts, and more.

2. The "Golden Triangle" Airport, a small facility off US Highway 82, services three towns in the state: Starkville, Columbus, and West Point, Mississippi.

Index

HOWARD BALL

is professor emeritus of political science at the University of Vermont.
He specializes in civil liberties, civil rights, constitutional law, and
American government. He is the author or co-author of over
thirty books, including *Of Power and Right: Hugo Black,
William O. Douglas, and America's Constitutional Revolution* and
The Supreme Court in the Intimate Lives of Americans.

Lightning Source UK Ltd.
Milton Keynes UK
UKHW021949180221
378955UK00003B/116

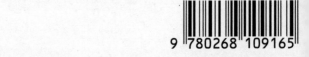